SOFTWARE ENGINEERING STANDARDS

A USER'S ROAD MAP

by

James W. Moore

IEEE

COMPUTER SOCIETY

Los Alamitos, California

Washington ● Brussels ● Tokyo

Library of Congress Cataloging-in-Publication Data

Moore, James W., 1948–
   Software engineering standards: a user's road map / James W. Moore.
     p. cm.
   Includes bibliographical references and index.
   ISBN 0-8186-8008-3
   1. Software engineering—Standards.   I. Title.
QA76.758.M66   1998
005.1 ' 02 ' 18—dc21

                                                     97-29227
                                                      CIP

IEEE Computer Society Press Order Number BP08008
Library of Congress Number 97-29227
ISBN 0-8186-8008-3

Additional copies may be ordered from:

IEEE Computer Society Press	IEEE Service Center	IEEE Computer Society	IEEE Computer Society
Customer Service Center	445 Hoes Lane	13, Avenue de l'Aquilon	Ooshima Building
10662 Los Vaqueros Circle	P.O. Box 1331	B-1200 Brussels	2-19-1 Minami-Aoyama
P.O. Box 3014	Piscataway, NJ 08855-1331	BELGIUM	Minato-ku, Tokyo 107
Los Alamitos, CA 90720-1314	Tel: +1-908-981-1393	Tel: +32-2-770-2198	JAPAN
Tel: +1-714-821-8380	Fax: +1-908-981-9667	Fax: +32-2-770-8505	Tel: +81-3-3408-3118
Fax: +1-714-821-4641	mis.custserv@computer.org	euro.ofc@computer.org	Fax: +81-3-3408-3553
Email: cs.books@computer.org			tokyo.ofc@computer.org

Publisher: Matt Loeb
Developmental Editor: Cheryl Baltes
Advertising/Promotions: Tom Fink
Production Editor: Lisa O'Conner
Cover Design: Walzak Advertising and Design, Inc.

Printed in the United States of America by BookCrafters

To a liberal arts education,
particularly
to my English teachers

PREFACE

In recent years, it has become widely accepted that improved software development *processes* will result in improved software development *products*. Because of the difficulty in directly measuring product quality, interest has increasingly turned to process improvement as the key to reducing cost, schedule, and risk as well as improving product quality. To improve their development process, many developers have rightly focused on the adoption of industry-wide "best practices" and their incorporation into strong institutionally internalized development processes.

As the craft of software development creeps closer to the status of an engineering discipline, many important practices have been captured in consensus standards. On the other hand, the inherent nature of software to cut across other disciplines and the slow consolidation of knowledge (as opposed to the rapid creation of technology) over the 50-year history of computing has resulted in a standardized body of knowledge that is both distributed and diffused. Today's user of software engineering standards is presented with a bewildering array of choices, more than 300 standards developed and maintained by more than 50 different organizations, all approaching software engineering from different viewpoints and contexts. The standards are inconsistent, overlapping, and occasionally contradictory. To make matters worse, even within a particular organization's collection, the evolution of technology and practice during the accumulation of the constituent standards may lead to awkward discontinuities among the standards.

These obstacles to the use of software engineering standards remain despite growing interest and need. Under the pressure of competition, litigation, and regulation, commercial organizations are pressed to improve their software engineering processes. Challenged to better assimilate rapidly changing information technology, governmental organizations are abandoning their own software engineering standards to adopt the presumably more current commercial standards.

Standards development organizations are aware of these difficulties and the needs and are making progress toward their solution with improved planning and coordination mechanisms. Two standards bodies, in particular, are leading the way. The Software Engineering Standards Committee (SESC) of the Computer Society, the largest of the 35 societies organized under the umbrella of the

Institute of Electrical and Electronic Engineers (IEEE), develops and maintains a collection of approximately 50 standards which grows at the rate of 5 or so per year. SESC has undertaken a set of strategic planning initiatives that will reorganize and reshape its collection into a unified body of standards. The key international organization is Subcommittee 7 of Joint Technical Committee 1, created by the International Organization for Standardization (ISO) and the International Electrotechnical Commission (IEC) for the purpose of standardization within the scope of Information Technology. Generally known as ISO/IEC JTC1/SC7, this subcommittee has created a Business Planning Group with the responsibility to develop an integrated "product plan" for the evolution of its collection.

This book is also part of the solution. Written with the cooperation of the IEEE SESC and the US Technical Advisory Group (TAG) to ISO/IEC JTC1/SC7, the text will describe the important standards and the plans and strategies that underlay and interrelate them. Although focus will be placed on the two principal bodies for software engineering standardization, SESC and SC7, related standards from other organizations will be selectively described. In particular, those standards that form a context for software engineering (such as quality management, project management, system engineering, dependability, and safety) will be considered.

Although the book may be read straight through, readers are encouraged to skip around to find topics of interest. Cross-referencing is provided to assist the reader who samples the contents. In fact, some material is inevitably repetitive because an important goal of the book is to provide different viewpoints of the same collections of standards.

The text is intended to appeal to the users of software engineering standards, that is, those individuals and organizations whose work is the creation and maintenance of software systems of the highest quality (and sometimes the highest difficulty). It is anticipated that the typical reader would be a senior technical professional or a manager with a background in software development.

Secondarily, the book should be useful to standards-writers, those professionals who are working on new or revised software engineering standards intended to fit within the existing bodies of such standards. It is hoped that an exposition of fundamental and unifying principles and the scope and relationships of existing standards would ease the difficult job of converting experience into standards.

Finally, the book should be useful to students in the emerging discipline of software engineering, who need access to a largely non-existent codified body of knowledge for the software discipline.

The introductory chapter provides an overview of important concepts of software engineering and the standards that codify them. The first topic addresses a basic issue in software engineering—is it really engineering or simply a quixotic ideal? The answer is necessarily mixed, because craft-based software development is progressing, albeit slowly and painfully, to the status of an engineering discipline. The chapter goes on to describe the scope, roles, and use of software engineering standards, the organizations that make them, and some future trends in their development.

Chapter 2 provides concepts and diagramming conventions useful in the remainder of the book. Two types of diagrams are used to guide the reader in designating and selecting standards to pursue specific goals. The first type of diagram provides a layered view of standards and is intended to illustrate the relationships among standards within a particular collection or portion of a collection. The second type of diagram, the road map, is central to the purpose of this book; the road maps illustrate the external relationships among selected standards, even those from different collections. They assist the reader in finding the way from a compelling need at the periphery of information technology to the software engineering standards that can assist in the satisfaction of that need. The second chapter also abstracts the whole of software engineering into a few simple objects, for example, process and product, and illustrates the relationships among those objects. This concept is used to illustrate the key relationships among the objects of software engineering, relationships that motivate the remainder of the book.

Chapters 3 and 4 provide overviews of some relevant US and international, respectively, Standards Development Organizations (SDO), with particular focus on IEEE SESC and ISO/IEC JTC1/SC7. The organization of each SDO is described and its current collection of standards is listed, as well as those standards expected in the near future. Layer diagrams are used to explain the relationships of the standards in the collection. Finally, strategic plans of the SDOs to evolve and improve their collections are described. In contrast with later chapters, these two chapters illustrate the relationships among the standards *within* the collections.

Chapters 5-10 draw relationships among the collections of the SDOs. Using the road map diagrams, each chapter begins at a point of departure in a different context and leads the reader to the selection of software engineering standards appropriate for achieving goals relevant to that context. For example, Chapter 6 begins with a presumption that the user already has a strong base (or a strong desire to improve) in quality management. The road map for that chapter will explain how to select software engineering standards to assist in that goal. Other chapters begin from the viewpoints of project management (Chapter 7), system engineering (Chapter 8), dependability (Chapter 9), and safety (Chapter 10). Chapter 5 is a little different, starting with the base of computing terminology drawn from computer science.

The next four chapters, Chapters 11-14, are also guides to selecting standards, but instead of beginning on the periphery of software engineering, they begin inside. Each one focuses on one of the objects of software engineering–resource (Chapter 11), product (Chapter 12), process (Chapter 13), and customer (Chapter 14)– identified in Chapter 2. The intent is to provide quick access to information relevant to those seeking to improve their practices related to one or more of those objects. These chapters focus specifically on the standards created and maintained by IEEE SESC and by SC7.

Chapter 15 provides descriptions of important alternatives to the standards described in the main body of the text. For reasons of regulation or custom, some users are required to apply sector-dependent standards for software engineering. A few important sector-dependent standards are described and related to the larger body of standards in the remainder of the book.

Two Appendices, A and B, provide useful reference information. Appendix A is a list of all of the standards and drafts mentioned in the book. Appendix B tells where the standards can be purchased and provides contact information for each of the standards-developers discussed in the text. Appendices C, D, and E are a glossary, a list of references, and an index, respectively.

Although the book pays great attention to integrated (and not-so-integrated) collections of standards, it is not my intention to encourage readers to adopt collections in their entirety—quite the opposite. By analyzing the collections, exposing key relationships, and regrouping them in various ways, I hope to provide the insights that allow readers to select standards to fill their specific needs with precision.

Throughout the text, I have not hesitated to elide portions of the names and numbers of standards to lighten the reading. For example, IEEE Std 1228-1994 may be variously termed IEEE Std 1228, IEEE 1228, or even simply 1228 when the context is clear. Tables at the beginning of each chapter or section generally give the complete designation of each standard mentioned in the chapter. In addition, I have often omitted the ubiquitous term, "Information Technology," from the titles of standards.

As you might imagine, during the year or so required to write and publish a book of this kind, it is challenging to track and consistently represent the ever-changing status of draft standards. Despite my best efforts, I suspect that some mistakes have crept into the text. I have paid particular attention to the accuracy of Appendix A; it is probably the more accurate in the case of any inconsistencies found in the body of the book.

Just prior to publication of this book, IEC decided to retroactively renumber their standards for consistency with CENELEC, their European regional counterpart. The renumbering adds 60,000 to the number of each IEC standard—including the ones that are already published. For example, IEC 880 will be renumbered as IEC 60880. Because of the large supply of existing standards, the change will take many years to completely implement. This text continues to use the old numbers.

Although I must bear the responsibility for the accuracy and usefulness of the text, I must also state my appreciation to many others who provided me with advice, assistance and support in writing this book. I gratefully acknowledge the forbearance of my son, David, and my wife, Barbara, who coped with my nearly complete withdrawal from normal family life. Two of the information analysts, Mary Przewlocki and Mary Maroney, in the library of The MITRE Corporation were simply superb in tracking down obscure books and articles on demand (and almost instantly). I appreciate the assistance of Jim French, Chris Denham, John Harauz, Robert Hegland, Dave Kitson, Jeanie Kitson, and Dorothy Wallace in providing me with timely access to standards, drafts, and other important documents. The Standards Information Center at the National Institute of Standards and Technology was a vital resource. Finally, any user or student of software engineering standards should benefit, as I did, from the excellent book by Stan Magee and Leonard Tripp [Magee97].

I am grateful to the people of the IEEE Computer Society Press, Bill Sanders and Lisa O'Conner, for their care and diligence in dealing with a first-time author, and to Joseph Pomerance, the copy editor, for reminding me of many rules of writing that I had too long forgotten.

Peer reviewers for the book were suggested by Leonard Tripp, Chairman of the IEEE SESC and Chairman of the US TAG to ISO/IEC JTC1/SC7. All of the peer reviewers gave valuable help, but two stand out for making particularly insightful comments and providing continuing counsel—John Harauz and David Kiang. Other peer reviewers included: Paul Croll, Perry DeWeese, Robin Fralick, Jim French, Nancy George, David Kitson, Dorothy Kuckuck, Tom Kurihara, Jerry Lake, Dennis Lawrence, Stan Magee, David Maibor, Peter Poon, Ken Ptack, Gary Robinson, Norman Schneidewind, and Raghu Singh.

As a result of its review, the Executive Committee of the SESC approved a resolution "endorsing and recommending" the text. I appreciate their vote of confidence.

I am fortunate to have benefited from the trust and cooperation of the SESC and other organizations in sharing their plans. In particular, I appreciate the encouragement and support of Leonard Tripp in pointing out the need for the book and encouraging its successful completion. Furthermore, I gratefully acknowledge the interest of my employer, The MITRE Corporation, in supporting my participation in some of the standardization activities described in this text.

Jim Moore
1 September 1997
Potomac, Maryland

TABLE OF CONTENTS

LIST OF FIGURES

LIST OF TABLES

INTRODUCTION

On an outside wall of the thirteenth century Town Hall in Rothenburg-ob-der-Tauber, Germany hangs an equally old iron *standard* used to measure the length of loaves of bread. Subject to punishment were bakers who made their loaves too short—for cheating their customers—as were those who made their loaves too long—for raising unrealistic expectations. The goal of this chapter is to provide general material about software engineering and software engineering standards and to address the reader's expectations regarding the usefulness of the standards.

Software Engineering

The Institute of Electrical and Electronics Engineers defines *software engineering*, in IEEE Std 610.12, as:

> *(1) The application of a systematic, disciplined, quantifiable approach to the development, operation and maintenance of software, that is, the application of engineering to software. (2) The study of approaches as in (1).*

Most of the standards to be considered are *practice* standards rather than *product* standards, concerned with the regulation of the practice of software engineering rather than the interfaces of the products produced.

Is it Engineering?

One could be excused for denying the premise of this book. Software engineering is not among the 36 engineering professions licensed in the United States. Furthermore, 48 states have laws forbidding an unlicensed individual from advertising as an "engineer." The state of Texas has prohibited its universities from offering master's degrees in software engineering and the state of New Jersey has considered legislation requiring the licensing of all software professionals [Jones95].

Nevertheless, in deference to common usage, this book will use the term "software engineering"; readers may choose to view the term as a statement of a goal or ideal rather than as a statement of a fact.

Engineering can be viewed as a closed feedback loop as shown in Figure 1. An engineering *process* consists of related activities performed in response to a statement of *needs* and consuming *resources* to produce a *product*. In order to manage or improve the process, one must exert *control*. Control is a decision-making mechanism that considers *goals* and *constraints* in the formulation of *action* that is intended to direct or modify the process. The decision to take action is based on *measurements,* quantitative evidence

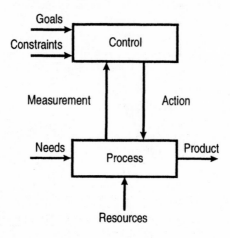

Figure 1. A model of engineering. (Source: [SESC93].)

regarding the state of the process. Measurements can be made of conditions inside the process, products of the process, and the satisfaction of users of the products [SESC93]. We would expect software engineering standards to contribute to the implementation of such a model with respect to the development, operation, and maintenance of software systems.

Indeed, we will find standards related to the process, product, and resources involved in the software discipline. We will find standards describing the treatment of needs in software development, not only as requirements and specifications, but articulating less formal needs from more remote stakeholders. We will find standards describing management plans, measurements, and actions for the purpose of controlling the ongoing processes. Finally, we will find methods to articulate goals and constraints, even informal ones, to guide the managers.

So, even if the software discipline has not yet formalized the empirical underpinnings of an engineering discipline, we will find that, in many ways, it is acting as if it has.

Relationship to Other Disciplines

Software engineering occupies a position intermediate between, on the one hand, the mathematical and physical disciplines *of computer science and technology* and, on the other hand, the requirements of the particular *application domains* applying the findings of the former to solve problems of the latter (Figure 2). The techniques for the engineering of software can be viewed, in part, as specializations of those of more general disciplines, such as *project management, system engineering,* and *quality management.* Furthermore, a software project must implement requirements imposed by cross-cutting disciplines like *dependability* (a term more general than *reliability*) and *safety.* These contextual disciplines are

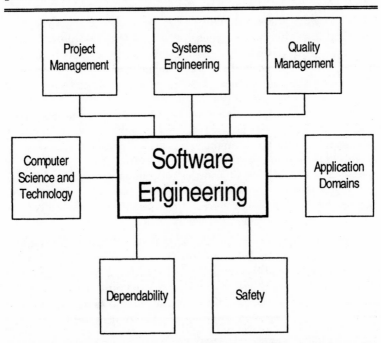

Figure 2. Relationship of software engineering to other disciplines.

important to the book because subsequent chapters will use them as entry points for selecting appropriate software engineering standards.

Fundamental Principles

The engineering style of education deals with rapidly changing technology by teaching fundamentals; students are provided little choice regarding their curriculum. As a consequence, there is a set of things that we can expect every engineer to know [Parnas95]. The teaching material is based on a common, principle-based body of knowledge, codified by some more-or-less officially designated organization, often enforced by licensing requirements.

Relating to the engineering style of education, Tom Gilb [Gilb96] offers a definition of engineering that he credits to Billy Koen:

> *Engineering is the use of* principles *to find designs that will meet multiple competing objectives, within limited resources and other constraints, under conditions of uncertainty.*

In other fields, practice standards can be traced to a body of fundamental scientific and engineering *principles* that constrain the standards. A trivial example is that mechanical engineering standards are constrained by the three-dimensional geometry of physical objects. The codification of software engineering standards is faced by particular challenges in this area. First, the subject of the standards—software—is inherently intangible and unconstrained by the common laws of physics. Second, the discipline is relatively new, compared to other engineering disciplines, and many of its important concepts remain immature. Third, there is not yet a commonly accepted body of knowledge[1] that can serve as a foundation, nor any body empowered to develop it [Abran96]. Finally, unlike product interface standards, there are few market forces to cause convergence on selected technologies.

This has caused some problems. Unfettered by any integrating forces of principles or dominant products, most software engineering standards are ad hoc recordings of individual practices claimed to be "best." This is not bad when each standard is considered in isolation, but when the standards are considered as a body, we find them to be *dis*-integrated, capriciously different in detail, overlap-

---

[1]There have been some attempts, though; [Davis95] is a catalog of principles.

ping and occasionally contradictory. These characteristics put the erstwhile adopter of the corpus of standards into a difficult situation, because the adopters must themselves develop some mechanism to rationalize, explain, and relate the various standards chosen for implementation.

Part of the solution to the problem is the adoption of a framework of vocabulary, key relationships and other constraints to which each individual standard must adhere. In fact, IEEE Software Engineering Standards Committee (SESC) and its international counterpart, ISO/IEC JTC1/SC7, have taken steps in this direction, efforts that are described elsewhere in this book. Perhaps a more basic requirement is for the identification of a set of *fundamental principles* that would serve to explain and motivate the provisions of the various standards. IEEE SESC is initiating this step.

Figure 3 shows a notional depiction of the role of principle standards. The principles of software engineering would be regarded as selected, adapted and specialized from the principles of engineering in general. The provisions of practice standards would be motivated by the software engineering principles and would be traceable to those principles. So-called "best practices" would be viewed as the detailed implementation of the provisions of the practice standards. Viewed in the other direction, practice standards would be regarded as descriptions of observed, effective best practices and the principles as abstractions of the practice standards. The principles found to be relevant beyond the scope of software engineering (perhaps those related to complexity, for example) might be considered as general principles of engineering.

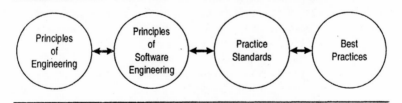

Figure 3. Relationship of principles and practice.

In this model, we can view practice standards as existing in a tension between the consolidating and integrating forces exerted by the principles and the expansive and innovative forces exerted by the recognition of new, effective practices.

IEEE SESC has initiated an effort to identify fundamental principles for software engineering. A workshop at the 1996 Software Engineering Standards Forum considered candidate principles and developed a set of criteria to be applied to candidates [Jabir97]. A Delphi experiment involving a number of notable experts in software engineering identified an initial working set of principles during 1997. A follow-up workshop held at the 1997 International Software Engineering Standards Symposium reviewed the results of the Delphi experiment and produced a working set of principles. More refinement is planned.

Software Engineering Standards

For the purposes of this book, the characterization of standards provided in [SESC93] is helpful:

> A standard can be: (1) an object or measure of comparison that defines or represents the magnitude of a unit; (2) a characterization that establishes allowable tolerances or constraints for categories of items; and (3) a degree or level of required excellence or attainment. Standards are definitional in nature, established either to further understanding and interaction, or to acknowledge observed (or desired norms) of exhibited characteristics or behavior.

Most of the standards described in this book have been developed by Standards Developing Organizations (SDO) operating on the principles of consensus development and voluntary adoption. For the purposes of this book, the organizations are regarded as national (US, with a few exceptions) or international. It must be noted, however, that even this basic distinction over-simplifies the actual situation.[2] Many major standards developers, for example, the IEEE, include members from many nations, any of whom may contribute to the development of standards. The resulting standards may be adopted by anyone, anywhere on the globe. Nevertheless, for purposes of international standardization, these trans-national organizations are regarded as national entities and required to participate via the designated national body. For example, IEEE contributions to international standardization are administered by the American National Standards Institute (ANSI)

---

[2]It turns out that almost every general statement made about standardization is an oversimplification. It seems that nearly every organization and every project involves special circumstances that make it exceptional in some regard. The term *standards organization* may be a not-so-funny oxymoron.

despite the fact that the standards were developed by members from many nations.

Some notable characteristics of standards developed by US organizations are listed in [Cargill97]:

- They have been written by a committee of anyone who could attend the meetings.

- They have undergone public scrutiny.

- All technical comments have received responses.

- They are a product of consensus within the committee and within an industry segment or professional community.

Subject to procedures administered by the American National Standards Institute (ANSI), such a standard may be designated as an "American National Standard." Policies of the US government[3] provide that these national standards may be used in federal procurements [Cargill97].

Scope of Software Engineering Standards

Software engineering standards cover a remarkable variety of topics. ISO/IEC DTR 14399 (Version 3.0) lists 21 subject areas. For the purpose of organizing their book [Magee97], Stan Magee and Leonard Tripp organized 29 subjects into the three categories adapted for Table 1.

Table 1. Scope of Software Engineering Standardization

Process	Technique or Tool	Applicability
Acquisition	CASE tools	General
Requirements definition	Languages & notations	Defense
Design	Metrics	Financial
Code and test	Privacy	Medical
Integration	Process improvement	Nuclear
Maintenance & operations	Reliability	Process control
Configuration management	Safety	Scientific
Documentation	Security	Shrink-wrap
Project management	Software reuse	Transportation
Quality assurance	Vocabulary	
Verification and validation		

---

[3]OMB Circular A119.

Importance of Software Engineering Standards

To consider the importance of software engineering standards, one must consider the uses to which they are put and the benefits that accrue from their application.

Improving the Product

Nearly all of the standards discussed in this book are voluntary, that is, an organization makes its own decision, without coercion, to adopt the standard. (This contrasts with regulatory standards, imposed by processes similar to law, and mandated standards, such as military standards, required as a precondition of doing business with a dominant customer.) Organizations often adopt these standards because they improve their products, or improve the perception of their products in a competitive marketplace. Alternatively, the standards may improve the organization's business processes, allowing them to make their products more cost-effectively.

Examples of benefits that standards may provide in this regard are the following:

- Some standards are simply statements regarding subjects in which the uniformity provided by agreement is more important than the gains to be made by small, but local, improvements. Standards on terminology, e.g. IEEE Std 610.12, and notations, e.g. the draft IEEE standards on the IDEF notation, are examples.

- Some standards provide a nomenclature for complex concepts, which, absent standardization, could exhibit detailed differences in characteristics which might ultimately prove crucial. For example, IEEE Std 1028 provides minimum, essential characteristics for the type of review known as an *inspection*.

- Some standards, in the absence of scientific proof of validity, provide criteria for measurement and evaluation techniques that are at least validated by consensus wisdom. For example, IEEE Std 1061 provides a methodology for metrics that can be used as early indicators of later results.

- Some standards record a community consensus of "best practices," that is, techniques broadly regarded as generally effective. For example, IEEE Std 1008 provides requirements and recommendations for the unit testing of code.

- Some standards provide a unified and systematic treatment of the so-called "ilities" in a manner that cuts across the organization of many enterprises, hence effecting consistent internal treatment. An example is IEEE Std 730 on software quality assurance.

- Some standards provide a framework for communication with customers and suppliers, reducing misunderstanding, and shortening the time (and text) needed to reach agreement. An important example is IEEE/EIA Std 12207 on software life cycle processes.

- Some standards share techniques that can lead to qualitative improvements in developing software better, faster, or less expensively, for example, IEEE Std 1044 on software anomaly classification.

To be sure, not all observers agree that software engineering standards have been successful. [Pfleeger94] says that the "standards lack objective assessment criteria, involve more process than product, and are not always based on rigorous experimental results." [Fenton96] finds "no evidence that any of the existing standards are effective [in improving] the quality of the resulting software products cost-effectively." [Schneidewind96], though, points to success stories such as the organization that has produced nearly error-free code for the space shuttle, in part, through use of software engineering standards. All parties would agree, though, that improvement is desirable.

Protecting the Buyer

With many products, buyers can make appropriate decisions based on advertising literature, previous experience with the seller or direct examination. The increasing complexity of technology-based products, however, inevitably causes essential characteristics to remain hidden until after purchase. Standards can play a role when they provide accurate information regarding the suitability of products for specific uses [Brobeck96]. The product quality standards of ISO/IEC JTC1/SC7/WG6 are aimed in this direction. For the most complex of systems, the application of standards by the developer can serve to increase the buyer's confidence in the seller's methods for coping with that complexity. The standards applied by the avionics and nuclear industries are examples.

Protecting the Business

Courts in the United States have used voluntary standards to establish a supplier's "duty of care." Failure to adhere to standards does not necessary establish negligence but may be considered as evidence when dealing with issues like product safety and liability [Peach94, p. 322]. On the other hand, adherence to the appropriate standards is a strong defense that the supplier was not negligent in its development practices and has taken due care to deliver a product that is safe and fit for its intended use. The introduction of evidence that a product meets a voluntary standard is admissible in 47 of the 50 states [Batik92]. Increasingly, companies are developing liability prevention programs that incorporate voluntary standards as key parts.[4] IEEE Std 1228 for software safety plans, might be appropriate for such usage.

Florida Power and Light (a winner of the prestigious Deming Award in 1990 [Batik92]), not only applies software engineering standards but sometimes performs causal analysis back to the standards themselves when failures are noted. A major credit reporting firm has applied the entire corpus of IEEE SESC standards to its organizational software development processes to further bolster its defenses against claims of reckless development, maintenance, and operation of its databases and their accompanying software.

Even in contractual situations, the appropriate application of standards protects both parties by dividing up responsibilities, clarifying terminology, and defining expected practices. Examples of standards appropriate for this purpose include IEEE/EIA 12207 and EIA/IEEE J-Std-016.

Increasing Professional Discipline

Even if the practice of software is not yet a proper engineering discipline, it is moving in that direction. A body of practice standards is an essential step because it would serve to define the

---

[4]Of course, the writers of standards assume some liability for their product—the standard. In a famous case, the Sunshine Mine used, for thermal insulation, a foam material incidentally described as "fireproof" in a standard of the American Society for Testing and Materials (ASTM). A fire at the mine was blamed partly on the poorly written standard and ASTM was named as a co-defendant in the lawsuit. Although the lawsuit eventually was dropped, ASTM and other standards organizations have taken steps to protect themselves, and their voluntary participants [Batik92].

methods to be expected in the responsible practice of software engineering. An example might the software verification and validation (V & V) standard, IEEE Std 1012. A joint task force of the IEEE Computer Society and the ACM is currently investigating other steps necessary to move toward the goal [Jones95].

Introducing Technology

Finally, the Software Engineering Institute notes that standards play a vital role in technology transition. "Standards provide users with common terminology and a framework for communicating about technologies across organizational boundaries. Such communications is particularly critical to acceptance by late adopters." Furthermore, codification of technologies prepares them for adoption [Pollak96]. Examples might include the recommended practices on Computer-Aided Software Engineering (CASE) tool selection and adoption developed by IEEE SESC and now under consideration by ISO/IEC JTC1/SC7.

History

Although *software engineering* may not yet be a recognized branch of engineering, the roots of an organized discipline began to emerge in the 1960s and use of the term itself dates back to the now-famous 1968 North Atlantic Treaty Organization (NATO) conference.

Perhaps because of government's inherent need to conduct its business in a procedural manner, early US software engineering standards were written by organizations within the federal government. In 1973, a task force of the National Bureau of Standards concluded that such standards were feasible. Accordingly, three years later, Federal Information Processing Standard Publication (FIPS Pub.) 38, *Guidelines for Documentation of Computer Programs and Automated Systems*, was published. It was organized around the production of 10 documents: functional requirements; data requirements; system/subsystem specifications; program specifications; database specifications; user manual; operations manual; program maintenance manual; test plan; and test analysis report. Meanwhile, in 1974, the US Navy initiated the development of its Mil-Std 1679, Weapons System Software Development, one of the first standards treating the usage, control, and management of embedded computer resources [SESC93].

IEEE activity began in 1976 with the creation of the Software Engineering Standards Subcommittee (SESS). Its first standard, IEEE Std 730, Standard for a Quality Assurance Plan, was approved for trial use in 1979 and full use 2 years later. Like FIPS Pub. 38, it was (and remains) oriented toward the documentation requirements, only implicitly placing requirements on the under-lying processes.

International standardization activities related to software oc-curred in various technical committees of the International Organi-zation for Standardization (ISO) and the International Electrotech-nical Commission (IEC), depending upon the application area. ISO and IEC agreed in 1987 to form Joint Technical Committee 1 (JTC1) to deal with the area of *information technology* (IT). Never-theless, we will see that important work strongly related to IT con-tinues in committees of ISO and IEC.

Makers of Software Engineering Standards

The need for software engineering standards has been filled by an amount that some would regard as exceeding the requirement. An authoritative source [Magee97] identifies 315 standards created and maintained by 55 different international, national, sector, and professional organizations; Magee is selective—others identify more.

IEEE SESC alone maintains about 50 standards, if we count "parts" individually. Its planned 1998 collection will be packaged in four volumes comprising a total of about 2,300 pages. The chairman of the SESC, Leonard Tripp, has estimated that the typical SESC standard takes 2 to 4 years to develop and costs (in the labor and travel of volunteers) between $2,000 and $10,000 per page [SESC93].

At the international level, the process is even longer and more expensive. One estimate [Spring95] says that ISO standardization typically exceeds 7 years in duration and the attentive reader will find that at least one family of standards described in this book has been in development for 14 years so far.

At the center of software engineering standardization in the United States is the Software Engineering Standards Committee (SESC) of the IEEE Computer Society. Its collection has grown from 1 in 1981 to about 50 by the end of 1997 and continues to grow at the rate of five or so per year. The size and growth of the collec-tion has exposed many stresses and SESC has been taking the ini-tiative to address the problems apparent in the world-wide corpus of process standards.

The counterpart of SESC in the international forum is ISO/IEC JTC1/SC7. It inherited an obsolescent set of mainframe-oriented practice standards (on subjects like flowcharts and sequential record processing) when it was formed in 1987 but has turned its attention toward more significant contributions, such as its 1995 standard for software life cycle processes, ISO/IEC 12207. SESC participates in SC7 through its membership in the US Technical Advisory Group (TAG) that formulates national positions and selects the delegation for meetings of SC7.

These two organizations are not alone in their work. Other relevant standards have been written by US organizations including the American Institute for Aeronautics and Astronautics (AIAA), the Electronic Industries Association (EIA), and the Power Engineering Society of the IEEE; national organizations like the Canadian Standards Association (CSA) and Standards Australia; and committees of international organizations, like ISO TC176 (quality), IEC TC56 (dependability), and IEC SC45A and 65A (safety). Important contributions have been made by organizations that are not formally accredited to develop standards, including the International Council on Systems Engineering (INCOSE), the Project Management Institute (PMI), and the Reuse Library Interoperability Group (RIG). Even this list is far from complete; [Magee97] lists 55 organizations that have developed relevant standards—and its authors were selective.

Components of the US federal government sometimes write specifications to regulate their own procurement practices. The role of the Department of Defense is well-known, particularly with respect to development process standards, but the National Aeronautics and Space Administration (NASA) and the Federal Aviation Agency (FAA) have also written standards.

The most influential government agency in information technology standardization, though, has been the Computer Systems Laboratory (CSL) of the National Institute of Standards and Technology (NIST), "where much of the technology infrastructure that is necessary to the United States is either created or validated." NIST is a 1988 renaming of the National Bureau of Standards, formed in 1901. The Computer Systems Laboratory specializes in information technology; it was formed in 1966, as a result of the Brooks Act, to help resolve the problems of incompatible computer systems in the federal government, the world's largest purchases of information technology, by making procurement practices more uniform and enlightened. This was accomplished largely through the creation of the famous Federal Information Processing Standards (FIPS) [Cargill97].

The FIPS publications provided important guidance to government managers on how to make open systems procurements. Complementary processor validation programs ensured that suppliers of open systems met their claims regarding adherence to standards. Process standards were not ignored—NIST/CSL played important roles in the development of standards for life cycle process and high-integrity systems. In recent months, though, CSL has redirected its priorities to specifically targeted efforts, like the National Information Infrastructure.

Roles of Software Engineering Standards

Software engineering standards can play a variety of important roles for an organization. Some of those roles are:

- *Naming*: A standard can provide a succinct name for a complicated concept. Particularly when two parties are contracting for a complex item, it is helpful to have a standard specifying the details. For example, is it easier to judge the adequacy of a 20-page explanation of a supplier's verification and validation procedures or a simple claim that they conform to IEEE Std 1012?

- *Best Practices*: Sometimes organizations want to adopt software development practices that are agreed by the community to represent "best of breed." Practice standards describe practices that are consensually agreed to be sound.

- *Badging*: Organizations need a way to assert (in a supportable fashion) that their institutional practices conform to a constellation of best principles and practices. The need is met by "badges," formulated by expert authorities and sometimes independently certified, for example, ISO 9000 and SEI Capability Maturity Model "levels." This usage is so important that we can expect to see new badges in the near future [Moore95].

- *Contractual Agreement*: In a complex information technology procurement, it is helpful and efficient to decouple complex technological issues from the business aspects of the agreement. Standards such as IEEE/EIA 12207 provide this service by setting norms which may be referenced rather than described in a contract.

Organizational Goals for Using Software Engineering Standards

Not all organizations will have the same goals in the adoption of software engineering standards.[5] Some possibilities are listed here along with the needs that software engineering standards may fill in the achievement of the goals.

Improve and Evaluate Software Competency. An organization may desire processes and measures to calibrate its ability to produce software that is competitive in some or all of the following areas:

- *Quality*: Analyze trends in product and process quality for software organizations.

- *Customer Satisfaction*: Measure the extent to which software satisfies the customers' needs.

- *Cycle Time and Productivity*: Track progress toward goals for software cycle time and productivity improvement.

- *Process Maturity*: Assess progress relative to industry software process benchmarks.

- *Technology*: Assess the application of technology within the organization.

Provide Framework and Terminology for Two-Party Agreements. An organization that specializes in buying or selling software services under contract may desire a uniform framework for defining the relationship and respective responsibilities of the acquirer and the supplier for software and systems containing software, a framework that transcends the scope of any particular contract:

- *Acquisition Process*: Provide the essential actions and criteria to be used by an organization in planning and executing an acquisition for software or software-related services.

- *Supply Process*: Provide the essential actions and criteria to be used by an organization in supplying software or software-related services to an acquirer.

---

[5]The material in this section is based on an untitled point paper written by Leonard Tripp.

- *Life Cycle Processes*: Provide the process requirements to be met during the life cycle (definition, development, deployment, operation, etc.) of software or systems containing software.

- *Life Cycle Deliverables*: Provide the requirements for information to be passed between the supplier and the acquirer during the performance of software life cycle processes.

Evaluate Products of Software Engineering Activities. An organization may need to formulate criteria, processes, and measures to determine the adequacy of a software product to fulfill its mission.

- *External Measurements*: Measurements of completed software products to evaluate the achievement of development goals.

- *Internal Measurements*: Measurement of incomplete software artifacts and development processes to provide early indicators of the achievement of development goals.

Assure High Integrity Levels for Software. An organization may need to develop software for critical applications where safety and dependability are important to protect lives or property.

- *Planning*: A framework to determine that appropriate resources and appropriate controls are provided to ensure treatment of concerns of criticality.

- *Achievement*: Provisions for ensuring that critical requirements for safety and dependability are appropriately treated throughout the providing of the software service

- *Assessment*: Verifiable measurement of the extent to which criticality goals have been achieved.

Trends

Some trends for the future of software engineering standardization are becoming apparent, particularly in the collections of the major organizations involved in developing these standards.

The absence of a firm, empirical and scientific foundation for software engineering standards has been a continuing vulnerability, one that has not gone unnoticed by its critics, for example, [Fenton96] and [Pfleeger94]. With the continuing maturation of the field, attempts are being made to address this problem. Notable efforts include:

- The series of workshops and other projects, mentioned above, to develop fundamental principles.

- Standardization efforts cooperative with related but more mature disciplines such as systems engineering and project management.

- The so-called "SPICE trials" (more properly termed as the Software Process Improvement and dEtermination project), efforts to empirically validate the process assessment mechanisms of the planned ISO/IEC 15504 series of standards [Emam95].

Little progress toward a coherent discipline can be made when each standard is an individual island of practice unrelated to its peers. Recent years, though, have seen a trend toward the recognition of key standards that provide a framework which may be elaborated by other, more detailed ones. Examples include:

- The broadly recognized quality management framework of the ISO 9000 standards.

- The life cycle process framework of the ISO/IEC 12207 standard on software life cycle processes.

- Cooperative liaison efforts among standards committees concerned with cross-cutting areas like functional safety, dependability, quality, and software engineering.

No one should be surprised at disrespect of software engineering standards if the various collections do not respect and build upon the contributions of other collections. Recent years have seen huge steps toward the harmonization of the important collections. For example:

- SESC standards have been used as the basis upon which SC7 standards have been drafted. On the other hand, SESC has voted to adopt newer SC7 standards to replace their own standards with a similar scope.

- ISO TC176 and IEC TC56 share a single standard, under two numbers, specifying the relationship between quality management and dependability.

- SESC has adopted policies designating various international standards, such as ISO/IEC 12207 and the ISO 9000 series as key standards with which its own must harmonize.

- A major accomplishment of the US adaptation of the ISO/IEC 12207 standard has been the addition of an annex explaining how SESC standards may be used to accomplish the requirements of the 12207 standard. SESC plans a "block change" of those standards during the next 2 years to increase the precision of the fit.

The great success of the SEI Capability Maturity Model and the ISO 9000 quality management standards provide ample indication of the need for "badges" summarizing achievement of important capabilities. It is appropriate for executive managers to deal with badges in order to set corporate level objectives and allocate resources while properly delegating technical activity. Before the end of the millennium, we can expect to see an SESC badge summarizing the enterprise-level achievement of a core set of software engineering practices [Moore95].

Using This Book

Recognizing the unique nature of every enterprise, this text "slices and dices" the important collections of software engineering standards in a variety of ways. The chapters describing the collections usually organize their constituent standards in ways suggested by the creators of the collections. The chapters describing the context of software engineering allow one to select software engineering standards by building on recognized contextual strengths of an organization, or by remedying notable contextual weaknesses. The chapters describing the objects of software engineering present the opportunity to consider standards addressing a single object, such as process, of the discipline.

Throughout, emphasis is placed on the idea that two extreme policies should be avoided: (1) software engineering standards are not isolated islands of practice that should be individually adopted; and (2) software engineering standards (even a single SDO's collection) are not a monolithic whole whereby a commitment to one requires a commitment to all of them. Instead, the book provides a middle course, allowing the selection of coherent subsets of standards, suitable for the achievement of goals specific to an organization.

WAYS TO VIEW
RELATIONSHIPS OF
STANDARDS

2

This chapter briefly describes two types of diagrams that are used throughout the book to discuss the relationships among the various standards. It also describes a set of software engineering "objects" that are used to classify the various standards.

A Layered View of Standards

One way to describe a collection of standards is with a layer diagram that proceeds from general considerations at the top and specific, detailed concerns at the bottom. Each layer is character- ized by the nature of the direction given by a standard at that level and their relationships to standards on other levels. A few organi- zations are already using this layered approach, including IEEE SESC and IEC TC56.[6] So, in some cases, it will be easy to fit the standards into the layered view. In other cases, judgment will be applied to superimpose the layering on a collection structured in some other way.

Figure 4 is an example of a layer diagram using a subset of the ISO 9000 series of standards as an example. Fundamental con- cepts are found at the top two levels. The top layer provides essen- tial terminology, vocabulary, and unifying concepts used by other standards in the collection. Typically, the documents in the top layer are standards. In many cases, the documents occupying this level are an integral part of the collection being described; in other cases, they are adopted from related collections. On the other hand, the second layer is typically a guide—often a single guide. It provides overall advice on how the other documents of the collection may be applied.

The third layer may consist of standards or guides. These documents specify the principles and objectives pursued by the col-

---

[6]In fact, TC56 developed the predecessor of the layer diagram, the "toolbox concept," to describe its own collection.

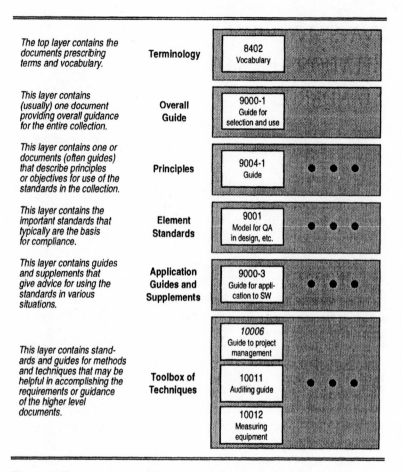

The top layer contains the documents prescribing terms and vocabulary.	**Terminology**	**8402** Vocabulary
This layer contains (usually) one document providing overall guidance for the entire collection.	**Overall Guide**	**9000-1** Guide for selection and use
This layer contains one or documents (often guides) that describe principles or objectives for use of the standards in the collection.	**Principles**	**9004-1** Guide • • •
This layer contains the important standards that typically are the basis for compliance.	**Element Standards**	**9001** Model for QA in design, etc. • • •
This layer contains guides and supplements that give advice for using the standards in various situations.	**Application Guides and Supplements**	**9000-3** Guide for application to SW • • •
This layer contains standards and guides for methods and techniques that may be helpful in accomplishing the requirements or guidance of the higher level documents.	**Toolbox of Techniques**	**10006** Guide to project management **10011** Auditing guide **10012** Measuring equipment • • •

Figure 4. Format of layer diagram using a subset of ISO 9000 as an example.

lection being described. There may be several such documents, specific to different subject areas of standards in the collection.

For those assessing conformance, the "meat" of a collection is found at the fourth level. These are the element standards that provide the basis for conformance. Often, there are several of these documents, depending on how the standards organization has chosen to subdivide their area of interest.

The fifth layer is a set of application guides and supplements. These documents interpret and elaborate how the element standards may be applied in various situations. In many cases, they are structured to provide insight regarding the intentions of the standards organization in creating the element standards. Sometimes they are descriptive rather than prescriptive. They should be used cautiously—in some cases, they have been mistakenly applied as replacements rather than supplements for the element standards.

The bottom layer may be regarded as a toolbox of techniques. These documents may be standards or guides and are intended to specify detailed requirements for specific techniques or methods that are referenced in the element standards. For example, an element standard might prescribe that reviews should be used to assess the progress of a software project. The toolbox level might provide one or more documents specifying detailed procedures for such reviews. One way to think of the tool box level is as a collection of subroutines that may be invoked from any of the other standards in the collection.

In some cases, it will be useful to mention incomplete standards that will eventually fit into a layered model. An incomplete standard is distinguished by italicization of its number, for example, 10006 in the example figure.

Layer diagrams are used throughout the book, typically to describe a collection of standards belonging to a single organization and to explain the relationships among the individual standards within the collection.

A Road Map View of Standards

The road map view is intended to assist readers in finding their way from a subject or concern outside of software engineering, that is, a contextual discipline, to those software engineering standards that directly contribute to the support of that discipline. Like the layer diagrams, the road maps will proceed from general concerns at the top to detailed standards at the bottom. Unlike the layer diagrams, a road map does not depict a single collection but instead make selections from one or more collections.

Another important difference is that the road maps are more selective than the layer diagrams. The intent of the layer diagram is to depict how every relevant standard within the collection of interest fits into the framework. On the other hand, the road maps are selective in several ways. First, only standards with a traceable relationship to software engineering are included. Second, only the significant relationships are depicted; even standards that are normatively referenced may be omitted if their contribution is minor relative to the ones that are shown. Finally, there is no attempt to integrate *all* of the contextual disciplines into one grand web of relationships. Each road map is intended to selectively explain the contributions of each individual discipline. It is left to the reader's good sense to conclude that, for example, both the quality management and the safety disciplines may be simultaneously applicable. This is not only convenient, but necessary. Only the business goals of a particular organization can determine, for example, if quality management is to be regarded as subsumed by project management or the other way around.

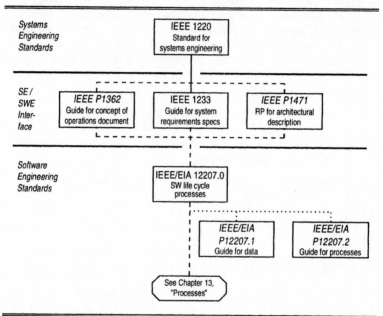

Figure 5. Example road map diagram.

The appearance of the lines between the boxes indicates the nature of the relationships between the standards. A solid line indicates a normative reference, that is, one of the documents specifically references the other one as a means of satisfying a requirement. A dotted line indicates that one document provides guidance to applying the other one. A dashed line means that, in the judgment of the author, the lower document would support implementing the requirements or accomplishing the intent of the upper one. Occasionally, an octagonal box is used to mark a relationship to another diagram. As in the layer diagram, italics are used to distinguish documents that are not yet completed. Figure 5 (borrowed from a later chapter) is an example, showing the connection from systems engineering standards to software engineering standards.

The road maps are used primarily in the six chapters describing the context of software engineering. They assist the reader in finding their way from a particular context to the software engineering standards supporting achievement of goals relevant to that context.

An Object-Oriented View of Standards

Another way to look at standards is to consider the "objects" of software engineering. By convention, software engineering is performed by a *project* consisting of a collection of *agents*, each having specified responsibilities. These agents interact with *customers* and use *resources* to perform *processes* producing *products*. Many of the standards deal with the objects and relationships shown in Figure 6.

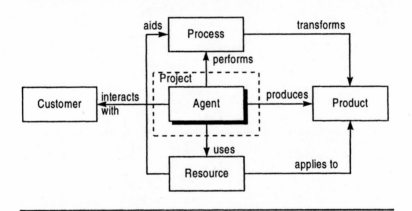

Figure 6. Objects of software engineering. (Source: Adapted from [SESC95])

SESC has chosen to organize its collection of standards around the four objects (Resource, Product, Process, and Customer) at the perimeter of the figure. In fact, the 1998 edition of the collection will be published as a set of four volumes with each volume devoted to one of the objects. Correspondingly, four chapters of this book, Chapters 11 through 14, address those objects.

US Standards Organizations

3

Unlike most countries, in the United States literally hundreds of trade associations, professional societies and other groups are permitted to make standards. Thousands of individuals and organizations voluntarily contribute their efforts to the development of standards. Most of these standards are developed as part of a voluntary system that is based on principles of due process, openness, and consensus [Baron95]. An important goal of the process is public confidence, not measured by market success, but by being "above reproach" in terms of being fairly developed and supported by consensus [Gibson95].

This chapter describes some[7] of the US organizations that make standards relevant to software engineering. A brief history of each organization will be provided along with an overview of its internal structure. Its collection of standards (at least those relevant to this book) will be summarized as well as its procedures for creating standards.

Because the IEEE Computer Society's Software Engineering Standards Committee is the principal US provider of software engineering standards, it will be treated in greater detail. The description will include the ways in which it has superimposed an organization upon its collection and its strategic plans for increasing the breadth and integration of its collection.

American National Standards Institute (ANSI)

The most important thing to know about the American National Standards Institute (ANSI) is *that it does not make standards*. It does provide other important services to the community of US standards developing organizations (SDO) [ANSI92].

---

[7][Magee97] references many more.

The successor of the American Engineering Standards Committee, formed in 1918, and the American Standards Association,[8] formed in 1928, ANSI is a private, non-profit, member-funded organization, that coordinates the development of voluntary US national standards and serves as the US national body to international standards organizations such as ISO and IEC [Cargill89]. ANSI is a federation of more than a thousand companies, hundreds of SDOs, and a few dozen government agencies.

The SDOs that are members of ANSI have the opportunity to submit their own standards for ANSI's approval as "American National Standards." A requirement of their membership is to follow an accredited process for the production of standards that is fair, consensus-based, and open to participation by all materially interested parties. Approval of a standard by ANSI implies only that the development process was judged to be properly applied; no technical judgment is involved. ANSI does not even check that the standard is within the scope of the submitting organization or that it is consistent with other national standards; it relies on declarations by the submitting organization.

Accredited standards developers may follow any one of three basic processes for the creation of standards:

- The Accredited Organization method is used by organizations, like the IEEE, that include standards-making among their various activities. "Usually an industry trade group or association of industry experts or participants, the [organization] often has extant standards that are based upon the methodologies of its profession or discipline" [Cargill97].

- The Accredited Standards Committee method is used for standing committees, like the National Committee for Information Technology Standards (NCITS),[9] of materially interested parties drawn from otherwise diverse backgrounds or organizations. "The ASC is formed for the specific purpose of creating standards in a contentious environment" [Cargill97].

- The Accredited Canvass method is typically used by small organizations which have documented an existing or planned practice and wish to have it recognized as a na-

---

[8]Those with long memories will recall the abbreviation, ASA, as a designation for film speed.

[9]Formerly known as X3.

tional standard. "The assumption is that a consensus on the proposed standard is extant; what is being sought is confirmation of consensus of impacted parties, and a demonstration of honest interest and intent in the standard" [Cargill97].

An organization using any of these methods may write their own procedures or use model procedures provided by ANSI. In any case, approval of the procedures is a requirement for ANSI accreditation.

ANSI provides a method for public notification that an accredited organization plans to develop a standard in a particular area. Using the Project Initiation Notification System (PINS), the developer places a notice in the ANSI publication, *Standards Reporter*.

On the completion of a standard, the developer submits it to the ANSI Board of Standards Review (BSR). Notification of this step is published in *Standards Reporter*, providing interested parties 4 months to make comment on the submission and appeal[10] if they feel that due process has not been observed. If no appeal is successfully pursued, BSR designates the document as an ANSI standard.

Different SDOs place varying value on the ANSI label. The American Institute of Aeronautics and Astronautics (AIAA) and the Electronic Industries Association (EIA), for example, are generally careful to prefix their designation of an approved standard with the label "ANSI". On the other hand, IEEE simply adds a legend to the cover saying that the document is "An American National Standard." Not all standards are submitted to ANSI for processing. The American Society for Testing and Materials (ASTM), a prolific SDO, submits few of its standards. Furthermore, some standards developers do not even belong to ANSI. One source, [Batik92], counted 571 US standards making organizations, of which only 260 belonged to ANSI.

ANSI serves as the US member body for participation in the International Organization for Standardization (ISO) and the International Electrotechnical Commission (IEC); all US Technical Advisory Groups (TAG) to these organizations operate under the procedures of ANSI. In some cases, ANSI itself administers the TAG; in other cases, administration is delegated to an SDO.

ANSI is the US distributor of the international standards developed by ISO and IEC, and European regional standards devel-

---

[10]Formal appeal is rare. It is more common for the submitting organization to revise the submission to deal with any comments.

oped by the European Committee for Standardization (CEN)[11] and the European Committee for Electrotechnical Standardization (CENELEC). Furthermore, ANSI receives a portion of the revenues resulting from the sales of American National Standards. This revenue is important for operating their standards activities. In all, ANSI finances about 28 percent of its operation from publication revenue.[12]

Some of the member organizations ([Magee97] lists additional ones) of ANSI responsible for the creation of standards relevant to software engineering are discussed in the following sections.

American Institute of Aeronautics and Astronautics (AIAA)

The American Institute of Aeronautics and Astronautics (AIAA) is the principal professional society serving the aerospace profession and counts 30,000 members worldwide. Its standards are oriented toward the particular requirements of aerospace but are sometimes applied more generally. Standards are created in Committees on Standards (COS) under the policy supervision of a Standards Executive Council (SEC) and the operational supervision of a Standards Technical Council (STC). The AIAA standards program is accredited by ANSI and AIAA participates in international standards activities [AIAA96].

Each of the 21 COS is assigned a particular scope of standards activity. To draft a standard within that scope, a COS creates an ad hoc Standards Working Group (SWG) consisting of experts from both inside and outside AIAA. The COS relevant to this book is Software Systems, responsible for the standardization of application-specific characteristics of computer software originating in aerospace.[13]

---

[11]The "N" stands for "normalisation," the French word for "standardization."

[12]Other SDOs also finance their standards development operations through sales of the documents. In some cases, the financial support is crucial. For example, ASTM receives 80 percent of its revenue in this manner [Cargill97].

[13]In addition, the Artificial Intelligence committee writes standards to promote the use of artificial intelligence and knowledge-based systems with emphasis on vocabulary, life cycle development, validation and verification, and software tools. The currently inactive Space-based Observation Systems COS was chartered for the

A draft standard is circulated to the members of the appropriate COS in a letter ballot. Changes are made in response to negative votes and the members are then permitted to change their vote upon recirculation of the draft. Most documents require a two-thirds vote for approval. If health, safety, or mission-critical issues are involved, the threshold for approval is raised to 90 percent along with a requirement to explain why any votes remain negative [AIAA92].

Public review of proposed standards actions coincides with COS balloting and is invited by notices published in *Aerospace America* and *ANSI Standards Action*. In some cases, the COS may supplement the public review with a review by selected interested parties or even with public hearings and workshops.

Following successful balloting, and approval by the STC, documents are submitted to ANSI for designation as national standards.

AIAA produces three types of standards documents; the letter prefixing the document's number indicates the type [AIAA92]:

- Standards (S): Documents that establish engineering and technical requirements for processes, procedures, practices, and methods. They contain the provisions necessary to verify compliance.

- Recommended Practices (R): Documents that contain authoritative engineering, technical or design information and data relating to processes, procedures, practices, and methods. They may evolve into standards through application and industry practice.

- Guides (G): Documents that contain technical information in support of Standards and Recommended Practices. Guides provide instructions and data for the application of standards and recommended practices, procedures, and methods. Handbooks are in this category as well as preliminary standards and recommended practices.

AIAA standards groups can also publish Special Project Reports (SP), sometimes as precursors to the other forms of documents, sometimes as proposed government standards or specifications. Special Project Reports are not subjected to the full consen-

---

standardization of planning and operational capabilities to help make satellite observation systems more effective; it was the original developer of AIAA R-013.

sus formation process. Any standard, recommended practice, or guide is reviewed once every 5 years by the committee that created it to determine if it should be revised, updated, reaffirmed, or canceled.

Some AIAA standards relevant to the subject of this book are listed in Table 2.

Table 2. AIAA Standards Relevant to Software Engineering

Standard	Title
AIAA G-010-1993	Guide for reusable software: Assessment criteria for aerospace applications
AIAA G-043-1992	Guide for the preparation of operations concept documents
AIAA R-013-1992	Recommended practice for software reliability

Electronic Industries Association (EIA)

Founded in 1924, the Electronic Industries Association (EIA) is a trade association representing a broad range of companies involved in US electronics manufacturing ranging from companies that produce small electronic parts to multinational corporations that design and manufacture complex systems used by industry, defense, space, and consumers. Although EIA is organized into groups along electronic product and market lines, its standards activities are supervised by a single staff organization, the Engineering Department Executive Committee (EDEC), reporting to the EIA Board of Governors. EIA is accredited by ANSI and participates in international standardization activities [EIA96].

EIA standards are developed within its 200 or so Engineering Committees and their subcommittees. Drafts are developed privately and are approved within the committee by a Committee Letter Ballot. If the document is intended to become an ANSI standard, the draft is then circulated as an industry-wide ballot, known as a "Standards Proposal," the so-called "Pink Ballot." Interested parties may purchase a copy of the ballot and cast a vote including comments. Comments are resolved and the draft is improved until an industry consensus is reached. The result is reviewed by EDEC to ensure that the requirements for due process have been met and then the standard is forwarded to the ANSI Board of Standards Review (BSR) for approval as a national standard. A national standard must be reviewed for currency every 5 years and may be reaffirmed, revised, or withdrawn.

EIA has a mechanism, called an "Interim Standard" (IS),[14] for the trial use of standards that are intended to be quickly revised.

Activities of two of EIA's groups are relevant to this book, the Electronic Information Group (EIG) and the Government Division. Within EIG, the CASE Data Interchange Format (CDIF) Division produces standards for the interchange of data among various computer-aided software and systems engineering tools (CASE) tools. Some of these standards are being promoted to international status through the work of ISO/IEC JTC1/SC7/WG11.

The members of EIA's Government Division are companies whose products are primarily designed and manufactured for the government market. Its Engineering and Operations Council (EOC) has the mission of promoting concurrent engineering approaches to technical issues and includes the 13 "G-Panel" engineering committees that develop some of the standards relevant to this book. Three of those committees are:

- G-33, Data and Configuration Management Committee

- G-34, Software Committee

- G-47, Systems Engineering Committee

Because of the Government Division's deep interest in the federal marketplace, its standards activities have been closely coordinated with the military standards of the Department of Defense (DoD). When the DoD announced in 1994 its intention to decrease reliance on military standards and correspondingly increase the emphasis on commercial standards, EIA launched several programs to cast the best of the military standards into commercial form. In many cases, this has resulted in the creation of an interim standard (IS), a quick rewrite of the military standard, followed by a longer-term project to create a true commercial standard. Table 3 lists some of the current and planned EIA standards along with their military ancestors.

The table indicates that IEEE is cooperating with EIA in the development of J-Std-016. In addition, EIA is cooperating with the IEEE in the US adaptation of ISO/IEC 12207, a standard to be designated as IEEE/EIA 12207.

---

[14]EIA's use of "IS" for Interim Standard should not be confused with ISO's use of "IS" to mean International Standard. This book will avoid the latter usage.

Table 3. Current and Planned EIA Standards Related to Software
Engineering

Mil-Std Predecessor	Interim EIA Standard	Title of Interim Standard	Project for Planned Standard	EIA Committee
Mil-Std 973	EIA/IS-649	Configuration management	PN-3721	G-33
Mil-Std 498	EIA/IS-640	Software development— Acquirer-supplier agreement (EIA/IEEE J-Std-016)	PN-3764	G-34
Mil-Std 499B	EIA/IS-632	Systems engineering	PN-3537	G-47

Institute of Electrical and Electronics Engineers (IEEE)

The Institute of Electrical and Electronics Engineers (IEEE) is the world's largest technical professional society with membership numbering more than 320,000 individuals in nearly 150 countries. The organization claims to publish nearly 25 percent of the world's technical papers in the scope described by its name [IEEE97].

The IEEE is organized into 37 Technical Societies, some of which are active in developing standards, including the Computer Society and the Power Engineering Society. Organizations at three different levels within the IEEE are responsible for the development of standards. First, at the IEEE level, the Standards Board is responsible for the encouragement, coordination and supervision of all IEEE standards activities. Second, a number of "sponsors" have a defined scope of interest in which they may develop standards; most sponsors are within the various Technical Societies. Finally, "working groups" are ad hoc committees that are authorized to draft or revise a standard falling within the scope of a particular sponsor. Because IEEE is a professional society, participants in IEEE standards-making generally represent only themselves, not their employers or any other organization.

IEEE produces three types of standards (with a lowercase "s") documents—Standards (with a capital "S"), Recommended Practices, and Guides. The different types of standards are differentiated by the degree of prescription in their normative requirements. IEEE Standards contain mandatory requirements, generally characterized by the use of the verb "shall." Recommended Practices (RP) present procedures and positions preferred by the IEEE; they are characterized by the use of the verb "should." Guides suggest alternative approaches to good practice but generally refrain from clear-cut recommendations; they are characterized by the use of the verb "may" [IEEE97a]. It is important to note, though, that any of the three documents can contain any of the three verb forms. Therefore it is possible to claim conformance with any of the three types of documents, although, in the case of a Guide or even an RP, the claim may not be a strong one.

IEEE can produce any of the three types of documents on a "Trial Use" basis. Trial Use standards are approved for a period of two years. At the end of this period, they may be administratively promoted to full use or returned to the sponsor for revision based on comments received during the trial use period.

The numbering of IEEE standards can seem a little complicated. In principle (although there are exceptions), the base number assigned to an IEEE standard has no meaning and the number's relationship to other numbers is not meant to suggest any relationships among the standards. Relationships among standards may be indicated by appending a part number to the base number. For example, standard "123.1" would be related to the "123" standard. It is also possible to add a supplement to an existing standard with the intention that the supplement eventually will be merged with the base standard. Supplements are indicated by appending a letter to the number. For example, standard "123a" would be regarded as a supplement, a logical part of, the "123" standard.

Standards development projects which have not yet reached final approval are indicated by the presence of a "P" before the number, indicating that the number denotes a "project" rather than a completed standard. One may also find the notation "(R)" following the number of an IEEE standard; this simply denotes a project to revise an existing standard.

The formal IEEE process for developing a standard is delimited by two actions of the IEEE Standards Board: approval of the Project Authorization Request (PAR), resulting in the assignment of a P-number to the project; and approval of the final standard for publication, at which point the "P" is removed from the number. The duration of the intervening period is generally limited to 4 years, although extensions may be granted. During this period the sponsor is responsible for developing a document satisfying the purpose, scope and other characteristics described in the PAR. Typically, the sponsor accomplishes this goal by creating a Working Group, within which individuals openly and publicly collaborate on a consensus basis to create a draft of a suitable standard. Following the preparation of the draft, a *sponsor ballot* is conducted among a larger group (perhaps the entire membership of the sponsor) to broaden the consensus and improve of the draft. The sponsor ballot may be repeated if necessary as the document is improved to address the concerns of the balloting group. A draft document cannot pass sponsor ballot unless 75 percent of the ballots are returned and the document is approved by 75 percent of those voting. (In practice, higher rates of approval are often demanded by the Standards Board.) Following successful sponsor ballot, the standard is submitted to the IEEE Standards Board for approval and publication.

Approved IEEE standards are usually submitted to ANSI for endorsement as US national standards. Approval is typically routine. IEEE standards are sometimes submitted to international bodies as a basis for their own standardization activities. In turn, IEEE sometimes adopts international standards—with or without adaptation to the specific concerns of IEEE.

An approved IEEE standard has a life of 5 years. At the end of that time it must be reviewed with one of three results: withdrawal, reaffirmation (without change), or revision. Revision is performed by a working group using a process very similar to that for writing a new standard [IEEE95].

IEEE Computer Society Software Engineering Standards Committee (SESC)

The IEEE Computer Society is the largest association for computer professionals in the world. Founded 50 years ago, it is now the largest of the technical societies of IEEE, an organization involved in standards-making for nearly 100 years.

Any Computer Society standards project is assigned to one of a dozen or so sponsors; a project transcending the scope of any particular sponsor is supervised by the Standards Coordinating Committee, the parent body of the sponsor groups. For software engineering standards, the sponsor is the Software Engineering Standards Committee (SESC).

History

SESC traces its roots back two decades to the creation of the Software Engineering Standards Subcommittee (SESS) in 1976. Its first standard, IEEE Std 730, Software Quality Assurance, was published on a trial use basis 3 years later. By 1997, the collection had grown to 44 documents. In addition to the development of standards, SESC sponsors or cooperates in annual US or international conferences and workshops regarding software engineering standards.

SESC cooperates with international standards-making as a member of the US Technical Advisory Group (TAG) to ISO/IEC JTC1/SC7. (In addition, IEEE is the organization responsible for administering the TAG.)

Through Memoranda of Agreement or other mechanisms, SESC cooperates with other international and US standards-related organizations such as EIA, PMI, Standards Australia, and the US Department of Defense. SESC also works closely with the Technical Council on Software Engineering (TCSE) of the IEEE Computer Society.

Organization

The mission of SESC [SESC96] is:

> *To develop and maintain a family of software engineering standards that are relevant, coherent, comprehensive and effective in use. These standards are for use by practitioners, organizations, and educators to improve the effectiveness and efficiency of their software engineering processes, to improve communications between acquirers and suppliers, and to improve the quality of delivered software and systems containing software.*

The management of SESC is performed by a Chair and an Executive Committee that meets periodically to conduct the business of the SESC. In addition, SESC has an elected five-member Management Board. Each member of the Management Board serves as the point-of-contact for several of the working groups, planning groups, steering committees, etc.

Like most sponsors, the drafting of standards documents in SESC is performed by working groups. In other sponsors, working groups are formed at the recognition of a "good idea" by a number of interested people. Although good ideas remain welcome, SESC has formed a number of planning groups to systematically investigate areas that are strongly related within the discipline as well as areas that cut across other areas of software engineering. The planning groups active during 1996 are listed in Table 4. Each planning group surveys user needs, the existing base of standards, and technological trends in arriving at recommendations to create new standards, adopt or revise existing ones, or withdraw obsolescent ones. Working groups are often initiated as the result of planning group recommendations.

Table 4. SESC Planning Groups in 1996

Architecture	Software Reliability
Formal Methods	Software Reuse
Integral Processes	Software Safety
Object-Oriented Methods	Software Testing
Process Maturity	Specification Processes
Process Measurement	Software Risk Management
Software Criticality	User Documentation

To ensure that each working group remains consistent with its PAR and with planning group recommendations, a series of milestone reviews examine the progress of the working group. During 1996, approximately a dozen working groups were engaged in the drafting of new standards and another ten or so were revising existing standards.

To deal with multiple working groups working in closely related areas, the SESC has developed the concept of a Steering Committee and has applied it for the first time in 1996. The Reuse Steering Committee will execute the recommendations of the Reuse Planning Group by coordinating half a dozen working groups in areas related to software reuse and reuse libraries.

Current Collection of SESC

The SESC currently maintains the inventory of nearly fifty standards listed in several tables beginning at Table 5. The tables classify the standards into several categories used by the SESC's most recent program plan [SESC97]. The identification of each IEEE standard carries the date on which it was originally approved. The date of reaffirmation, if any, is indicated with an "R" and enclosed in parentheses.

Table 5. Current IEEE SESC Standards for Project Management

IEEE Standard	Title
IEEE Std 1044-1993	Standard classification for software anomalies
IEEE Std 1044.1-1995	Guide to classification for software anomalies
IEEE Std 1058.1-1987 (R1993)	Standard for software project management plans

The first category of standards, shown in Table 5, are the SESC standards for the management of software projects. Table 6 lists the IEEE standards that specify the contents of various plans useful in software development. It should be noted that process requirements are often implicit in the required contents of the plans.

Table 6. Current IEEE SESC Standards for Plans

IEEE Standard	Title
IEEE Std 730-1989	Standard for software quality assurance plans
IEEE Std 730.1-1995	Guide for software quality assurance planning
IEEE Std 828-1990	Standard for software configuration management plans
IEEE Std 1012-1986 (R1992)	Standard for software verification and validation plans
IEEE Std 1228-1994	Standard for software safety plans
See also IEEE Std 1058.1 under project management.	

Table 7. Current IEEE SESC Standards for Life Cycle Processes

IEEE Standard	Title
IEEE Std 1074-1995	Standard for developing software life cycle processes
IEEE Std 1074.1-1995	Guide for developing software life cycle processes
IEEE Std 1220-1994	(Trial-use) Standard for the application and management of the systems engineering process
IEEE/EIA Std 12207.0-1996	Standard for software life cycle processes
EIA/IEEE J-Std-016-1995	(Trial use) Standard software life cycle processes—Software development: Acquirer-supplier agreement

Table 8. Current IEEE SESC Standards for Individual Processes

IEEE Standard	Title
IEEE Std 1008-1987 (R1993)	Standard for software unit testing
IEEE Std 1028-1988 (R1993)	Standard for software reviews and audits
IEEE Std 1042-1987 (R1993)	Guide to software configuration management
IEEE Std 1059-1993	Guide for software verification and validation plans
IEEE Std 1062-1993	Recommended practice for software acquisition
IEEE Std 1219-1992	Standard for software maintenance
IEEE Std 1298-1992	Software quality management system—Part 1: Requirements [Adoption of the Australian AS 3563.1-1991]

The SESC standards shown in Table 7 prescribe requirements for software life cycle processes. More detailed requirements for some of the life cycle processes are specified in the standards listed in Table 8.

Table 9. Current IEEE SESC Standards for Documentation

IEEE Standard	Title
IEEE Std 829-1983 (R1991)	Standard for software test documentation
IEEE Std 830-1993	Recommended practice for software requirements specifications
IEEE Std 1016-1987 (R1993)	Recommended practice for software design descriptions
IEEE Std 1016.1-1993	Guide to software design descriptions
IEEE Std 1063-1987 (R1993)	Standard for software user documentation
IEEE Std 1233-1996	Guide for developing system requirements specifications

Table 10. Current IEEE SESC Standards for Measurement

IEEE Standard	Title
IEEE Std 982.1-1988	Standard dictionary of measures to produce reliable software
IEEE Std 982.2-1988	Guide for the use of standard dictionary of measures to produce reliable software
IEEE Std 1045-1992	Standard for software productivity metrics
IEEE Std 1061-1992	Standard for a software quality metrics methodology

Table 11. Current IEEE SESC Standards for Tools

IEEE Standard	Title
IEEE Std 1175-1992	Standard reference model for computing system tool interconnections
IEEE Std 1209-1992	Recommend practice for the evaluation and selection of CASE tools
IEEE Std 1348-1995	Recommended practice for the adoption of computer-aided software engineering (CASE) tools

Some SESC standards, shown in Table 9, provide requirements for the documentation of software systems. Interest is growing in systematic measurement of the processes and products of software development. The SESC standards listed in Table 10 are useful for that purpose.

Tooling is often regarded as important to development productivity, but the tools must work together. The standards listed in Table 11 provide assistance in this area.

SESC provides a suite of standards related to reuse library interoperability, so that users are easily able to find and utilize the resources of several libraries. These standards are listed in Table 12.

Table 12. Current IEEE SESC Standards for Reuse

IEEE Standard	Title
IEEE Std 1420.1-1995	Software reuse—Data model for reuse library interoperability: Basic interoperability data model (BIDM)
IEEE Std 1420.1a-1996	Supplement to software reuse—Data model for reuse library interoperability: Asset certification framework
IEEE Std 1430-1996	Guide to software reuse—Concept of operations for interoperating reuse libraries

Finally, Table 13 lists SESC standards providing a glossary of software engineering terms and a taxonomy of software engineering standards.

Table 13. Other Current IEEE SESC Standards

IEEE Standard	Title
IEEE Std 610.12-1990	Standard glossary of software engineering terminology
IEEE Std 1002-1987 (R1992)	Standard taxonomy for software engineering standards

Planned Collection of SESC

IEEE SESC has a number of projects underway to revise and extend their collection, as shown in Table 14 through Table 23 [SESC97]. (Following the general convention for tables and figures in this book, the numbers of any draft standards are noted by the use of italics in these tables.) An IEEE project may be established to write a new standard, revise an existing standard, reaffirm an existing standard without changes, or withdraw an existing one. SESC generally avoids reaffirmation ballots because a successful reaffirmation inherently requires ignoring comments that would improve the document.

Table 14 shows that the planned revision of the 1058.1 standard on project management may be renumbered. Since only one part exists, the part number ".1," is unnecessary. SESC is also considering adopting as an IEEE standard the Project Management Institute's, Guide to the Project Management Body of Knowledge.

Table 14. Planned IEEE SESC Standards for Project Management

Project	Revision or New	Planned Title
P1058.1 (R)	Rev*	Standard for software project management plans
P1491	New	Adoption of the PMI standard, Guide to the project management body of knowledge
*This revision of 1058.1 may be given the number 1058.		

The currently ongoing revision of the 1012 standard on Software Verification and Validation (V & V) plans, listed in Table 15, will describe how V & V activities are affected by the "criticality" of the planned software, that is, the risks of failure and the consequences of failure.

Table 15. Planned IEEE SESC Standards for Plans

Project	Revision or New	Planned Title
P1012 (R)	Rev	Standard for software verification and validation plans
See also P1058.1 (R) under project management.		

Table 16. Planned IEEE SESC Standards for the Life Cycle

Project	Revision or New	Planned Title
P1074 (R)	Rev	Standard for developing software life cycle processes
P1220 (R)	Rev*	Standard for the application and management of the systems engineering process
P12207.1 (P1448.1)	New†	Guide—Software life cycle processes—Life cycle data
P12207.2 (P1448.2)	New†	Guide—Software life cycle processes—Implementation considerations
*The transition to a full-use standard involves revision to accommodate comments received during the trial use period. †Under development jointly with EIA. The IEEE project number is 1448 even though the standard will ultimately be designated as 12207.		

The revisions to the collection of the life cycle standards, Table 16, will complete a set providing comprehensive standards for planning and implementing system and software life cycle processes encompassing operations and maintenance as well as acquisition, supply and development. The planned revision to the 1028 standard for reviews (see Table 17) will change the standard to better integrate into the process structure of 12207.

Table 17. Planned IEEE SESC Standards for Processes

Project	Revision or New	Planned Title
P1028 (R)	Rev	Standard for software review processes

A new standard for Concept of Operation documents, listed in Table 18, will extend the standardized suite of software documents to the interface of systems engineering with software engineering.

Table 18. Planned IEEE SESC Standards for Documentation

Project	Revision or New	Planned Title
P1362	New	System definition—Concept of operation document

Table 19 shows that IEEE plans to revise its documents regarding software reliability measures. The intention is to add criteria for inclusion in the dictionary, examine the existing items for conformance to the criteria, and add new items that have appeared in the literature since the documents were last published.

Table 19. Planned IEEE SESC Standards for Measurement

Project	Revision or New	Planned Title
P982.1(R)	Rev	Standard dictionary of measures to produce reliable software
P982.2(R)	Rev	Guide for the use of standard dictionary of measures to produce reliable software

The new notation standards, listed in Table 20, will provide standard specifications for the popular IDEF0 modeling notation and the IDEF1X97 extension of that notation. Work has also begun on a method or notation for describing system and software architectures.

Table 20. Planned IEEE SESC Standards for Notation

Project	Revision or New	Planned Title
P1320.1	New	Standard syntax and semantics for the integrated computer aided manufacturing (ICAM) definition language—function modeling (IDEF0)
P1320.1.1	New	Standard user's manual for the ICAM function modeling method (IDEF0)
P1320.2	New	Standard Syntax and semantics for the ICAM definition language—Information modeling extended (IDEF1X97)
P1320.2.1	New	Standard User's Manual for the ICAM definition language—Information modeling method (IDEF1X97)
P1471	New	Recommended practice for system design—Architectural description

Table 21 indicates that the 1175 standard for the interconnection of tools will be revised. SESC is also considering the adoption of ISO/IEC 14102 on CASE tool selection.

Table 21. Planned IEEE SESC Standards for Tools

Project	Revision or New	Planned Title
P1175 (R)	Rev	Standard reference model for computing system tool interconnection
P1462	New	Adoption of ISO/IEC 14102, Guideline for the evaluation and selection of CASE tools

Table 22. Planned IEEE SESC Standards for Reuse

Project	Revision or New	Planned Title
P1420.1b	New	Software reuse—Data model for reuse library interoperability: Intellectual property rights framework
P1420.2	New	Software reuse—Data model for reuse library interoperability: Bindings to HTML and SGML
P1420.3	New	Software reuse—Data model for reuse library interoperability: Model extensions

The new standards listed in Table 22 will complete the planned suite of reuse library interoperability standards by extending the data model to encompass information about intellectual property rights, by explaining how the model may be represented in Hypertext Markup Language (HTML) and Standard Generalized Markup Language (SGML), and by explaining how additional extensions to the model may be made.

Table 23 depicts a change in the management of the glossary of software engineering terms. IEEE Std 610 will continue to be an overall glossary of computing and Part 12 of that standard will continue to deal with software engineering. SESC, however, will create and maintain its own standard, 729, to record new glossary entries as they are coined in new and revised SESC standards. Periodically, the contents of 729 will be considered for "promotion" into IEEE Std 610.

Table 23. Other Planned IEEE SESC Standards

Project	Revision or New	Planned Title
P729	New	Standard for software engineering—Fundamental terms
P1465	New	Adoption of ISO/IEC 12119, Software packages—Quality requirements and testing

The table also shows that IEEE is considering the adoption of ISO/IEC 12119, prescribing requirements for consumer software packages, including their documentation.

Organization of the SESC Collection

The SESC collection has grown large enough that users can no longer be expected to intuitively perceive the relationships among the various component standards. In attempting to articulate overall organizing concepts as well as relationships to other collections of standards, the SESC strategy statement [SESC95] formulated the diagram of Figure 7. The various parts of the figure may look familiar to the reader—they roughly mirror the organization of this book. In fact, this book is intended for use as the "Overall Guide" shown in the figure. The boxes to the left of the dashed line are, with the exception of "Software Engineering," the various "Contexts" that are described in Chapters 5-10. The shaded box in the right-hand portion of Figure 7 is the inspiration for the layer diagrams that are used throughout this book, for other disciplines as well as for software engineering standards. The four shaded columns correspond to the "Objects" of software engineering that were introduced in Figure 6; those objects are the subjects of Chapters 11-14. Unlike the SESC figure, this book does not treat the ISO/IEC JTC1 software engineering standards as part of the context, but (somewhat idealistically) as part of the same collection as the SESC standards.

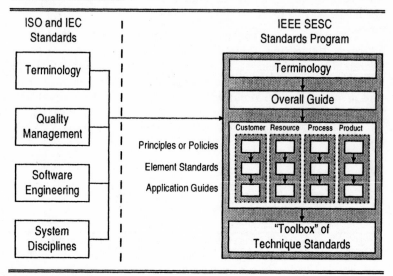

Figure 7. Elements of the SESC program plan. (Source: Adapted from [SESC95].)

Of course, it is quicker to plan an architecture than to implement it, and standards are no exception. This elegant architecture of standards remains an objective for the SESC rather than a reality. Figure 8 depicts the current (and near-term planned) state of the outer layers of the architecture. The inner layers will be detailed in the four diagrams that follow. As in all of the diagrams and tables in this book, the use of italics indicates that a document is only a draft.

It is important to note that this architecture has been superimposed on the SESC collection. In some cases, it is a "force fit." As SESC continues its strategic efforts, the architecture will be more neatly and completed populated.

There are two important terminology standards plus one that is now mainly of historical interest. IEEE 610 is a multi-part glossary of engineering terminology; Part 12 is the section specific to software engineering. Previously, the various parts of this glossary were administered in a decentralized fashion by the various sponsors—an arrangement that valued currency above consistency. IEEE has now decided to administer the standard centrally. SESC has decided that it needs an additional glossary to responsively capture its own evolving terminology and to form the basis for submissions to the more slowly evolving 610.12. That additional glossary will be designated 729. IEEE 1002 was an early attempt at a strategic organization of the SESC collection—an approach now largely superceded by others.

IEEE 1044 and its companion guide, 1044.1, provide a method for classifying software anomalies. The method is clearly applicable during software integration and for tracking failures after operational deployment of the software. Some users, though, might find it useful throughout the development and maintenance cycles. Therefore, it is positioned in the "toolbox" of broadly applicable techniques.

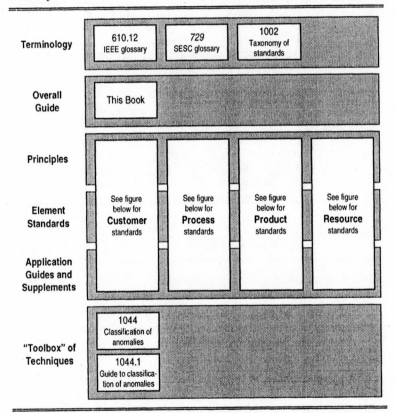

Figure 8. Outer layers of the SESC collection.

The customer "stack" of the SESC collection is depicted in Figure 9. SESC strategy documents, for example, [SESC96a], subdivide the subject into several areas: two-party agreement, contractor and supplier selection, and system stakeholders.

Aside from military standards, customer-oriented standards for software are a relatively new phenomenon, so this part of the collection is small. As explained in the chapter on customer interaction, Chapter 14, the US adaptation of ISO/IEC 12207 is a key standard prescribing the relationship of a software project to its customer. The initial part of this standard, IEEE/EIA Std 12207.0, has added material prescribing objectives for the software life cycle processes, including the acquisition and supply processes. The planned Parts 1 and 2 of the standard (shown in italics to note their draft status) are guides providing additional material related to life cycle data and process implementation.

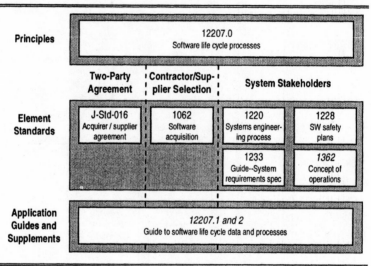

Figure 9. Inner layers of the customer "stack" of the SESC collection.

EIA/IEEE J-Std-016 is a "demilitarized" version of a Defense Department standard and focuses directly on the nature of the relationship of the developer to the customer in a complex software development program.

The process stack of the SESC collection is shown in Figure 10. (Incomplete drafts are marked by italics.) The process objectives of 12207.0 are the source of the principles that many of the standards would detail. For purposes of summary exposition at this point, four categories of process standards have been abstracted from the eight categories used in [SESC96a]. The category of General Processes encompasses the overall software life cycle (SWLC) as well as closely related enveloping processes such as systems engineering and project management. The Primary Processes are from ISO/IEC

12207: acquisition, supply, development, operation, and mainte-nance. The Supporting Processes contribute to the execution of the primary processes. Finally, Process Measurement cuts across all of these processes. The relationships among these standards will be explained in the chapter on processes, Chapter 13.

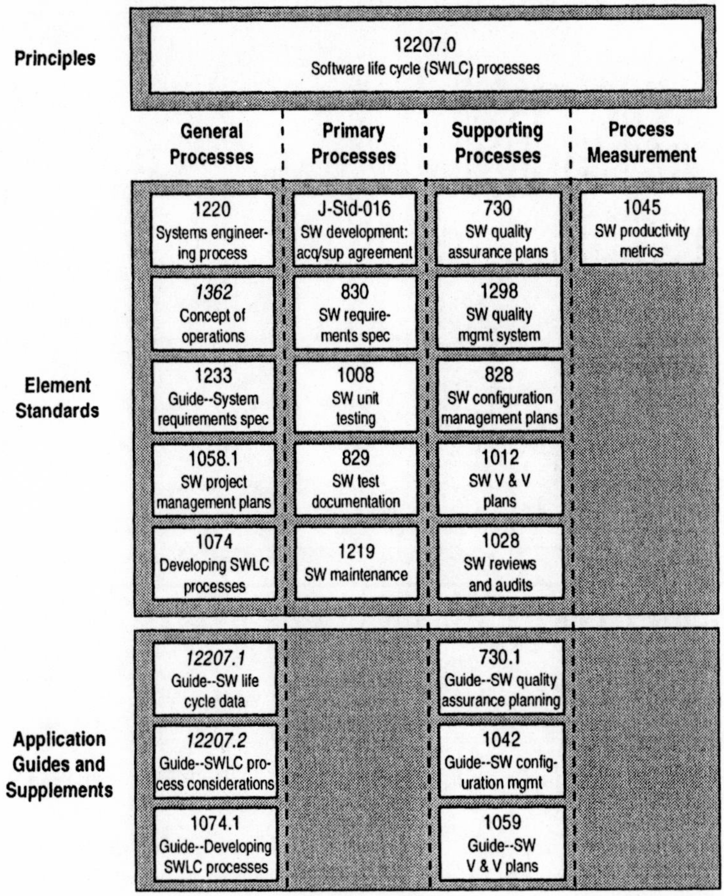

	General Processes	Primary Processes	Supporting Processes	Process Measurement
Principles	12207.0 Software life cycle (SWLC) processes			
Element Standards	1220 Systems engineering process	J-Std-016 SW development: acq/sup agreement	730 SW quality assurance plans	1045 SW productivity metrics
	1362 Concept of operations	830 SW requirements spec	1298 SW quality mgmt system	
	1233 Guide--System requirements spec	1008 SW unit testing	828 SW configuration management plans	
	1058.1 SW project management plans	829 SW test documentation	1012 SW V & V plans	
	1074 Developing SWLC processes	1219 SW maintenance	1028 SW reviews and audits	
Application Guides and Supplements	12207.1 Guide--SW life cycle data		730.1 Guide--SW quality assurance planning	
	12207.2 Guide--SWLC process considerations		1042 Guide--SW configuration mgmt	
	1074.1 Guide--Developing SWLC processes		1059 Guide--SW V & V plans	

Figure 10. Inner layers of the process "stack" of the SESC collection.

Figure 11 shows the Product "stack" of the SESC collection. Software engineering standards have traditionally focused on proc-ess standards, so it is not surprising that this section of the collec-tion is relatively sparse. There is no standard providing overall principles. The element standards and their guides have been force-fitted into four categories: Characteristics, Product Measurement, Product Evaluation Process, and End-Item Specification. Many of these documents are listed in other stacks, but are also listed here because they have something to contribute to this relatively new area of emphasis. Chapter 12, on software engineering product standards, explores this area more deeply.

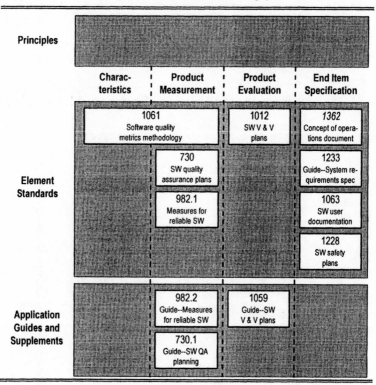

Figure 11. Inner layers of the product "stack" of the SESC collection.

Finally, Figure 12, illustrates the Resource "stack" of the SESC collection. (Standards existing only as drafts are noted with italics.) This category encompasses several independently written standards that are grouped into four sets: Data Storage and Interchange, Notation, Reuse Libraries, and Tools and Environments. Prospects are good for increased integration of these standards. The 1420 family, along with 1430, will provide an integrated collection of standards for the interoperation of software reuse libraries. Similarly, the 1320 family, will provide standards and guides for using the IDEF0 and IDEF1X97 notations for both data and process description. The Computer-Aided Software Engineering (CASE) tools standards are being developed in close cooperation with a working group of ISO/IEC JTC1/SC7 with the goal of consistency within the standards and between the two standards organizations. It is reasonable to expect that each of these families may someday contribute a document at the principle level. The relationships among these standards are more completely described in the chapter on resources, Chapter 11.

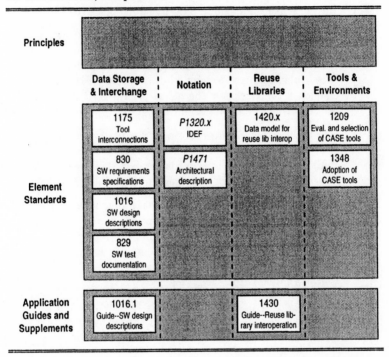

Figure 12. Inner layers of the resource "stack" of the SESC collection.

Strategic Plans

Because of the broad scope of SESC, and because of the desire to better integrate the body of knowledge for software engineering, SESC has adopted a number of management structures and planning instruments to supplement those typically used by sponsors.

Beginning early in the decade of the 1990s, the SESC initiated a set of long-range planning activities with the ultimate intention of reorganizing itself and its collection to better achieve its mission:

- A survey of existing software engineering standards that discovered 220 standards, guides, handbooks and other normative documents maintained by 46 different organizations worldwide [SESC94].

- A master plan that examined the need for practice standardization from the customer viewpoint, resulting in the formulation of: 370 customer expectations allocated to 18 different classes of customers; a set of 58 general requirements and constraints for software engineering standards; and a planning framework of 26 software engineering processes encompassing a total of 165 objectives [SESC93].

- A conceptual model for practice standards designating four key concepts of customer, resource, process, and product; a fifth concept, project, that applies the other four; and the key relationships among the concepts [SESC95]. This model is the basis for the object-oriented view of software engineering standards used throughout this book.

- Designation of four program elements, corresponding to the four key concepts, and a forced distribution of the existing inventory of standards among those program elements for purposes of management [SESC95, SESC96a].

- A planning framework that, externally, relates the program elements to over-arching standards and international standards, and, internally, explains the role of policy standards, element standards, guides, and technique standards [SESC95]. This model is the basis for layered view of standards applied throughout this book.

- Strategic product plans for both SESC and related international standards that provide a context for planning at a level higher than individual standard development efforts [SESC96a].

These strategic efforts will never actually end. The rapidly changing environment of information technology serves to destabilize long-range plans as quickly as they can be developed. So, in a very real sense, the SESC collection will never reach a goal of complete integration; it can only more closely pursue an always moving target.

For the foreseeable future (the remainder of this decade), SESC plans a set of specific strategies to provide users with a more integrated and usable collection:

- Architectural coherence

- Uniform process framework based on ISO/IEC 12207

- Emphasis on organizationally adopted processes

- Strategic alliances with related disciplines

- A clearer relationship between system and software disciplines

Architectural coherence: As SESC manages the evolution of its collection, it will apply its planning and management methods to better ensure that revised and new standards fit more neatly and clearly into the architecture described in the preceding section. In particular, emphasis will be placed on the creation of the "policy and principles" standards that serve to motivate and explain the other standards in each category of the collection.

Uniform process framework: Fundamental to the coherence of the collection is agreement on the terminology for the processes that contribute to the life cycle of software and systems development. Formal standards and accepted practice have for a long time been in substantive agreement on this framework but documents have exhibited capricious and bothersome differences in terminology. SESC has decided to adopt the process framework provided by ISO/IEC 12207 and to apply that framework in all new and revised standards.

Organizational processes: It has become clear that the most capable of organizations do not invent new software processes for each new project. Instead, they have a sound basis of organizational processes that are adapted and applied to the specific requirements of each new project. Therefore, the focus for the application of best practices, including software engineering standards, must be at the organizational level rather than at the project level. Furthermore, best practices must be specified and applied, not individually, but rather as a coordinated collection. To meet this need, SESC plans the development of a new concept of conformance, a concept that applies at the organizational level to the adoption of a coordinated body of standard practices that encompass the entire software systems life cycle.

Strategic alliances: As the integrated suite of software engineering standards becomes more comprehensive, it is inevitable that it intersects with other disciplines. We must address the question of whether, for example, to write a narrow standard regarding software project management or to adopt an existing, broader standard on general project management. SESC has chosen to seek out strategic alliances with organizations writing standards in the various areas that form the context of software engineering. Many of these standards are described in Chapters 5-10 of this book, the chapters concerning the context of software engineering.

System-software relationships: The extension of SESC standards to increasingly complex systems has served to emphasize the importance of the relationships between systems and software engineering. Some SESC efforts, such as the Concept of Operations document and the System Requirements Specification, directly address this interface when concepts are well understood. Some of the interfaces, though, are the subject of disagreement. For example, SESC planning efforts have shown that responsible professionals disagree on whether the concept of "software safety" makes any sense—some claiming that only system-level analysis is meaningful and others claiming that a body of software techniques should be articulated and systematically applied in conjunction with the system analysis. In the face of such fundamental disagreements, progress is made slowly and relationships must be carefully articulated. Despite the obstacles, the body of standardized knowledge is growing. IEEE 1228 is a start on the unification of a codified body of knowledge for the software aspects of systems safety. Recent Nuclear Regulatory Commission (NRC) regulations have recognized the role that software standards may play in assuring sound systems design.

IEEE Power Engineering Society Nuclear Power Engineering Committee

The scope of the IEEE's Power Engineering Society encompasses all engineering aspects of the safe, reliable, and economic generation, transmission, distribution, conversion, measurement, and control of electrical energy. The creation of appropriate standards is clearly an important activity. The sponsor for these activities is the Power Engineering Society Standards Coordinating Committee. The standards are actually drafted, though, by any of 14 Technical Committees within the Society's Technical Council. This text is specifically concerned with the Nuclear Power Engineering Committee which has drafted relevant standards concerning the use of software within the systems of nuclear power plants. The standards relevant to this book are listed in Table 24.

Table 24. IEEE Nuclear Power Engineering Standards Relevant to Software Engineering

IEEE Standard	Title
603-1991	Standard criteria for safety systems for nuclear power generating stations
7-4.3.2-1993	Standard criteria for digital computers in safety systems of nuclear power generating stations

IEEE Std 603 provides general requirements for safety systems while IEEE Std 7-4.3.2 expands on the general requirements for those cases when computers and software are used in the safety systems [Matras95].

International Council on Systems Engineering (INCOSE)

The International Council on Systems Engineering (INCOSE) is an international organization formed to develop, nurture, and enhance the system engineering approach to multi-disciplinary system development. Although it is not an accredited US standards development organization, it does inform its members regarding the development of relevant standards and encourages them to participate. As of April 1996, INCOSE had formed six Technical Committees, further subdivided into Working Groups and Interest Groups. The Standards and Handbook Working Group of the Systems Engineering Management Technical Committee has the responsibilities to: collect and disseminate information on relevant standards; formulate and coordinate INCOSE positions on those standards; and recommend INCOSE endorsement of standards representing "World Class Systems Engineering." This Working Group holds membership and sends representatives to the EIA committee drafting the revision of the current EIA/IS-632 standard for systems engineering [INCOSE97].

Project Management Institute (PMI)

The Project Management Institute (PMI) was founded in 1969 to promote professionalism in project management. It has since grown to a world-wide membership of nearly 25,000. It provides educational programs, a professional certification program called the Project Management Professional (PMP), and a code of ethics. PMI members can choose to join any of 16 specific interest groups (SIGs) including, for example: Aerospace and Defense; Government; and Information Systems [PMI97].

An enduring interest of PMI has been the collection of a generally accepted body of knowledge which is tangibly represented by their 1996 standard, A Guide to the Project Management Body of Knowledge [PMI96], a revision of a slightly differently titled document first published 9 years prior. Although PMI uses an open, consensus-based process, it is not accredited by ANSI to develop national standards, instead representing its interests through accredited standards committee XK36.3 [Toth96]. Recently, PMI entered into a memorandum of agreement with the IEEE Computer Society to adopt its Guide as an IEEE standard.

Reuse Library Interoperability Group (RIG)

The Reuse Library Interoperability Group (RIG) was formed in 1991 as a volunteer, consensus-based organization to draft standards for the interoperability of software reuse libraries (*not* the same thing as the interoperability of the software components in the library). Because RIG was not an accredited standards developer, it entered into an agreement in 1994 with the IEEE SESC for processing RIG proposals into formal IEEE standards. By the end of 1996, the RIG deemed its mission to have been completed and transferred the responsibility for maintenance of the standards to the newly formed Reuse Steering Committee of the SESC. The various IEEE standards and projects with the base numbers 1420 and 1430 are the result of specifications submitted to SESC by the RIG.

INTERNATIONAL STANDARDS ORGANIZATIONS

4

International standards organizations are increasingly important because of the growth of global marketplaces. The two organizations most relevant to software engineering are the International Electrotechnical Commission (IEC) and the International Organization for Standardization (ISO).[15] For purposes of standardizing *information technology*, they have formed a Joint Technical Committee. Nevertheless, several disciplines related to information technology remain within one or the other of the two parent organizations.

In addition, one national organization from outside the United States, the Canadian Standards Association, will be briefly described at the end of this chapter.

International Electrotechnical Commission (IEC)

The International Electrotechnical Commission was formed in 1906 with the mission "to promote, through its members, international cooperation on all questions of standardization and related matters, such as the assessment of conformity to standards, in the fields of electricity, electronics and related technologies." Its products are international standards and technical reports [IEC96].

The members of IEC and its committees are National Committees representing nations. At year-end 1996, 52 nations held some form of membership in IEC. (In the United States, the National

---

[15]The third international standards organization, the International Telecommunications Union (ITU), deals exclusively with telecommunications. Unlike ISO and IEC, it is a *treaty* organization, hence representing governments rather than the private sector.

Committee is a part of ANSI.) Individual countries adopt IEC standards by using them as the basis for national standards.

IEC is managed by a Council that delegates the management of standards activities to a Committee of Action. The technical work of the IEC is conducted by Technical Committees (TC) that are, for management purposes, categorized into three groups: general subjects and industrial electrotechnics; electronics, components, and applications of information technology; and safety, measurements, and consumer goods. Four advisory committees, including an Advisory Committee on Safety, coordinate activities that may transcend the individual TCs.

Technical Committees may form Subcommittees (SC) to deal with designated portions of their scope. National Committees select the TCs and SCs in which they desire to actively participate. Smaller Working Groups (WG) are appointed by TCs or SCs for the purpose of drafting documents. WG members act as individual experts rather than as representatives of their National Committees.

Generally, a project progresses through six formal stages, that are sometimes designated by number, possibly preceded by an informal stage [ISO/IEC97]:

0. In the *preliminary* stage, any TC or SC can perform informal work on a new idea by simply voting a preliminary work item (PWI) into its own work program.

1. Formal additions to the TC or SC program of work are considered in a *proposal* stage. Typically, a new work item proposal (NP) originates with a National Committee. Its acceptance requires a majority vote of the relevant TC or SC along with a commitment of active support by five or more of the National Committees participating in the TC or SC. On approval, it is sometimes called a new work item (NWI).

2. During the *preparatory* stage, a WG is formed and a project editor designated to produce a Working Draft (WD). When suitable for comment, the WD is sent to the IEC Central Office for registration.

3. Now designated as a Committee Draft (CD), the document is circulated, in the *committee* stage, among the members of the appropriate SC or TC for technical comment. When consensus is achieved, the revised document is registered by the IEC Central Office.

4. During the *enquiry* stage, the Committee Draft for Vote (CDV) is circulated by the Central Office to the National Committees participating in the TC or SC. Although formal procedures permit technical comment at this stage, actual practice discourages it. Af-

ter the incorporation of balloting comments, the revised draft is registered by the Central Office as representing the consensus of the TC or SC.

5. In the *approval* stage, the Central Office circulates the revised document, now called a Final Draft International Standard (FDIS) to all National Committees for a 2-month vote on acceptance.

6. The final stage, *publication*, concludes with the actual issuing of the standard by the Central Office.

Documents in progress carry a three-part number indicating the originating TC or SC, a sequence number, and code summarizing the stage of processing. For example, "56/347/CD" would be the 347th document prepared by TC56, a document at the Committee Draft stage of processing. Project numbers are sometimes more informative than document numbers. They also have a three part number indicating the responsible TC or SC, the number assigned for the eventual standard, and a sequence of numbers assigning part numbers, amendment numbers, etc. For example, project 49/1178-3-1/A2/f1 would refer, reading right to left, to the first fragment of the second amendment of standard IEC 1178-3-1, as assigned to TC49.

It should be noted that IEC processing of a document is sometimes coordinated with the European Committee for Electrotechnical Standardization (CENELEC), composed of 18 European National Committees. This can lead to powerful results because it is mandatory that CENELEC standards be adopted as national standards within the member countries. Ironically, this consequence may sometimes cause a National Committee to vote affirmatively in IEC but negatively on the same document in CENELEC.[16]

National Committees participate in the TCs and the SCs of IEC by appointing delegations to attend their meetings. The national delegation is appointed by the US Technical Advisor (TA) designated for the committee. The TA is supported by a Technical Advisory Group (TAG) which also forms national positions on anticipated issues.

---

[16]Late in the writing of this book, IEC changed its numbering system to add 60,000 to the numbers of all of its standards, including the ones already published. For example, IEC 1078 will now be known as IEC 61078. The change was made to align numbering with CENELEC. This book continues to use the "old" numbers.

IEC TC56—Dependability

IEC TC56 is assigned the scope of "dependability," a term coined in 1989, intended to be non-quantifiable and broader than the more familiar "reliability." The scope includes "availability, reliability, maintainability and maintenance support" as well as their supporting technologies. Originally formed in 1965, the committee's mission was broadened in 1990 to address dependability in a generic manner cutting across the responsibilities of all other ISO and IEC technical committees [TC56-95]. Accordingly, the TC conducts liaison with several other groups relevant to this book, including ISO TC176 (Quality Management) and ISO/IEC JTC1/SC7 (Software Engineering).

Table 25. Working Groups of IEC TC56

Working Group	Name	Scope
WG1	Terms and Definitions	Terminology and mathematical expressions for reliability, maintainability, and availability terms
WG3	Equipment Reliability Verification	Specifying and testing reliability of equipment and electronic hardware
WG4	Verification and Evaluation Procedures	Methods and procedures for quantitative evaluation of test and field data, and statistical estimation of reliability characteristics
WG6	Maintainability	All aspects of maintainability and maintenance support including their integration into the system development process
WG7	Component Reliability	Reliability of electronic components
WG8	Dependability Management	Management of a dependability programme, harmonized with ISO 9000 and other standards
WG10	Software Aspects	Application of dependability to software
WG11	Human Aspects of Reliability	Human aspects of reliability with particular emphasis on human involvement in industrial and commercial processes
WG12	Risk Analysis	Analysis techniques for technological risk, specifically excluding insurance, actuarial, legal, and financial risks
WG13	Project Risk Management	Management of technical risks in projects

The TC is organized into ten Working Groups as shown in Table 25. (Because IEC uses WGs only for drafting specific documents, the scope descriptions have been generalized from their current document assignments.) Traditionally, TC56 dealt with hardware and systems issues, but the increased use of software led to the formation of WG10 with the responsibility to "provide guide-lines on assessing the integrity of the design and performance re-lated aspects of systems which contain both hardware and soft-ware." [Kiang95]

Current Collection of IEC TC56

TC56 is responsible for the maintenance of 45 standards; the ones relevant to software engineering, as well as a few of general interest, are listed in Table 26.

Table 26. IEC TC56 Dependability Standards Relevant to Software

IEC Standard	Title
IEC 50-191 (1990)	International Electrotechnical Vocabulary—Chapter 191: De-pendability and quality of service*
IEC 300-1 (1993)	Dependability management—Part 1: Dependability programme management†
IEC 300-2 (1995)	Dependability management—Part 2: Dependability programme elements and tasks
IEC 300-3-1 (1991)	Dependability management—Part 3: Application guide—Section 1: Analysis techniques for dependability: Guide on methodology
IEC 300-3-2 (1993)	Dependability management—Part 3: Application guide—Section 2: Collection of dependability data from the field
IEC 300-3-3 (1995)	Dependability management—Part 3: Application guide—Section 3: Life cycle costing
IEC 300-3-4 (1996)	Dependability management—Part 3: Application guide—Section 4: Guide to the specification of dependability requirements
IEC 300-3-9 (1995)	Dependability management—Part 3: Application guide—Section 9: Risk analysis of technological systems
IEC 812 (1985)	Analysis techniques for system reliability—Procedure for failure mode and effects analysis (FMEA)
IEC 1025 (1990)	Fault tree analysis (FTA)
IEC 1078 (1991)	Analysis techniques for dependability—Reliability block diagram method
*This document is maintained by IEC TC1, Terminology, in cooperation with TC56. †This document is the same as ISO 9000-4.	

Planned Collection of IEC TC56

The current work program of TC56 includes the development of 33 additional documents. The application of dependability man-agement techniques to software is a vital interest to TC56 and sev-eral relevant standards are under preparation as shown in Table 27. (Following the convention for tables in this book, draft stan-dards are noted in italics.) Aside from terminology, the work is being performed in WG10, which shares a convener and operates jointly with ISO/IEC JTC1/SC7/WG9, the software engineering working group concerned with software integrity.

Table 27. Planned Software-Related Additions to the Collection of IEC TC56

Planned Standard, Current Draft (Date)	Title	WG
IEC 300-3-6, FDIS (96-10)	Dependability management—Part 3: Application guide—Section 6: Software aspects of dependability	WG10
IEC 1703, CD (96-10)	Mathematical expressions for reliability, maintainability and maintenance support terms	WG1
IEC 1704, CD (95-06)	Guide to test methods for reliability assessment of software	WG10
IEC 1713, CD (96-05)	Guide to software dependability through the software life cycle processes	WG10
IEC 1714, CD (94-09)	Software maintainability and maintenance aspects of a dependability programme	WG10
IEC 1719, NP (94-02)	Guide to measures (metrics) to be used for the quantitative dependability assessment of software	WG10
IEC 1720, NP (94-02)	Guide to techniques and tools for achieving confidence in software	WG10

Organization of IEC TC56 Collection

IEC construes the term "dependability" to encompass reliability, availability, and maintainability of equipment and systems. Through the joint work of IEC TC56/WG10 and ISO/IEC JTC1/SC7/WG9, the general dependability aspects of the TC56 standards have been specialized to deal with software aspects. The layer diagram[17] of Figure 13 depicts the relevant portion of the TC56 collection [SC7WG9-96]. (As usual in the diagrams of this book, the numbers of draft standards are shown in italics.

The top layer shows two important terminology standards. The first, IEC 50-191, is actually the 191st chapter of IEC's vocabulary standard. It is maintained by IEC TC1 in cooperation with TC56/WG1; it provides the overall terminology of dependability.

---

[17]The "toolbox" concept formulated by TC56 in 1987 [TC56-95] was the original motivation for the layer diagrams used to describe the various collections. Of course, TC56 cannot be held responsible for the author's use of the concept.

TC56/WG1 is also developing a new document, IEC 1703, specifying standard mathematical expressions for many terms related to reliability, availability, and maintainability. Together, these two documents will provide a uniform terminology for the TC56 standards.

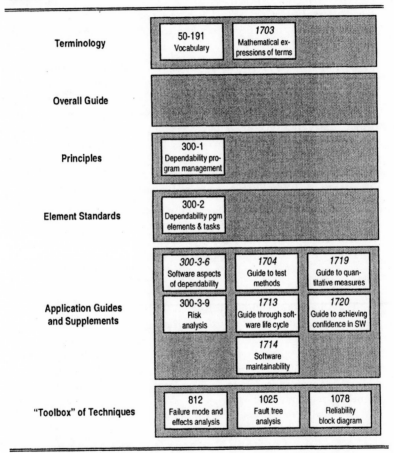

Figure 13. Layer chart of TC56 dependability standards related to software.

The next layer is vacant; TC56 has not written a guide to its overall collection of standards. This deserves some explanation. TC56 regards its collection as integrally related to the ISO 9000 series of standards via a shared document; IEC 300-1, Dependability Management—Part 1: Dependability Programme Management, is the same document as ISO 9000-4, Quality Management and Quality Assurance Standards—Part 4: Guide to Dependability Programme Management. Furthermore, the quality management vocabulary, 8402, now includes "dependability" and other important terms. Therefore, their overall guide as the same as that of ISO TC176.[18]

The "principles" layer is populated by only one standard relevant to this discussion. IEC 300-1 provides overall guidelines for a dependability management program in the framework of a generic product life cycle.

The standard at the next layer, IEC 300-2, enumerates the various elements and tasks of a dependability program and relates them to the product life cycle phases defined in IEC 300-1. All of the dependability standards described so far have been generic rather than tailored to software; the tailoring occurs in the series of standards planned for the next layer. IEC 300-3-6 will describe the software-specific aspects of a dependability program and will be supported by more detailed guidance planned in five additional documents. IEC 300-3-9 describes risk analysis techniques.

All of these standards are supported by underlying analysis techniques. IEC 812 describes failure mode and effects analysis. IEC 1025 describes methods for fault tree analysis, and IEC 1078 describes the reliability block diagram method.

Strategic Plans

TC56 has successfully shifted its focus from traditional hardware-centric reliability toward the broader viewpoint of dependability. Current and imminent standards provide appropriate linkage to quality management standards and to software engineering standards [TC56-95]. The current collection, though, is weak in addressing system-level issues. New work is needed to provide appropriate methods and metrics for the prediction, demonstration, and monitoring of system-level reliability [Kiang97a].

IEC SC45A—Nuclear Reactor Instrumentation

IEC TC45 has the responsibility for electrical and electronic equipment used for the instrumentation of nuclear applications. One of its subcommittees, SC45A, responsible for nuclear reactor

---

[18]In fact, TC176 did not actually contribute to the shared document and will probably relinquish its share of the maintenance responsibility to TC56. Some are concerned that the "Year 2000" strategy of TC176 may sever the relationship between the two committees. A relationship stronger than simple liaison may be necessary.

instrumentation, has been active in writing standards regarding software used in those systems.

The SC currently has seven Working Groups, as shown in Table 28, with names descriptive of their scope. As one would expect from the name, WG3 is the working group most active in applying safety principles to software.

Table 28. Working Groups of IEC SC45A

Working Group	Name
WG2	Nuclear reactor measurement, control and safety instrumentation
WG3	Application of digital processors to safety in nuclear power plants
WG4	Radiation monitoring
WG5	Special process measurements
WG6	Reactor shutdown without access to the main control room
WG7	Reliability of electrical equipment in reactor safety systems
WG8	Control rooms

Current Collection of IEC SC45A

SC45A has completed 48 standards. Of that number, the ones listed in Table 29 are specifically related to software or provide a more general framework into which the software-related standards must fit.

Table 29. Some of the Standards of IEC SC45A

IEC Standard	Title
IEC 557 (1982)	IEC terminology in the nuclear reactor field
IEC 643 (1979)	Application of digital computers to nuclear reactor instrumentation and control
IEC 880 (1986)	Software for computers in the safety systems of nuclear power stations
IEC 987 (1989)	Programmed digital computers important to safety for nuclear power stations
IEC 1226 (1993)	Nuclear power plants—Instrumentation and control systems important for safety—Classification

Planned Collection of IEC SC45A

Software is playing a greater role in the operation of nuclear power plants. Even in the United States (conservatively regulated in comparison to other countries) software is now beginning to appear in safety systems.[19] SC45A standards-making has been active in this area. Of the 19 projects under way in SC45A, the ones listed in Table 30 are either of general importance or specifically related to software. (Because all are drafts, all are noted with italics.)

Table 30. Planned General and Safety-Related Additions to the
        Collection of IEC SC45A

Planned Standard, Current Draft (Date)	Title	WG
IEC 880-1, CDV (96-11)	Supplement 1 to IEC 880, Software for computers important to safety for nuclear power plants	WG3
IEC 880-2, NWI (87-12)	Supplement 2 to IEC 880, Software for computers important to safety for nuclear power plants	WG3
IEC 1513, CD (93-11)	General requirements for computer-based systems important to safety in nuclear power plants	WG3
IEC 1838, NP	Supplement to IEC 1226, Risk-based classification	WG7

Organization of IEC SC45A Collection

SC45A has not organized its collection using the layered model used by some of the other committees discussed in this book. Nevertheless, the layer diagram, shown in Figure 14, is useful to understand the relationships among the standards.[20] (Draft standards are noted with italics in the diagram.)

Terminology in this field is maintained by SC45A itself in the form of the IEC 557 standard. The terminology is supplemented by the two standards depicted as techniques. IEC 1226 specifies a classification scheme (based on the consequences of failures) used to categorize three levels of software; category A has the most severe consequences. (The committee is considering the development of a companion risk-based classification scheme, 1838, but work

---

[19]In the jargon of nuclear power, "safety systems" have critical importance. *Safety systems* (also known as "Category A" systems), such as reactor protection systems, are differentiated from the less critical *safety-related systems*. The term "systems important to safety" is generic.

[20]The layer diagram depicts only voluntary IEC standards and omits the Safety Guides, regulatory in nature, written by the International Atomic Energy Agency. Although the guides are beyond the scope of this book, they are, nevertheless, notable because many of the IEC standards have been written to implement the provisions of the Safety Guides.

has been delayed on the grounds that it might prove to be redundant with IEC 300-3-9 developed by TC56.) The categories defined by 1226 are fundamental to determining the applicability of other software standards in the collection [Leret95].

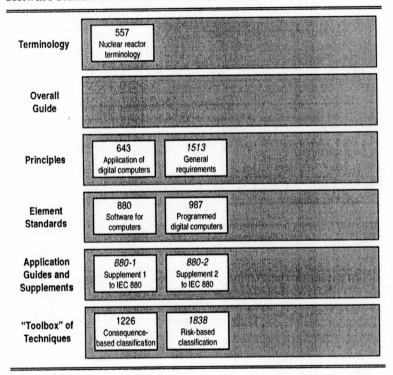

Figure 14. Layer chart of general and software safety standards in the SC45A collection.

The planned 1513 standard will play a unifying role by dealing with requirements at a system level, hence its informal name "chapeau" ("hat" in French). Also shown at the level of principles is IEC 643, dating back to 1979, and covering the general application of digital computers to reactors, but excluding protection systems.

Of the element standards, IEC 880 prescribes the requirements for computers in safety systems (category A systems) of nuclear power stations. IEC 987 provides the complementary hardware requirements.

IEC 880 is a broad standard covering material such as the development life cycle, design and coding, testing, documentation, and language processors. Nevertheless it has been criticized for inadequate treatment of topics such as formal methods, support engineering tools, and configuration management. Furthermore, it is applicable only to category A software. To address the weaknesses, SC45A has created a list of topics that will be treated in the two planned supplements.

Table 31. Working Groups of IEC SC65A

Working Group	Name	Scope
WG2	Service Conditions	Establish classes concerning climatic and other conditions to which control systems may be subjected during operation and storage
WG4	Electromagnetic Interference	Prepare guidance documents and standards proposals regarding electromagnetic interference problems for process measurement and control systems
WG8	Evaluation of System properties	Define properties for process measurement and control systems and to recommend methodologies for their assessment
WG9	Safe Software	Study and make recommendations regarding new work on the subject of safe and reliable software
WG10	Functional Safety of Programmable Electronic Systems (PES)	Prepare standards and guidance regarding functional safety requirements for PES and other safety-related systems for process industries
WG11	Batch Control Systems	Develop glossary and a functional model for batch control systems

Table 32. Some of the Standards of IEC SC65A

IEC Standard	Title
IEC 1069-1 (1991)	Industrial-process measurement and control—Evaluation of system properties for the purpose of system assessment—Part 1: General considerations and methodology
IEC 1069-2 (1993)	Industrial-process measurement and control—Evaluation of system properties for the purpose of system assessment—Part 2: Assessment methodology
IEC 1069-3 (1996)	Industrial-process measurement and control—Evaluation of system properties for the purpose of system assessment—Part 3: Assessment of system functionality
IEC 1069-5 (1994)	Industrial-process measurement and control—Evaluation of system properties for the purpose of system assessment—Part 5: Assessment of system dependability

IEC SC65A—Industrial Process Control

IEC SC65A, a subcommittee of TC65, is assigned the "system aspects" of its parent TC's responsibility for "industrial process measurement and control." SC65A has used this scope to pursue a number of issues related to the safety of software-intensive systems. The SC has formed the six Working Groups shown in Table 31.

Table 33. Planned General and Safety-Related Additions to the Collection of IEC SC65A

Planned Standard, Current Draft (Date)	Title	WG
IEC 1069-4, FDIS (97-03)	Industrial process measurement and control—Evaluation of system properties for the purpose of system assessment—Part 4: Assessment of system performance	WG8
IEC 1069-6, CDV (96-12)	Industrial process measurement and control—Evaluation of system properties for the purpose of system assessment—Part 6: Assessment of system operability	WG8
IEC 1069-7, CD (96-12)	Industrial process measurement and control—Evaluation of system properties for the purpose of system assessment—Part 7: Assessment of system safety	WG8
IEC 1069-8, CD (96-12)	Industrial process measurement and control—Evaluation of system properties for the purpose of system assessment—Part 8: Assessment of not task related properties	WG8
IEC 1508-1, CDV (96-05)	Functional safety—Safety-related systems—Part 1: General requirements	WG10
IEC 1508-2, CD (96-05)	Functional safety—Safety-related systems—Part 2: Requirements for electrical/electronic/programmable electronic systems	WG10
IEC 1508-3, CDV (96-05)	Functional safety—Safety-related systems—Part 3: Software requirements	WG9
IEC 1508-4, CDV (96-05)	Functional safety—Safety-related systems—Part 4: Definitions and abbreviations of terms	WG10
IEC 1508-5, CDV (96-05)	Functional safety—Safety-related systems—Part 5: Guidelines on the application of Part 1	WG10
IEC 1508-6, CD (96-05)	Functional safety—Safety-related systems—Part 6: Guidelines on the application of Parts 2 and 3	WG10
IEC 1508-7, CD (96-05)	Functional safety—Safety-related systems—Part 7: Bibliography of techniques and measures	WG10

Current Collection of IEC SC65A

SC65A is responsible for the maintenance of 15 standards. None are specifically relevant to software engineering, but some of the general ones contribute to a framework into which the relevant standards will fit. Those general standards are listed in Table 32.

Planned Collection of IEC SC65A

The role of safety, particularly software safety, can better be perceived in the plans for the expansion of the collection of SC65A, shown in Table 33. (As in other tables, draft standards are noted with italics.) The current work program of SC65A includes the development of 20 additional documents. System safety is regarded as one of the relevant properties for system assessment. More specifically, a family of standards, 1508, is planned for the treatment of *functional safety*, that is, safety at the system level rather than at the equipment level [Harauz97a].

Organization of IEC SC65A Collection

Unlike some of the other standards groups discussed in this book, SC65A has not itself organized its collection into a layered model, so the depictions shown in the next two figures are necessarily approximations. For our purposes, we can view SC65A as maintaining two collections: one regarding the assessment of system properties in industrial process measurement and control systems, shown in Figure 15; and one regarding safety-related control systems involving programmable devices, shown in Figure 16. (Draft documents are distinguished by the use of italics.)

Despite occupying only three levels of the layered model, the SC65A collection for the assessment of the properties of process control systems seems well-organized. The IEC 1069 standard is used to assess properties of completed, perhaps off-the-shelf, systems and does not deal specifically with the design process [Leret95]. It does not have its own vocabulary document, instead relying on IEC's overall vocabulary, IEC 50, known as the International Electrotechnical Vocabulary (IEV). Part 1 of the standard prescribes general considerations and outlines the methodology for the assessment of system properties. Parts 3-8 specify the assessment of specific properties: functionality, performance, dependability, operability, safety, and other properties. (The dependability document makes normative references to the standards of TC56 discussed earlier in this chapter.) All make use of the detailed assessment methodology prescribed in Part 2.

The planned collection of standards for functional safety, shown in Figure 16, makes fuller use of the layered model. Part 4 of the planned IEC 1508 standard provides definitions and abbreviations for the entire set. Part 1 prescribes general requirements for safety management that are further elaborated in Part 2 into specific requirements primarily applicable to the hardware portions of the system. Software requirements are further specified in Part 3. Guidelines to the previous parts appear in Parts 5 and 6 and a bibliography of techniques and measures appears in Part 7 [Brazendale95]. SC65A has been working on the 1508 standards for fourteen years, an observation that suggests the difficulties in developing generic safety standards. When completed, we can expect the IEC 1508 standards to prescribe principles for the treatment of safety in other collections of standards.

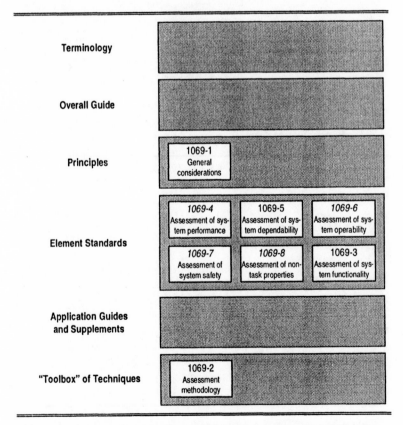

Figure 15. Layer chart of the SC65A collection of system assessment standards.

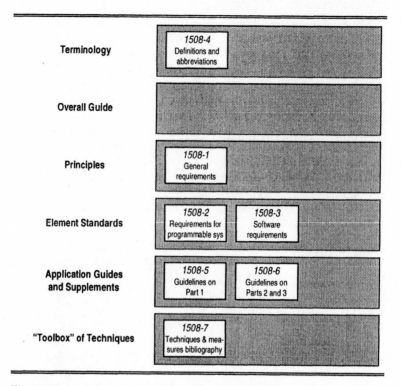

Terminology	*1508-4* Definitions and abbreviations
Overall Guide	
Principles	*1508-1* General requirements
Element Standards	*1508-2* Requirements for programmable sys / *1508-3* Software requirements
Application Guides and Supplements	*1508-5* Guidelines on Part 1 / *1508-6* Guidelines on Parts 2 and 3
"Toolbox" of Techniques	*1508-7* Techniques & measures bibliography

Figure 16. Layer chart of the planned software-related standards in the SC65A collection of functional safety standards.

International Organization for Standardization (ISO)

The most well-known international standards developer, the International Organization for Standardization (ISO),[21] is a non-governmental federation of national standards bodies, created in 1947 as a successor to the International Federation of the National Standardizing Associations, which had focused primarily on mechanical engineering. Its scope now includes standardization in all fields except electrical and electronic engineering, covered by IEC, and telecommunications, covered by the International Telecommunications Union (ITU). The mission of ISO is "to promote the

---

[21]The organization selected "ISO" as its abbreviation precisely because it is not an acronym for the name in any major language and because of the derivation from the Greek *isos* meaning "equal."

development of standardization and related activities in the world with a view to facilitating the international exchange of goods and services, and to developing cooperation in the spheres of intellectual, scientific, technological and economic activity" [ISO97]. The work of ISO has resulted in the development of 9,300 international standards comprising more than 170 thousand pages of English and French text [Cargill97].

The members of ISO are national bodies, typically representing countries. ISO standards are developed in a hierarchical organization of Technical Committees (TC), Subcommittees (SC), and Working Groups (WG), the lowest level at which documents are formally drafted. National body membership is distinct for each different ISO TC, SC and WG; national bodies select the levels and the organizations in which they choose to participate. The standardization operations of ISO are managed by a Technical Management Board that reports to the ISO Council.

Information Technology is a special case. Since ISO and IEC both view themselves as responsible for aspects of this area, they agreed in 1987 to cooperate by forming a Joint Technical Committee, JTC1, to develop information technology standards. JTC1 uses procedures distinct but similar to those of ISO.

The ISO standards development process is very similar to the IEC process, described earlier, except that the term Final Committee Draft (FCD) is used instead of CDV[22]. (Many existing drafts are permitted to follow an older process that used the term Draft International Standard, DIS, instead of FDIS.) Administrative documents are numbered differently from IEC practice; the ISO committee or subcommittee is given, followed by an "N" and a sequential number. For example, the 512th document (from some designated starting point) of ISO TC176 might be labeled as "ISO/TC176/N512." Documents designated in this manner range in importance from grand policy, through draft standards, to incidental items. To the casual observer, the "N" numbers are notable only because, prior the assignment of a project number, they may be the only way to identify important items, for example, project proposals [ISO/IEC95].

The US relationship to ISO is managed slightly differently than its relationship to IEC. Rather than having a US National Committee, ANSI itself is the US member body of ISO. The designation of delegates to ISO meetings and the formulation of US posi-

---

[22]The process has recently been changed and some older documents use a process with slightly different stages.

tions are controlled by Technical Advisory Groups (TAGs). Each TAG has both a chair and an administrator. In some cases, ANSI serves as the administrator; in others, the responsibility is delegated to another organization.

ISO TC176—Quality Management

Since their first publication in 1987, the ISO 9000 series has become, arguably, the most successful set of standards ever written in any area that affects information technology. World-wide, more than 135,000 organizations claim conformance to ISO 9000 [Kiang97], more than 80 countries have adopted them as national standards [Peach94], and more than 50 countries actively participate in developing the standards [Kiang97]. Although the standards have their origins in a regulated industry structure for the European Union, they have become, in fact, the baseline for quality management standards around the world. The principle underlying the standards is that an organization with a well-defined engineering process is more likely to produce products meeting the needs of its customers than a poorly managed organization. The ISO 9000 series of standards and guidelines specifies an approach to quality management intended to achieve this goal.

The ISO 9000 series of standards are developed and maintained by ISO Technical Committee 176. (In the United States, the standards have been adopted by the American Society for Quality Control and are designated with similar numbers, for example, ANSI/ASQC Q9001 corresponds to ISO 9001. Similar forms of adoption occur in several other countries.) Internally, TC176 is organized into three subcommittees: SC1, Concepts and terminology; SC2, Quality systems; and SC3, Supporting technology. Each subcommittee has several working groups, some that appear to have enduring missions and some that seem to be organized for particular tasks.

Current Collection of ISO TC176

The ISO 9000 standards were originally developed to deal with the wide variety of national quality standards that were hindering the development of a single market in the European Union. The organization of the collection has evolved as its mission has broadened.

In addition to the 8402 standard for terminology, two series of numbers have been reserved for the series and its future additions. The familiar 90xx series will continue to be used for the standards for quality management, systems, and assurance. The new 100xx series will be used for "quality technology" standards. The current collection is listed in Table 34.

Table 34. Current Collection of ISO TC176

Standard	Title
ISO 8402:1994	Quality management and quality assurance—Vocabulary
ISO 9000-1:1994	Quality management and quality assurance standards—Part 1: Guidelines for selection and use
ISO 9000-2:1993	Quality management and quality assurance standards—Part 2: Generic guidelines for the application of ISO 9001, ISO 9002 and ISO 9003
ISO 9000-3:1991	Quality management and quality assurance standards—Part 3: Guidelines for the application of ISO 9001 to the development, supply and maintenance of software
ISO 9000-4:1993	Quality management and quality assurance standards—Part 4: Guide to dependability programme management*
ISO 9001:1994	Quality systems—Model for quality assurance in design, development, production, installation, and servicing
ISO 9002:1994	Quality systems—Model for quality assurance in production, installation, and servicing
ISO 9003:1994	Quality systems—Model for quality assurance in final inspection and test
ISO 9004-1:1994	Quality management and quality systems—Part 1: Guidelines
ISO 9004-2:1991	Quality management and quality systems elements—Part 2: Guidelines for services
ISO 9004-3:1993	Quality management and quality systems elements—Part 3: Guidelines for processed materials
ISO 9004-4:1993	Quality management and quality systems elements—Part 4: Guidelines for quality improvement
ISO 10005:1995	Quality management—Guidelines for quality plans
ISO 10007: 1995	Quality management—Guidelines for configuration management
ISO 10011-1:1990	Guidelines for auditing quality systems—Part 1: Auditing
ISO 10011-2:1991	Guidelines for auditing quality systems—Part 2: Qualification criteria for quality systems auditors
ISO 10011-3:1991	Guidelines for auditing quality systems—Part 3: Management of audit programmes
ISO 10012-1:1992	Quality assurance requirements for measuring equipment—Part 1: Metrological confirmation system for measuring equipment
ISO 10013:1995	Guidelines for developing quality manuals
*This document is identical with IEC 300-1; responsibility for maintenance is shared with IEC TC56.	

Planned Collection of ISO TC176

Work continues in TC176 to complete the current generation of quality management standards. The work in progress is summarized in Table 35

Table 35. Standards Expected from ISO TC176

Standard	Title
ISO FDIS 9000-2	(Revision)
ISO FDIS 9000-3	(Revision)
ISO FDIS 10006	Quality management—Guidelines to quality in project management
ISO FDIS 10012-2	Quality assurance requirements for measuring equipment— Part 2: Guidelines for control of measurement process
ISO FDIS 10014	Guidelines for managing the economics of quality

Organization of ISO TC176 Collection

ISO 9000 is actually a series of standards and guidelines written generically to cover a wide variety of business endeavors. The series covers both *quality management*, the implementation of quality systems internal to an organization, and *quality assurance*, generic requirements for a customer's evaluation of a supplier's quality system.

According to Clause 6 of ISO 9000-1, the ISO 9000 series is intended to be used in four situations:

- Guidance on quality management for a single party

- Contractual, between two parties

- Second-party approval or registration

- Third-party certification and registration

In a sense, these situations can be viewed as a natural progression. The first usage provides guidance for an organization's improvement of its own internal quality management systems for the purpose of improving competitiveness in a cost-effective manner. The contractual usage permits a customer to specify a quality assurance model requiring that particular quality elements and processes be part of the supplier's quality system. Proceeding outside the context of any one particular contract, the third usage permits the customer to approve or register the organizational quality system of a regular supplier as conforming with the relevant standard. Finally, third party certification is a recognition of a supplier's conformance outside the context of the relationship with any particular customer.

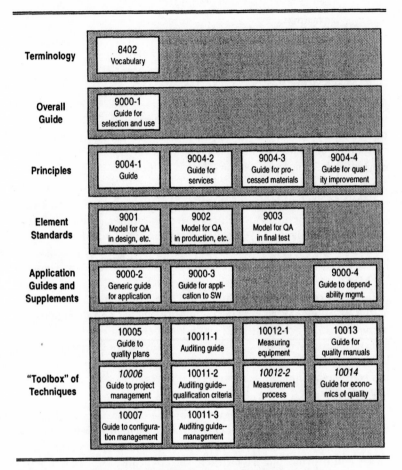

Figure 17. Layer chart of the ISO 9000 series of standards.

Figure 17 shows the ISO 9000 series of standards organized as a layered collection. Terminology for the series is collected in ISO 8402 but is not yet quite consistent across the various documents. The customer is called simply that—the *customer*—or occasionally, the *purchaser*. The organization implementing the quality system is called the *supplier,* or sometimes, the *organization* or the *contractor*. In turn, the organizations from which it makes purchases are called *subsuppliers* or *subcontractors*. The *product*, the item produced by the supplier for the customer, is defined as the "result of activities or processes." Clause 4.4 of ISO 9000-1 classifies products into four generic categories, although it is recognized that the offerings of most organization will fall into more than one category:

- Hardware
- Software (not just computer software)
- Processed material
- Service

Quality is defined as "the totality of characteristics of an entity that bear on its ability to satisfy stated or implied needs." Even in a contractual situation, not all relevant needs will be addressed in the statement of requirements. So, quality can also be viewed more generally as "fitness for use" or "fitness for purpose."[23]

The titles of the documents indicate that they deal with the subjects of quality *systems, management* and *assurance*, terms that should be distinguished. To produce high-quality products, a supplier would implement a *quality system* involving all life cycle processes that affect quality of the final product. *Quality management* refers to all activities of the overall management function that determine and implement the systems affecting product quality. Finally, *quality assurance* includes "all the planned and systematic activities implemented within the quality system and demonstrated as needed to provide adequate confidence that an entity will fulfill requirements for quality." Quality assurance plays a prominent role in the contractual situation because it provides the customer with the confidence that the company's quality system will provide satisfactory products.

At the second level of Figure 17 is the document providing the overview of the series; ISO 9000-1 (formerly called ISO 9000) is the overall guide that describes the relationships among the other standards and provides advice on their selection and use. It is a guidance document rather than a conformance document and de-

---

[23]Ironically, considering the success of the ISO 9000 standards, the desired definitions of *quality* and related terms remain a matter of discussion within TC176. One proposal is to use *quality requirement* as the fundamental concept and to define it as "expectation or need expressed as a set of technical characteristics and their values." "Quality" would then be defined as the "extent to which the quality requirement is met" [TC176-96]. Such a change might upset some of the relationships built from other standards to the ISO 9000 series; there is some concern within ISO/IEC JTC1/SC7, for example.

scribes the basic quality objectives of an organization, emphasizing a process-based viewpoint.

The 9004 documents at the third level are also guidance documents, describing the principles for an organization's internal quality management and their implementation of quality systems. ISO 9004-1 (formerly 9004) is the overall guide at this level and deals with subjects not yet treated in the conformance documents, subjects like quality economics, product safety, and liability. Organizations that desire, but do not need to demonstrate, quality management may find their needs satisfied by 9004-1 and the other documents discussed so far. Of particular interest to software developers, 9004-1 introduces the concept of configuration management, a subject that will receive additional treatment in another document. Parts 2 and 3 of 9004 are guides specialized to two of the product categories mentioned previously, services and processed materials. Part 4 provides advice for continuous quality improvement.

All of the documents discussed so far have been guides and all have addressed the organization's internal processes. At the fourth level, though, are the element standards, ISO 9001, 9002, and 9003. These are conformance documents, addressing quality assurance, and requiring compliance in a two-party contractual situation or the third-party registration situation. Essentially, by introducing the *quality manual*, they require an organization to "document what it does, do what it documents, review the process and change it when necessary" [Peach94]. ISO 9001 is the broadest of the three; it includes all of the elements of the other two as well as addressing design and development capabilities not described in the others. This standard is applicable to contracts specifically requiring a design effort. ISO 9002 omits design activities and is applicable in situations where the customer provides detailed designs and specification for execution by the supplier. Finally, ISO 9003 is the narrowest document; it applies to situations where the product can be evaluated by testing and inspection. For software development, 9001 is the appropriate document. After all, from the manufacturing viewpoint that characterizes the 9000 series, all of software development counts as design (as distinguished from production).

At the next level is another set of guidance documents that explain how to interpret and apply the conformance documents in various situations. ISO 9000-2 provides generic guidance and is particularly intended as assistance in the early stages of implementing a quality program. ISO 9000-3 is perhaps the most important document for software engineers because it provides guidance

on the application of 9001 to software development and maintenance. The 9000-4 standard provides guidance for the assurance of
the dependability characteristics of a product; it may be applicable
to software forming part of a system intended to exhibit a high level
of dependability.

Finally, the bottom level is a set of "tools," *supporting technologies* in the jargon of TC176, that may be helpful in implementing a
quality program. ISO 10005 and 10007 are guides to quality planning and configuration management. The three parts of the 10011
document provide guidance on implementing the audits recommended by 9000-1. Part 1 of ISO 10012 (as well as additional
forthcoming parts) deals with measurement equipment. Finally,
the 10013 guide provides detailed guidance for how to write the
quality manual that is the fundamental documentation of the organization's quality system.

Strategic Plans

A document called Vision 2000 [Marquadt91] outlined the
plans of TC176 for the 1990s. The committee perceives the marketplace for its standards as having three segmenting dimensions:

- Generic product categories: hardware, software, processed
  materials, services. Typically, the offering of any organization falls in two or more of these categories.

- Complexity. The existing model of three alternative standards plus guidance documents is deemed as adequate for
  most situations. The still unmet needs of large organizations that purchase complex products may require modest
  additions and revisions of the existing 9000 series contractual standards.

- Contractual versus non-contractual. The circa 1994 revision and restructuring is presumed to have dealt satisfactorily with this distinction.

The long-range strategy of TC176 is to write guideline documents addressing these various needs. They feel that this will ob-
viate the need for sector-specific supplementary or derived standards dealing with generic quality issues. Nevertheless, the auto-
mobile industry and the medical device industry (ISO TC210) have
been pressing for quality standards that are more specific and more
understandable for their particular needs [Kiang97].

Global competitiveness will lead to a greater intermingling of
the four generic product categories in the offerings of large organizations. Therefore, the plan for the "Year 2000 Family"

[TC176-96a] calls for the three standards, 9001, 9002, and 9003, to be integrated into a single document providing comprehensive requirements for quality assurance. Corresponding to it (and thoroughly consistent with it) would be a single guidance document, 9004, providing principles for quality management. The current vocabulary, 8402, would be merged with the current 9000-1, to produce an overall guide to concepts and terminology, 9000. Several of the guides of particular interest to software engineers (9000-2, 9000-3, 10005, and 10007) would become Part 1 of 9004. TC176 would relinquish its share of the responsibility for maintaining the dependability document, 9000-4, leaving the sole responsibility to IEC TC56. The result would be a document set sharply reduced in number and more tightly integrated [Kiang97, TC176-96b].

In overall terms, we can see an evolution in the goals of the ISO 9000 series. The original 1987 version of ISO 9001 was focused on the two-party contractual situation. The revision in 1994 shifted toward emphasis on third-party registration of quality compliance for the purpose of encouraging international trade. The planned revision aims for implementation of comprehensive quality management systems at the enterprise level [Kiang97].

ISO/IEC JTC1

As computing technology evolved, it became clear that the scope for the standardization work of both ISO and IEC overlapped in many areas related to the emerging technologies. In 1987, the two organizations decided to coordinate their efforts by the creation of a new Joint Technical Committee, JTC1, with responsibility for work related to "standardization in the field of information technology" [ISO/IEC95].[24] Although JTC1 also assumed the work programs of IEC TC47B and TC83, most of its activity was a continuation of work formerly performed by ISO TC97, dating back to 1960 [Cargill97].

Membership in JTC1 and its subcommittees is held by nations rather than individuals. Participating Members have voting privileges while Observing Members are authorized to attend meetings and to contribute and receive documents. Liaison membership permits both external and internal (other ISO, IEC and JTC1 committees) organizations to participate without voting.

---

[24]JTC1 also has an agreement for collaboration with the third international standards body, the International Telecommunications Union (ITU) [Gibson95].

JTC1 is organized into subcommittees, each dealing with related areas of work, as shown in Table 36 [ISO/IEC97a]. The SC are further subdivided into Working Groups (WG).

Table 36. JTC1 Subcommittees

Subcommittee	Scope
SGFS	Special group on functional standardization
SC1	Vocabulary
SC2	Coded character sets
SC6	Telecommunications and information exchange between systems
SC7	Software engineering
SC11	Flexible magnetic media for digital data interchange
SC14	Data element principles
SC17	Identification cards and related devices
SC18	Document processing and related communications
SC21	Open systems interconnection, data management, and open distributed processing
SC22	Programming languages, their environments, and system software interfaces
SC23	Optical disk cartridges for information exchange
SC24	Computer graphics and image processing
SC25	Interconnection of information technology equipment
SC26	Microprocessor systems
SC27	IT security techniques
SC28	Office equipment
SC29	Coding of audio, picture, multimedia, and hypermedia information
SC30	Open electronic data interchange
SC31	Automatic identification and data capture techniques

JTC1 uses procedures similar to those of ISO, but in some cases, the technical work is pushed down one level deeper in the hierarchical structure, for example, JTC1 Subcommittees often perform work analogous to ISO Technical Committees.

JTC1 produces two main types of products: international standards (IS) and technical reports (TR). Each completed IS is reviewed for currency every 5 years resulting in a decision to retain, revise, or withdraw. There are three types of technical reports: a type 1 TR is a document which, although worthwhile, failed to reach consensus as an IS; a type 2 TR is a document on a subject that remains technically immature and on which IS development continues; and a type 3 TR provides material not suitable for a standard but is otherwise of interest, for example, models, frameworks, guidance. Type 1 and 2 technical reports are reviewed after

3 years with the expectation that they may be revised and designated as standards [Rehesaar96].

The JTC1 development process follows the same six stages previous described for ISO. Each of the key stages has a maximum allowed duration as well as a de facto minimum duration as a consequence of the frequency of meetings. The average duration of the process has been decreasing in recent years and is now about 40 months, two-thirds of the time required by the average ISO committee [Gibson95].

US interests in the business of JTC1 are represented by a Technical Advisory Group (TAG) administered by the Information Technology Industry (ITI) Council under the procedures prescribed by ANSI, the US member body in JTC1. The hierarchical structure of JTC1 is mirrored by a family of TAGs representing US interests at the SC and at the WG levels. The family of US TAGs to JTC1

Table 37. Working Groups of JTC1/SC7

Working Group	Name	Scope
WG2	Systems Software Development	Documentation of software systems
WG4	Tools and Environments	Tools and computer-aided software/systems engineering (CASE) environments
WG6	Evaluation and Metrics	Software products evaluation and metrics for software products and processes
WG7	Life Cycle Management	Life cycle management
WG8	Support of Life Cycle Processes	Support of life cycle processes
WG9	Software Integrity	Software integrity (ensuring the containment or confinement of risk) at the system and system interface level
WG10	Software Process Assessment	Methods, practices and application of process assessment in software product procurement, development, delivery, operation, evolution, and related service support
WG11	Software Engineering Data Definition and Representation	Definition of the data used and produced by software engineering processes, its representation for communication by both humans and machines, and definition of data interchange formats
WG12	Functional Size Measurement	Establishment of a set of practical standards for functional size measurement, a general term for methods of sizing software from an external viewpoint

cooperate under the terms of a Memorandum of Agreement sponsored by the Information Systems Standards Board (ISSB) of ANSI [Gibson95].

ISO/IEC JTC1/SC7—Software Engineering

ISO/IEC JTC1/SC7 is the major source of international standards on software engineering. It was formed in 1987 from three existing technical committees and inherited their programs of

Table 38. Current Collection of ISO/IEC JTC1/SC7

Standard	Title
ISO/IEC 2382-1: 1993	Vocabulary—Part 1: Fundamental terms
ISO/IEC 2382-7: 1989	Vocabulary—Part 7: Computer programming
ISO/IEC 2382-20: 1990	Vocabulary—Part 20: System development
ISO/IEC TR 12382:1992	Permuted index of the vocabulary of information technology
ISO 5806:1984	Information processing—Specification of single-hit decision tables
ISO 5807:1985	Information processing—Documentation symbols and conventions for data, program and system flowcharts, program network charts and system resources charts
ISO 6592:1985	Information processing—Guidelines for the documentation of computer-based application systems
ISO 6593:1985	Information processing—Program flow for processing sequential files in terms of record groups
ISO/IEC 8631:1989	Program constructs and conventions for their representation
ISO 8790:1987	Information processing systems—Computer system configuration diagram symbols and conventions
ISO/IEC 9126:1991	Software product evaluation—Quality characteristics and guidelines for their use
ISO 9127:1988	Information processing systems—User documentation and cover information for consumer software packages
ISO/IEC TR 9294:1990	Guidelines for the management of software documentation
ISO/IEC 11411:1995	Representation for human communication of state transition of software
ISO/IEC 12119:1994	Software packages—Quality requirements and testing
ISO/IEC 12207:1995	Software life cycle processes
ISO/IEC 14102:1995	Guideline for the evaluation and selection of CASE tools
ISO/IEC 14568:1997	Diagram eXchange Language for tree-structured charts

work. The terms of reference for SC7 are defined as the "standardization of process, products, and technologies for the engineering of software and products or systems containing software" [SC7-96]. SC7 or its working groups maintain liaison with ISO TC176 (for software aspects of quality assurance), IEC TC56 (for software aspects of dependability), and IEC SC45A and 65A (for software aspects of safety).

Currently, there are nine active Working Groups within SC7 with scope delimited as shown in Table 37.[25] The subdivision of responsibilities is neither orthogonal nor exhaustive because WGs are formed as their need is perceived rather than in response to an integrated plan.

Current Collection of JTC1/SC7

When JTC1 was formed, SC7 inherited the responsibility for maintaining (and, in some cases, completing) various standards related to techniques and notations. The current collection, as shown in Table 38, represents this history [SC7-96]. Only in recent years has SC7 been free to focus on more fundamental issues. (The first four standards listed, the relevant vocabulary standards, are actually maintained by SC1.)

Planned Collection of JTC1/SC7

Using a planning horizon of 1999, SC7 expects to produce additional standards and revise existing ones as shown in Table 39 [SC7-96].

It should also be noted that WG9 is jointly working with IEC TC56 on the dependability standards listed in Table 27.

Organization of JTC1/SC7 Collection

Although most of SC7's current collection is a legacy of old notation standards, recent products (and current plans) have indicated an ambitious desire to deal with some of the key problems of software engineering standardization. Recently, the Business Planning Group of SC7 developed a Product Plan [SC7-96] intended to provide overall direction to SC7 standards development. That plan names four program elements similar to those named by SESC,

---

[25]As this chapter is written, it appears likely that SC7 will create a WG13 to develop a standard framework for software measurement.

Table 39. Standards Expected from ISO/IEC JTC1/SC7

Planned Standard and Current Status	Title	WG
DIS 6592	Guidelines for the documentation of computer-based application systems	WG2
CD 9126 CD 14598	Software product evaluation [a total of 9 parts]	WG6
DTR 12182	Categorization of software	WG9
CD 12220	Software life cycle process—Configuration management for software	WG8
DIS 14143-1	Functional size measurement—Part 1: Definition of concepts	WG12
DTR 14399	Mapping of relevant software engineering standards—Standards relevant to ISO/IEC JTC1/SC7—Software engineering	WG9
DTR 14471	Adoption of CASE tools	WG4
CD 14756	Measurement and rating of performance of computer-based software systems	WG6
DTR 14759	Software life cycle model tailored for mock-up and prototype	WG7
WD 14764	Software maintenance	WG7
DIS 15026	System and software integrity levels	WG9
DTR 15271	Guide for ISO/IEC 12207 (Software life cycle processes)	WG7
WD 15288	System life cycle processes	WG7
WD 15289	Guidelines for the content of software life cycle process information products	WG2
15474-15479	Software engineering data definition and inter-change [a total of 31 parts]	WG11
DTR 15504	Software process assessment [9 parts]	WG10

that is, *customer*, *process*, *product*, and, lastly, *technology*, a gener-alization of the term *resource* used by SESC.[26]

For the purposes of this book, the standards have been placed into a architecture similar to that of the SESC standards. Just as for SESC, this architecture is best viewed as an objective rather than a reality.

The different organizational principles of SESC and SC7 have led to some differences in the way standards are approached. Be-

---

[26]Some SC7 sources use the term "organization." Although this book will respect the different nomenclature adopted by SC7, it will treat all of these terms as synonymous.

cause SESC working groups are formed to create a single document, overall coordination must be superimposed on the individual documents that are created. On the other hand, SC7 working groups persist beyond the completion of single documents; they tend to create coordinated clusters of documents, often in the form of multiple parts of a single numbered standard. Of course, the problem remains of superimposing coordination on these clusters of standards. Nevertheless, the approach tends to be more successful in producing the principles and policy standards that play such an important role in an architecture.

Figure 18 depicts the outer layers of the architecture. (As usual, italicized numbers indicate standards that are planned for completion in the near future.) There are several vocabulary stan-

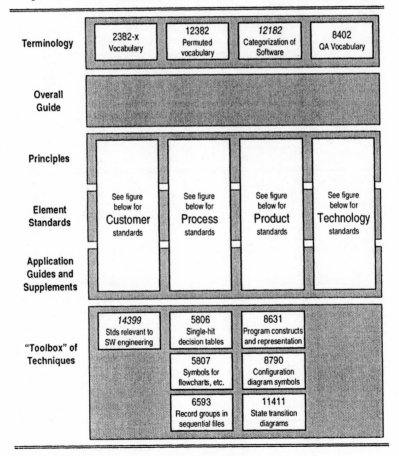

Figure 18. Outer layers of the SC7 collection.

dards; in addition to the multi-part information technology vocabulary of JTC1, the quality vocabulary adopted from ISO TC176 is also relevant. The planned 12182 document will define various categories for software characteristics; the categories will serve as terminology for future standards.

SC7 has not commissioned an overall guide to its collection of standards. This book will attempt to fill that role although no official endorsement from SC7 has been sought or granted.

Six legacy standards specifying basic software techniques (decision tables, flowcharts and other diagrams, record groups, program constructs, configuration diagrams, and state transition diagrams) are included in the toolbox for this collection. DTR 14399 provides summary lists of about 550 standards related to the efforts of SC7. The lists were developed by surveying member bodies and organizing the nominated standards into various categories.

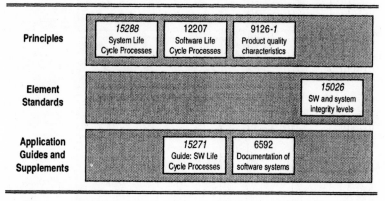

Figure 19. Inner layers of the customer "stack" of the SC7 collection.

The customer stack includes the standards and drafts shown in Figure 19. (Italics indicate the documents available in only draft form.) ISO/IEC 12207 already provides a framework and nomenclature for software life cycle processes that has been adopted by the SESC for its collection. Uniform application of this framework will do much to improve the coherency of both the SESC and SC7 collections. Having completed the 12207 standard, the same working group is attempting to accomplish an analogous task with the planned 15288 standard for *system* life cycle processes. WG7 plans to revise 12207 in coordination with the system standard. WG7 is also producing a guide to the application of the 12207 processes. Although also shown in the product stack, the current 9126 standard and its planned replacement, 9126-1, are shown here because they provide a framework for specifying and evaluating the characteristics that a customer desires in a software product. WG2 is revising 6592 to provide a profile of possible documents that might be produced as a result of software development. It would be useful in reaching agreement with a customer regarding the documents to be delivered.

The process stack of the SC7 collection is shown in Figure 20 as subdivided into three areas: system processes; software processes; and process assessment. (Drafts are indicated with italics.) The system and software process standards are repeated here. In addition, the 9294 technical report is a guide to the policies, procedures, and resources needed for effectively managing the production of software documentation. The process assessment category is populated with the planned nine-part set of technical reports.

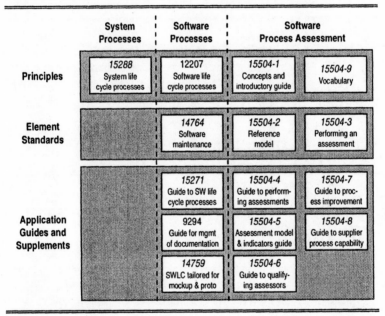

	System Processes	Software Processes	Software Process Assessment	
Principles	*15288* System life cycle processes	12207 Software life cycle processes	*15504-1* Concepts and introductory guide	*15504-9* Vocabulary
Element Standards		*14764* Software maintenance	*15504-2* Reference model	*15504-3* Performing an assessment
Application Guides and Supplements		*15271* Guide to SW life cycle processes	*15504-4* Guide to performing assessments	*15504-7* Guide to process improvement
		9294 Guide for mgmt of documentation	*15504-5* Assessment model & indicators guide	*15504-8* Guide to supplier process capability
		14759 SWLC tailored for mockup & proto	*15504-6* Guide to qualifying assessors	

Figure 20. Inner layers of the process "stack" of the SC7 collection.

The product standards of Figure 21 are placed into the same categories used by SESC. (Draft standards are indicated by the use of italics.) The concept of product evaluation, contrasted with the usual emphasis on software process, pervades this stack. An existing standard, 9126, provides a lexicon of product characteristics and attributes. The planned three-part revision will add metrics for the evaluation of those characteristics. The planned six-part standard, 14598, will specify the process of evaluating those characteristics. A planned standard, 15026, will specify the concepts of system and software integrity levels as important characteristics of software. The planned standard 14143 will specify software functional size measurements, more commonly known as *function points*. The planned 14756 standard will describe the measurement of software system performance using the *remote terminal emulator* technique. The 9127 standard specifies requirements for user documentation and cover information (visible through the "shrink wrap") of consumer software packages. The 12119 standard is based upon a European standard specifying product quality requirements for software packages, such as spreadsheets or word processors. SC7/WG6 is cooperating with ISO TC159 to draw a connection from the product quality standards to the usability and ergonomics work of that Technical Committee.

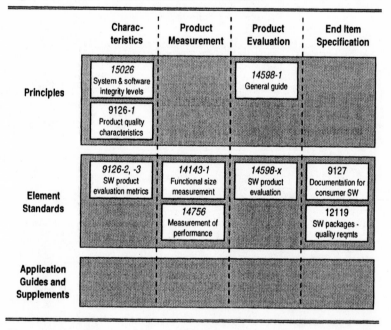

Figure 21. Inner layers of the product "stack" of the SC7 collection.

The technology stack, shown in Figure 22, is dominated by the Software Engineering Data Definition and Interchange (SEDDI) effort of WG11. (Most are unfinished and are marked by the use of italics.) WG11 is cooperating with the EIA to promote a large number of their CASE Data Interchange Format (CDIF) specifications to the status of international standards. The effort is ambitious— literally dozens of documents are planned. The planned 15289 standard will specify a wide variety of software life cycle "process information products," the documents used to effect transition among the processes, activities, and tasks of the life cycle. Finally, 14102 is the first standard in WG4's program for CASE tool evaluation and selection.

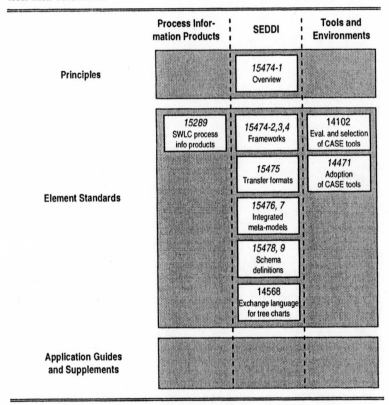

Figure 22. Inner layers of the technology "stack" of the SC7 collection.

Strategic Plans

SC7 is only now beginning to approach their work from a strategic viewpoint and a Strategic Planning Workshop is scheduled for June 1997. Some key documents [Tripp95, SC7-96] provide insight into the thinking of those responsible for the strategic plans.

Software engineering is viewed as existing within the context of several other disciplines. For example, from a process point of view, the origin of the software development process must interface with the requirements portion of the system engineering process and the completion of the software engineering process must achieve an interface with the integration portion of the system engineering process. The products of the software process must implement requirements imposed by various system-level disciplines including quality, safety and dependability.

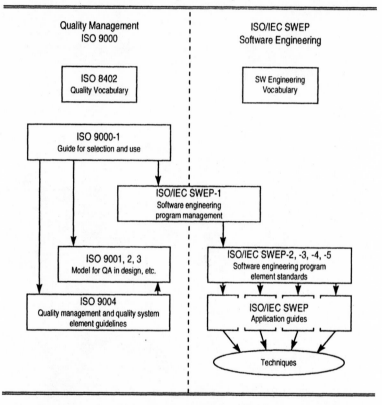

Figure 23. Strategic relationship of the SC7 software engineering program (SWEP) to the TC176 quality management program.

SC7 planning has also adopted some important architectural concepts for its Software Engineering Program (SWEP). We can see an example of those concepts in Figure 23, adapted from [Tripp95], depicting the strategic relationship to the ISO TC176 quality management standards. Although the content of the figure is interesting, the form of the drawing better illustrates the architectural concepts. A layered approach and a toolbox of techniques is apparent; TC56 is given credit for this approach. The attempt to achieve a structure parallel with that of the TC176 collection is also apparent. Finally, but not shown in this diagram, is an SC7 decision to use the ISO/IEC 12207 framework of processes as an organizing concept. All of these architectural concepts have been adopted for use throughout this book.

Canadian Standards Association

In Canada, the boundary between regulatory and voluntary standards is not as distinct as in the United States. Although the Canadian Standards Association is privately funded and staffed, its standards are frequently cited in Canadian federal and provincial law for the purposes of regulation [Cargill89].

CSA's continuing areas of interest, stable for about a decade, include:

- Communications and Information: Information Technology; Electromagnetic Compatibility; and Telecommunications

- Electrical and Electronics: Wiring Products; Industrial Products; Consumer and Commercial Products

- Energy: Renewable Energy; Energy Conservation; Fire Safety Equipment; Fuel Burning Equipment; and Nuclear Energy

- Business and Quality Management Systems: Quality Assurance; Basic Engineering; Protection of Personal Information

- Life Sciences: Health Care Technology; Dentistry; Public Safety; Occupational Health and Safety; Sports and Recreational Equipment

- Environmental Technology and Environmental Management Systems: Sustainable Forestry

- Construction: Building Materials and Products; Concrete; Forest Products; Plumbing Products; Industrial Building Construction; and Design of Structures

- Transportation and Distribution: including Materials Handling and Logistics; Oil and Gas Systems and Materials; and Offshore Structures

- Materials Technology: Welding; and Metals and Metal Products

Established in 1919, membership in CSA is open to any Canadian citizen, business, or organization; membership currently numbers about 9000. An elected Board of Directors governs the CSA with operations delegated to an appointed president. Funding is obtained through membership dues, an extensive certification program dealing with a wide variety of products, and contracts or grants for standards development. Standards are developed by Technical Committees—currently more than a thousand—and are accepted by the consensus of expert opinion. In all, CSA has published about 1,500 standards [CSA96].

Some CSA standards relevant to software quality management are described in Chapter 6.

Context of Software Engineering: Computer Science

Of course, the discipline of software engineering applies the findings of computer science toward the solution of engineering problems. Although that statement is unarguable in principle, its truth is less clear when one examines practice. Few standards provide normative guidance on subjects that are generally regarded to be part of computer science, a phenomenon that has not gone unnoticed. David Parnas has been particularly vocal on the subject, saying that if software engineering is to be regarded as a marriage between the science of software and the profession of engineering, "the marriage is unconsummated" [Parnas95].

To be fair, we should note that computer science results are well-represented in subjects such as language design, operating system design, and communications—all described in standards outside the scope of this book. Software engineers use these products, but the standards of practice that guide their usage can be traced more directly to general engineering disciplines than to computer science.

This chapter will briefly note the software engineering standards that do seem to be closely related to computer science. Most of these standards concern either terminology or relatively low-level techniques.

The first group of standards, listed in Table 40, are vocabularies of terms, many borrowed from computer science, that pertain to the discipline of software engineering. The primary ISO document is 2382, a 28 part vocabulary maintained by JTC1/SC1. All of the parts are relevant to software engineering, but the three most important parts are listed. The Technical Report is a permuted index to the vocabulary; it contains the same terms as 2382.

The most important IEEE standard of this group is IEEE Std 610, a multi-part vocabulary of which Part 12 concerns software engineering. Until recently, the various parts of 610 were controlled by the same sponsors that controlled the related standards. In 1996, though, the decision was made to manage IEEE 610 centrally

Table 40. Standards Containing Computer Science Terminology

Standard	Title
ISO/IEC 2382-1:1984	Data processing—Vocabulary—Section 01: Fundamental terms
ISO/IEC 2382-7:1989	Information technology—Vocabulary—Part 7: Computer programming
ISO/IEC 2382-20:1990	Information technology—Vocabulary—Part 20: System development
ISO/IEC TR 12382:1992	Permuted index of the vocabulary of information technology
IEEE Std 610.12:1990	Standard glossary of software engineering terminology
IEEE P729	Standard for software engineering—Fundamental terms

to improve the consistency of the overall document. Feeling a compelling need to manage its own terminology, SESC elected to initiate its own project, P729, to develop and maintain a standard containing fundamental terminology.[27] When IEEE Std 729 is completed, we can expect that its terminology will migrate into IEEE Std 610 as the latter standard is updated.

Table 41. Standards Containing Computer Science Taxonomies

Standard	Title
ISO/IEC DTR 12182	Categorization of software
ISO/IEC DTR 14399	Mapping of relevant software engineering standards
IEEE Std 1002-1987	Standard taxonomy for software engineering standards

The standards in the next group (Table 41) are taxonomies, based on computer science principles, that are relevant to software engineering standards. Draft Technical Report 12182 describes categories of software (including both products and data) that are produced by various software engineering processes. Draft TR 14399 lists various standards relevant to software engineering and categorizes them in various ways. IEEE Std 1002 is an interesting document classifying various possible roles for software engineering standards. (Both 14399 and 1002 are of greater interest to standards writers than to standards users.)

---

[27]Veterans of SESC will recall that 729 was the number formerly used for software engineering terminology standard until it was merged into IEEE Std 610.

The standards shown in Table 42 describe various techniques that would be familiar to computer scientists. In effect, these documents provide standard names for the techniques as well as settling some details that might otherwise be matters of disagreement. The ISO standards describe techniques that have been common in computer programming for perhaps 25 years:

- 5806 describes the technique of single-hit decision tables with particular emphasis on the documentation of computer-based systems.

- 5807 provides conventions for various types of flowcharts.

- 6593 describes techniques for the batch processing of sequential record files containing control breaks.

- 8631 is, in effect, a standard for structured programming, specifying the various constructs and how they may be combined.

- 11411 provides notations and conventions for expressing state transitions in interactive software, communication protocols, or command languages.

Most software engineers would agree that these standards seem more appropriate to another era of computing. Though still useful, they do not represent the complexity of problems confronting modern practitioners. They are best regarded as the legacy that SC7 inherited from the various other committees that operated in that era.

Table 42. Standards Describing Computer Science Techniques

Standard	Title
ISO 5806:1984	Specification of single-hit decision tables
ISO 5807:1985	Documentation symbols and conventions for data, program, and system flowcharts, program network charts and resource charts
ISO 6593:1985	Program flow for processing sequential files in terms of record groups
ISO/IEC 8631:1989	Program constructs and conventions for their representation
ISO/IEC 11411:1995	Representation for human communication of state transition of software
IEEE Std 1016:1987	Recommended practice for software design descriptions
IEEE Std 1016.1:1993	Guide to software design descriptions
AIAA G-010-1993	Guide for reusable software: Assessment criteria for aerospace application

IEEE Std 1016 and its guide recommend practices for software design descriptions and, implicitly, design itself. In particular, IEEE Std 1016.1 deals with design methods familiar to many computer scientists: function-oriented, data-oriented, real-time control-oriented, object-oriented, and formal language-oriented.

The AIAA G-010 standard provides engineering guidance for the use of reusable software components, a subject currently situated at the boundary between computer science theory and software engineering application. This standard covers a broad area including domain analysis, component assessment, and reuse libraries. Many of the component assessment guidelines are specific to the programming language Ada 83 (ISO/IEC 8652:1987).

CONTEXT OF SOFTWARE ENGINEERING: QUALITY MANAGEMENT

In the relevant bodies of standards, there are two different ways of viewing quality. The first, the approach taken by the famous ISO 9000 series, is to presume that product quality will be the natural result of developing strong quality management and quality assurance systems. The second, the approach taken by ISO/IEC 9126 and associated standards, is to directly define and measure product quality characteristics. Of course, both approaches are important and both are described. This chapter deals with the quality management approach taken by ISO 9000. The product quality standards are discussed in Chapter 12.

Throughout this chapter, references to "ISO 9000" refer to the entire collection of quality management standards maintained by ISO TC176. Because there is a standard designated by that number, any references to it will cite the specific part, for example, ISO 9000-1.

Quality Systems Standards

The ISO 9000 standards take a process-based view of the organization. The fundamental premise of the ISO 9000 standards is that a well-defined engineering process is more likely to create high-quality products than a poorly defined one. To implement a quality system an organization must define its processes and the interfaces among them. Of course, this premise corresponds exactly with accepted wisdom regarding the development of high-quality software. Many software engineers may be surprised to learn that practices they may have regarded as exclusive to software are regarded by ISO 9000 as general to all quality systems. Examples include configuration management, document control, product and process measurements, reviews, and audits. Even process improvement is described in ISO 9004-1. In fact, ISO 9000 has been criticized for aggregating all possible aspects of goodness under the label of "quality."

Table 43. Quality Assurance Standards Relevant to Software
Engineering

Standard	Title
ISO 8402: 1994	Quality management and quality assurance—Vocabulary
ISO 9000-1: 1994	Quality management and quality assurance standards—Part 1: Guidelines for selection and use
ISO 9000-2: 1993	Quality management and quality assurance standards—Part 2: Generic guidelines for the application of ISO 9001, ISO 9002 and ISO 9003
ISO 9000-3: 1991	Quality management and quality assurance standards—Part 3: Guidelines for the application of 9001 to the development, supply, installation and maintenance of computer software
ISO 9000-4: 1993	Quality management and quality assurance standards—Part 4: Guide to dependability programme management
ISO 9001: 1994	Quality systems—Model for quality assurance in design, development, production, installation, and servicing
ISO 9004-1: 1994	Quality management and quality system elements—Part 1: Guidelines
ISO 10005: 1995	Quality management—Guidelines for quality plans
ISO 10007: 1995	Quality management—Guidelines for configuration management
ISO 10013: 1996	Quality management—Guidelines for developing quality manuals

The quality management standards directly relevant to software quality assurance are listed in Table 43. The key document in the application of ISO 9000 to software is ISO 9000-3, a guidance document intended to bridge the gap between the manufacturing orientation of 9001 and the design-centered discipline of software development. The strategy followed by 9000-3 is to expand on the design portion of the 9001 document while leaving untouched the less relevant portions. The guidance introduces the concept of life-cycle but does not dictate the choice of a particular life cycle

Table 44. Software Engineering Standards Related to Quality
Management

Standard	Title
IEEE Std 730-1989	Standard for software quality assurance plans
IEEE Std 730.1-1995	Guide to software quality assurance planning
IEEE Std 1298-1992	Software quality management system—Part 1: Requirements

model. It also introduces activities, like configuration management, that occur independently of life cycle phases and recognizes the distinction between verification and validation (V & V). Refreshingly, clause 6.4.1 admits that there are "no universally accepted measure of software quality."

Table 44 lists the IEEE standards that are directly related to quality management. Additional standards, listed in Table 45, contain provisions supporting the objectives of quality management.

Because the quality management standards of ISO 9000 pervade all aspects of the discipline of software engineering, there are several important routes from the quality management standards to the software engineering standards. This section will consider the guidance provided by ISO 9000-3, its relationship to the IEEE

Table 45. SESC Standards Supporting the Objectives of Quality Management

Standard	Title
IEEE Std 828-1990	Standard for software configuration management plans
IEEE Std 829-1983	Standard for software test documentation
IEEE Std 830-1993	Recommended practice for software requirements specifications
IEEE Std 1008-1987	Standard for software unit testing
IEEE Std 1012-1986	Standard for software verification and validation plans
IEEE Std 1016-1987	Recommended practice for software design descriptions
IEEE Std 1016.1-1993	Guide to software design descriptions
IEEE Std 1028-1988	Standard for software reviews and audits
IEEE Std 1042-1987	Guide to software configuration management
IEEE Std 1044-1993	Standard classification for software anomalies
IEEE Std 1044.1-1995	Guide to classification for software anomalies
IEEE Std 1045-1992	Standard for software productivity metrics
IEEE Std 1058.1-1987	Standard for software project management plans
IEEE Std 1059-1993	Guide for software verification and validation plans
IEEE Std 1061-1992	Standard for a software quality metrics methodology
IEEE Std 1062-1993	Recommended practice for software acquisition
IEEE Std 1074-1995	Standard for developing software life cycle processes
IEEE Std 1074.1-1995	Guide for developing software life cycle processes
IEEE Std 1219-1992	Standard for software maintenance

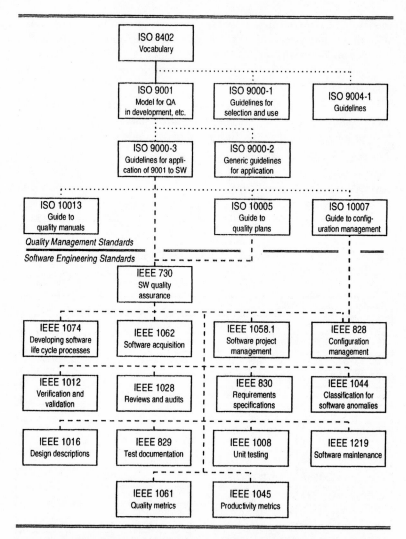

Figure 24. Road map from quality management standards to software engineering standards.

730 software quality assurance standard and from there to other relevant IEEE standards, as shown in Figure 24.

Not shown in this map are other important relationships from the ISO 9000 standards collection to standards of interest:

- The relationship to software life cycle process standards is described in Chapter 13.

- The relationship to dependability standards through a shared standard, IEC 300-1/ISO 9000-4, is described in Chapter 9.

- The relationship to the general discipline of configuration management is described as a topic of project management in Chapter 7.

- Software product quality standards are discussed in Chapter 12.

The collection of quality management standards maintained by ISO TC176 is described in Chapter 4. A subset of those standards is relevant to software engineering. ISO 8402 provides the quality management vocabulary needed to understand the terminology used in the other ISO 9000 standards. In addition, two guides, ISO 9000-1 and ISO 9004-1, provide overall guidance in selecting and applying the other standards. Three standards, ISO 9001, 9002 and 9003, provide normative requirements for quality systems. The one relevant to software engineering is ISO 9001 because only it covers a life cycle broad enough to include development processes. ISO 9000-2 provides generic guidance for applying all three of the normative standards, while ISO 9000-3 provides specific guidance in applying the provisions of ISO 9001 to software. ISO 10013 is a guide to preparing the organization's quality manual while ISO 10005 covers the development of a quality plan for a specific project. ISO 10007 provides guidance to the quality management aspects of configuration management.

The traditional bridge from quality management to software engineering is IEEE Std 730, which prescribes requirements for the quality assurance plan associated with a software project. Other IEEE standards may be useful in applying the provisions of IEEE 730.

ISO 9000-3 and IEEE Std 730

The mandatory requirements for quality assurance in the development of software are provided by ISO 9001. For everyone but "standards lawyers," though, the source for requirements is 9000-3 because, despite its being merely a guide, it applies the 9000 principles directly to the more familiar jargon of software development.

Table 46 is organized to assist the user in selecting software engineering standards relevant to the application of the "requirements" of the ISO 9000-3 guide. It shows detailed relationships between ISO 9000-3 and the other relevant standards. Each row corresponds to the clause (or related group of clauses) from ISO 9000-3 listed in the second column. An informative annex of ISO 9000-3 provides the cross-references to ISO 9001 listed in the first column. The third column lists the clauses of IEEE Std 730 relevant to the clause of ISO 9000-3. Finally, the right-most column lists other IEEE standards which might be helpful in applying the requirements of the corresponding clauses of 9000-3 and 730.[28]

In using IEEE Std 730 with ISO 9000-3, it must be remembered that the documents differ in two fundamental ways:

- ISO 9001 and 9000-3 (as well as the quality manual described in ISO 10013) are meant for application to an entire organization. Although ISO 9001 requires the preparation of quality plans for specific projects, it anticipates that the requirement will be largely satisfied by reference to organizational procedures. IEEE 730 is written for application to a single project.

- ISO 9000-3 describes an overall framework for quality assurance. IEEE 730 describes the content of a software quality assurance *plan* (SQAP); nevertheless, the prescribed content of the plan implies additional requirements comparable to the scope of ISO 9000-3.

ISO 9000-3 begins by describing management's responsibility for organizing a quality system framework. The specific clauses touch on policy and organization as well as requirements for verification and review; supplementary guidance is provided by ISO 10013. The corresponding clauses of IEEE 730 have similar scope but are intended to be project-specific rather than applying to an entire organization. On the other hand, clause 3.0 requires that the SQAP must be approved by the chief operating officer of each business unit having responsibility for execution of the plan, a requirement that would seem impractical outside of the context of an organizational quality program. IEEE 1058.1 describes project management plans and IEEE 1062 is a recommended practice for software acquisition. The management control requirements for verification and for reviews are described in IEEE 1012 and 1028, respectively.

---

[28]This discussion is based on the 1991 version of ISO 9000-3. As described below, a major revision of ISO 9000-3 is currently at the Final Draft International Standard stage.

Table 46. Cross-Reference from ISO 9000-3 to ISO 9001, IEEE Std 730 and Other Useful IEEE Standards.

ISO 9001 Clause	ISO 9003-1 Clause		IEEE Std 730 Clause		Other IEEE Stds
4.1	4.1	Management responsibility	3.0	Approval of SW Qual. Assurance Plan	1028
			3.3	Management	1058.1
			3.4.2.3/.4	SW V&V Plan/SW V&V Report	1012
			3.6.2	Reviews and audits	1062
4.2	4.2	Quality system	3.0	Software Quality Assurance Plan	1058.1
			3.4	Documentation	
4.17	4.3	Internal quality system audits	3.6.2.7	In-process audits	1028
4.14	4.4	Corrective action	3.8	Problem reporting and corrective action	1044
	5.1	General			
4.3	5.2	Contract review	none		
4.3 4.4	5.3	Purchaser's requirements specification	3.4.2.1	SW Requirements Specification	830
			3.6.2.1	SW Requirements Review	1028
4.4	5.4	Development planning	3.3	Management	1058.1
			3.4.3	SW Development Plan	1074
			3.5	Standards, practices, etc	828
			3.9	Tools, techniques and methodologies	829
			3.6.2.8	Managerial reviews	1028
			3.4.2.3/.4	SW V&V Plan/SW V&V Report	1012
4.2 4.4	5.5	Quality planning	3.0	Software Quality Assurance Plan	1061
			3.3	Management	1058.1
4.13 4.4 4.9	5.6	Design and implementation	3.4.2.2	SW Design Description	1028
			3.5	Standards, practices, etc	1016
			3.6	Reviews and audits	
			3.9	Tools, techniques and methodologies	
4.11 4.13 4.4 4.10	5.7	Testing and validation	3.4.2.3/.4	SW V&V Plan/SW V&V Report	829
			3.6.2.4	SW V&V Plan Review	1008
			3.7	Test	1012
4.15 4.10	5.8	Acceptance			
4.13 4.15 4.10	5.9	Replication, delivery and installation	3.6.2.5	Functional audit	
			3.6.2.6	Physical audit	
			3.11	Media control	
4.13 4.19	5.10	Maintenance	3.4.3	SW Maintenance Manual	1219 1044
4.12 4.13 4.4 4.5 4.8	6.1	Configuration management	3.4.2.6	SW Configuration Management Plan	828
			3.10	Code Control	
			3.11	Media control	
4.5	6.2	Document control	3.13	Records collection etc.	828
4.16	6.3	Quality records	3.13	Records collection etc.	1044
4.20 4.11 4.9	6.4	Measurement	3.5	Standards, practices, etc	1061
	6.5	Rules, practices, conventions	3.9	Tools, techniques and methodologies	1045
	6.6	Tools and techniques			1044
4.6 4.7	6.7	Purchasing	3.12	Supplier control	1062
	6.8	Included software product			
4.18	6.9	Training	3.14	Training	

Clause 4.2 of ISO 9000-3 requires planning and documentation of the quality system, a requirement met by the SQAP itself along with the documentation requirements of IEEE 730.

The next clause, 4.3, is not satisfied well by IEEE Std 730. That clause calls for internal audits of the quality system. The closest match in 730 calls for in-process reviews of the software design. Users could apply IEEE 1028 to meet that requirement.

A corrective action process is required by clause 4.4 of ISO 9000-3 and by clause 3.8 of IEEE 730. No IEEE standard prescribes a corrective action process but IEEE Std 1044 is helpful in classifying the types of anomalies to be tracked by such a system.

Clause 5.2 of ISO 9000-3 requires that the supplier should review received contracts. Apparently believing it obvious, the writers of IEEE 730 omitted this activity.

Requirements specification is the subject of ISO 9000-3 clause 5.3 and is premised on mutual cooperation between acquirer and supplier. IEEE 830 deals with the specification itself and IEEE 1028 provides a mechanism for reviewing the specification, both supporting clauses 3.4.2.1 and 3.6.2.1 of IEEE Std 730.

Clause 5.4 places requirements on a development plan. IEEE Std 730 and IEEE Std 1058.1 specify similar requirements. Several more IEEE standards are useful in detailing the requirements— 828 (Configuration Management), 829 (Test Documentation), 1012 (Verification and Validation), and 1028 (Reviews and Audits). In particular, clause 5.4.2.1 requires definition of a "disciplined process or methodology" including "development phases," inputs, outputs, and verification procedures. IEEE Std 1074, Developing Software Life Cycle Processes, would be particular helpful in satisfying these requirements.

The quality planning activities of ISO 9000-3 clause 5.5 are treated by the SQAP of IEEE 730 and by the project management plan of IEEE 1058.1. The quality metrics methodology described in IEEE 1061 would be helpful in setting quality objectives.

Clauses 5.6 and 5.7 of ISO 9000-3 focus on the design, implementation, and test activities central of software development. The recommended practice for software design descriptions in IEEE 1016 may be helpful. IEEE standards 1008 and 829 describe unit testing and test documentation, respectively. Of course, reviews and audits are described in IEEE Std 1028 and V & V is described in IEEE Std 1012.

The ISO 9000-3 requirements for acceptance test, set forth in clause 5.8, are rather general in nature and have no specific counterpart in the IEEE standards. The audit and media control requirements of IEEE 730 are helpful, but not sufficient, in meeting the replication, delivery, and installation requirements in clause 5.9 of 9000-3.

Clause 5.10 of 9000-3 provides an extensive list of quality requirements for the maintenance phase of the life cycle. While IEEE 730 itself makes only passing mention of maintenance, IEEE Std 1219 provides important and detailed requirements for implementing a conforming maintenance process.

Clauses 6.1 through 6.9 of ISO 9000-3 provide requirements for the "supporting activities," those that are not specific to a particular phase of the life cycle. Clauses 6.1 and 6.2 deal with the important subjects of configuration management and document control. Appropriate requirements for detailing these activities are found in IEEE Std 828, Software Configuration Management Plans.

The specific subject of quality records falls in clause 6.3 of ISO 9000-3. Although the IEEE standards do not directly address quality records in their full generality, the provisions of several of the standards could contribute, notably IEEE 1044 providing for the classification of detected software anomalies.

Clause 6.4 of 9000-3 prescribes measurements and clauses 6.5 and 6.6 urge the use of appropriate procedures and tooling to implement the quality system. IEEE Std 730 mentions some specific examples in clauses 3.5 and 3.9. Much more detail can be found in IEEE 1045 and 1061, the standards for productivity and quality metrics, respectively.

Requirements governing the supplier's purchases from vendors are provided in clauses 6.7 and 6.8 of ISO 9000-3. The IEEE 1062 recommended practice on software acquisition may be helpful in implementing these requirements.

Finally, ISO 9000-3 clause 6.9 deals with training. Aside from a mention in clause 3.14 of IEEE Std 730, the IEEE standards do not deal with this subject.

The Proposed Revision of ISO 9000-3

Some individuals in the software engineering community have expressed frustration because 9000-3 is arranged differently than ISO 9001. The relationship between the two is established by tables of cross-references whose entries are sometimes puzzling. (It is reported that the murky correspondence sometimes causes assessors to attempt to enforce the guidelines of 9000-3 as if they were mandatory requirements.) Responding to this concern, ISO TC176 recently agreed to restructure the 9000-3 guide in a manner matching the 9001 standard, making the relationships more apparent. In fact, the current draft repeats (inside boxes) the entire text of clause 4 of the 9001 standard, with guidance interspersed at appropriate points.

Table 47. Correspondence of DIS 9000-3 with Other Standards

DIS 9000-3 Clause	Title	References to Other ISO Standards	References to Clauses of ISO/IEC 12207	Useful IEEE Standards
4.1	Management responsibility			
4.2	Quality system	10013	6.3	
4.2.3	Quality planning	10005		730, 1061
4.3	Contract review		5.2.1, 5.2.6	
4.4	Design control			
4.4.1	General		5.2.5, 5.3	1074
4.4.2	Design and development planning		5.2.4	1058.1, 1045
4.4.3	Organizational and technical interfaces		5.2.6.1, 6.6.2	1028
4.4.4	Design input	9126	5.3.2, 5.3.4	830, 1233
4.4.5	Design output		5.3.3-10	1471, 1016, 1063
4.4.6	Design review		6.3.2.3, 6.6.3	1028
4.4.7	Design verification		5.3.9, 6.4	1012
4.4.8	Design validation		5.3.11, 6.5	1012
4.5	Document and data control		6.1	828
4.6	Purchasing		5.1	1062
4.8	Product identification and traceability	10007	6.2.1	828
4.9	Process control		7.1, 7.2	
4.10	Inspection and testing		5.3.5-5.3.11	829, 1008
4.11	Control of inspection, measuring and test equipment	10012		
4.13	Control of non-conforming product		6.8	1044
4.14	Corrective and preventive action		6.8, 7.3	1044
4.17	Internal quality audits	10011	6.7, 6.8, 7.3	
4.18	Training		7.4	
4.19	Servicing	9000-2	5.4.4, 5.5	1219

Another important change has been made in the draft. Cross-references to the ISO/IEC 12207 life cycle process standard have been provided. For users of IEEE standards, this has an important result. IEEE Std 730 will no longer be the most appropriate gateway from the quality management standards to the software engineering standards. Instead, 12207 will fill that role. In fact, DIS 9003-1 overtly reinterprets some of the jargon of ISO 9001 in terms of ISO/IEC 12207 language. For example, "design" and "development" in 9001 are mapped to "development" in 12207; "design and development planning" is interpreted to encompass the development and the supporting processes of 12207; and "servicing" is equated to "maintenance" in 12207. Using 12207 as a gateway is good news for those interested in implementing enterprise-level software engineering processes. The 12207 document is more appropriate than 730 in this regard, and fits better with the enterprise level quality processes required by the ISO 9000 series.

The new ISO 9000-3 is still in draft stage and changes may yet be made. Nevertheless, Table 47 provides some insight into how the mapping to software engineering will be simplified. The first two columns list clauses selected from DIS 9000-3; their titles and numbers are identical to clauses in ISO 9001. The next column lists references to other quality management standards provided by the text of ISO 9001 or DIS 9000-3. The fourth column lists references to clauses of ISO/IEC 12207 made in the DIS text of 9000-3, along with some additional references[29] that may be added before the document is approved. Finally, the fifth column suggests IEEE standards that may be useful in implementing the guidance set forth.

If the new ISO 9000-3 is published in something like its current form (and this seems likely to occur by the end of 1997), then IEEE Std 730 will have to be reevaluated. Certainly, its application, at least in the context of ISO 9000 compliance, will change—the best use of the standard will shift from prescribing quality assurance *planning* to prescribing the format and contents of a quality assurance *plan*. It seems likely that IEEE SESC will choose to revise the standard along these lines; perhaps it will become a map, similar in content to Table 47, describing the application of the various SESC standards in the context of ISO 9000.

An Alternative: AS 3563.1/IEEE Std 1298

For several years, IEEE Std 1298 has played a role similar to that planned for the revised 9000-3 guide. Concerned with the obscure correspondence between 9001 and the old 9000-3 guide, Stan-

---

[29]Many of the additions were suggested by [SC7-97].

dards Australia developed its own document, Software Quality Management System, Part 1: Requirements. The 1991 revision, AS 3563.1-1991, is structured to map directly to the key clauses of 9001. The IEEE has adopted this standard as IEEE Std 1298-1992, but ANSI declined to designate it as a national standard, because of the obvious overlap in scope with the American Society for Quality Control (ASQC) adoption of 9000-3.

The Australian experience in developing the document described above provides benefits for the rest of the world. The plan for the restructuring of 9000-3 is based largely on extensive comments provided by Standards Australia during the revision process.

When the revision of ISO 9000-3 is approved, it seems likely that IEEE will withdraw Std 1298. This short life expectancy would discourage the use of AS 3563.1/IEEE 1298 as a basis for developing organizational processes implementing the ISO 9000 quality management principles. On the other hand, organizations urgently interested in a single, self-contained document making the connection from quality management to software engineering may find that IEEE 1298 meets their short-term needs.

An Alternative: CAN/CSA-Q396

The combination of ISO 9001 and 9000-3 has been criticized for inadequately differentiating levels of software criticality and for providing inadequate support for the make-buy decision in obtaining software components of a system. To deal with these concerns, the Canadian Standards Association (CSA) has developed a series of documents that categorize software in two dimensions: critical versus non-critical, and developed versus pre-developed, as shown

Table 48. Canadian Standards for Software Quality Assurance

Standard	Title
CAN/CSA Q396.0 (1991)	Guide for selecting and applying the CAN/CSA-Q396-89 software quality assurance program standards
CAN/CSA Q396.1.1 (1989)	Quality assurance program for the development of software used in critical applications
CAN/CSA Q396.1.2 (1989)	Quality assurance program for previously developed software used in critical applications
CAN/CSA Q396.2.1 (1989)	Quality assurance program for the development of software used in non-critical applications
CAN/CSA Q396.2.2 (1989)	Quality assurance program for previously developed software used in non-critical applications

in Table 48 [Joannou95]. A separate standard occupies each of the four categories and an overall guide describes general subjects and provides guidance in selecting the appropriate standard. The guide provides extensive information regarding the relationships of the CSA standards to other standards, including the ISO 9000 series, IEEE 730, RTCA DO-178B, and other standards of interest.

On the other hand, the CAN/CSA Q396 standards fail to solve another problem of the 9000-3 standard. Though adequately dealing with the disciplines of quality management and software engineering, in any realistic situation, they fail to address the systems engineering problems involved in developing the system [Harauz97].

CONTEXT OF SOFTWARE ENGINEERING: PROJECT MANAGEMENT

Management involves the activities and tasks undertaken by people for the purpose of planning and controlling the activities of others in order to achieve objectives that could not be achieved by individual action. *Project management* is a system of management procedures, practices, technologies, skill, and experience applied to managing an engineering project [Thayer95].

Project Management Standards for Software

The most important tenet in the study of management is a principle called the *universality of management* [Fayol49, Koontz72] stating that:

- Management performs the same functions of planning, organizing, staffing, directing, and controlling regardless of the nature of the activity being managed.

- Management functions are characteristic duties of managers, but the specific practices, techniques and methods are particular to the nature of the activity being managed.

This concept permits us to apply general management principles to the particular needs of software project management [Thayer84]. The two standards, shown in Table 49, perform this specialization. The Program Management Institute's (PMI) document, often called the PMBOK Guide and currently in the process of being adopted as an IEEE standard, provides the principles. IEEE Std 1058.1 applies the principles to software project management.

One of the characteristic functions of management is controlling, which necessarily involves measurement of the processes being executed and products being produced. Standards helpful in the measurement of software engineering products and processes are listed in Table 50. The two draft ISO/IEC standards are shown in italics.

Table 49. Project Management Standards Relevant to Software Engineering

Standard	Title
PMI, 1996	A guide to the project management body of knowledge
IEEE Std 1058.1-1987	Standard for software project management plans

Table 50. Standards for Software Engineering Measurement

Standard	Title
IEEE Std 982.1-1988	Standard dictionary of measures to produce reliable software
IEEE Std 982.2-1988	Guide for the use of standard dictionary of measures to produce reliable software
IEEE Std 1044-1993	Standard classification for software anomalies
IEEE Std 1044.1-1995	Guide to classification for software anomalies
IEEE Std 1045-1992	Standard for software productivity metrics
IEEE Std 1061-1992	Standard for a software quality metrics methodology
ISO/IEC DIS 14143-1	Software measurement—Functional size measurement—Part 1: Definition of concepts
ISO/IEC CD 14756	Measurement and rating of performance of computer-based software systems

Table 51. Configuration Management Standards Relevant to Software Engineering

Standard	Title
ISO 10007:1995	Quality management—Guidelines for configuration management
EIA/IS-649 (1995)	National consensus standard for configuration management
IEEE Std 828-1990	Standard for software configuration management plans
IEEE Std 1042-1987	Guide to software configuration management
ISO/IEC CD 12220	Software life cycle process—Configuration management for software

To a software development project, one of the most important management control functions is configuration management (CM). Software CM, though, is a specialization of a more general discipline. Important CM standards are listed in Table 51. Italics mark standards available only in draft form.

As will be explained below, *planning* is one of the five characteristic functions of project management. The standards listed in Table 52 deal with plans for various activities specific to software engineering project management. Although these standards address *plans*, their import is not necessarily confined to the *planning* function of project management. Implicit within the requirements for the content of the plans are requirements for the controls on execution of those plans. Hence, it can be said that these standards also address *controlling*, another one of the five functions of management.

Table 52. Standards for Software Engineering Plans

Standard	Title
IEEE Std 730-1989	Standard for software quality assurance plans
IEEE Std 730.1-1995	Guide to software quality assurance planning
IEEE Std 828-1990	Standard for software configuration management plans
IEEE Std 1042-1987	Guide to software configuration management
IEEE Std 829-1983	Standard for software test documentation
IEEE Std 1012-1986	Standard for software verification and validation plans
IEEE Std 1059-1993	Guide for software verification and validation plans
IEEE Std 1228-1994	Standard for software safety plans
ISO/IEC TR 9294:1990	Guidelines for the management of software documentation
IEEE Std 1062-1993	Recommended practice for software acquisition

PMI Guide to the PMBOK

A project management road map is shown in Figure 25. (Two of the ISO/IEC documents are shown in italics because they are not yet approved standards.) Like the other road maps for the context of software engineering, it focuses on a single discipline, omitting important related disciplines, like quality management, that are depicted in their own road map diagrams.

The project management road map begins with the Guide to the Program Management Body of Knowledge (PMBOK). The Program Management Institute (PMI) defines the *Program Management Body of Knowledge* as the sum of knowledge within the profession of project management. The *PMBOK Guide* is intended to describe the subset of the PMBOK that is generally accepted and to provide a common lexicon for discussion of project management. The *PMBOK Guide* is used by the PMI in certification activities including accreditation of degree-granting educational programs and professional certification programs.

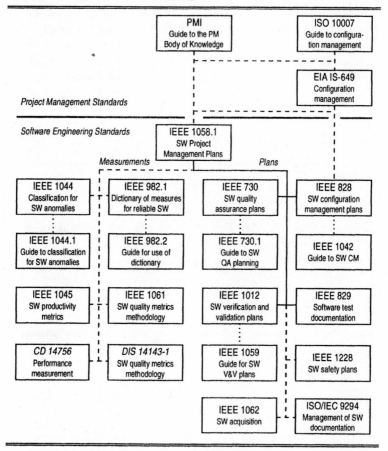

Figure 25. Road map from project management standards to software engineering standards.

The guide describes project management as an instance of general management—the planning, organizing, staffing, executing, and controlling the operations of an ongoing enterprise. Project management applies those techniques to the *project—a temporary endeavor undertaken to create a unique product or service*. The temporary nature of the project implies, of course, that each one has a definite beginning and an end.

The guide describes five types of management processes:

- *Initiating*—recognizing that a project or phase should begin and committing to do so,

- *Planning*—devising and maintaining a workable scheme to

Table 53. Project Management Knowledge Areas and Processes

Knowledge Area	Process
Project integration management	Project plan development Project plan execution Overall change control
Project scope management	Initiation Scope planning Scope definition Scope verification Scope change control
Project time management	Activity definition Activity sequencing Activity duration estimating Schedule development Schedule control
Project cost management	Resource planning Cost estimating Cost budgeting Cost control
Project quality management	Quality planning Quality assurance Quality control
Project human resource management	Organizational planning Staff acquisition Team development
Project communications management	Communications planning Information distribution Performance reporting Administrative closure
Project risk management	Risk identification Risk quantification Risk response development Risk response control
Project procurement management	Procurement planning Solicitation planning Solicitation Source selection Contract administration Contract close-out

accomplish the business need that the project was undertaken to address,

- *Executing*—coordinating people and other resources to carry out the plan,

- *Controlling*—ensuring that project objectives are met by monitoring and measuring progress and taking corrective action when necessary,

- *Closing*—formalizing acceptance of the project or phase and bringing it to an orderly end.

The guide then specializes those process types into 37 instances of processes that are each applied to nine program management knowledge areas, as shown in Table 53.

IEEE 1058.1—Software Project Management Plans

In the preface to the 1975 edition of The Mythical Man-Month, Fred Brooks says that managing a software project is more like other types of management than most programmers initially believe [Brooks95]. Although the IEEE standard for project management, 1058.1, was not originally written with the PMBOK Guide in mind, it can still be viewed as providing a specialization of the PMBOK processes.

IEEE Std 1058.1 describes the format and content of software project management plans. (Development of the plan would imply that many of the planning processes of the PMBOK have been completed.) The standard is intended to be applicable to software projects of any size or type. The plan specified by the standard is intended to subsume the software development plan described in IEEE Std 730, Software Quality Assurance Plans.

Table 54 shows the outline of the plan required by IEEE Std 1058.1. IEEE standards that are normatively referenced by 1058.1 or that otherwise seem helpful are noted.

Section 3.4 of the plan would describe the mechanisms for monitoring and controlling adherence to the plan. IEEE Std 1044 and its accompanying guide deal with the classification of software anomalies; statistics based on these classifications may be useful in monitoring the maturity and quality of the software product. IEEE 1045 describes a variety of productivity metrics that may be useful in monitoring progress.

Table 54. Cross-reference from IEEE 1058.1 to Other Standards

Outline of Software Project Management Plan	Normative Refs to IEEE Stds	Helpful Stds (IEEE except as noted)
1 Introduction		
1.1 Project overview		
1.2 Project deliverables		
1.3 Evolution of the plan		
1.4 Reference materials		
1.5 Definitions and acronyms		
2 Project organization		
2.1 Process model		
2.2 Organizational structure		
2.3 Organizational boundaries and interfaces		
2.4 Project responsibilities		
3 Managerial process		
3.1 Management objectives and priorities		
3.2 Assumptions, dependencies, and constraints		
3.3 Risk management		
3.4 Monitoring and controlling mechanisms		1044, 1044.1, 1045
3.5 Staffing plan		
4 Technical process		
4.1 Methods, tools and techniques		982.1, 982.2, ISO/IEC 14143, ISO/IEC 14756
4.2 Software documentation	829	ISO/IEC 9294
4.3 Project support functions		
• Quality assurance	730, 730.1	1061
• Configuration management	828, 1042	
• Verification and validation	1012, 1059	
5 Work packages, schedule, and budget		
5.1 Work packages		
5.2 Dependencies		
5.3 Resource requirements		
5.4 Budget and resource allocation		
5.5 Schedule		
6 Additional components		1062, 1228
6.1 Index		
6.2 Appendices		

Section 4.1 of the plan is intended to describe methods, tools, and techniques to be employed in the project. If reliability is an important consideration, it may be addressed in this portion of the plan. IEEE Std 982.1 and its guide, 982.2, may be useful. Candidate measurements of other characteristics can be found in ISO/IEC 14143-1, Functional Size Measurement, and ISO/IEC 14756, Measurement and Rating of Performance of Computer-Based Software Systems.

Section 4.2 of the plan would contain the plan for documenting the software project. IEEE 829 is a standard for software test documentation. ISO/IEC 9294 may be helpful as a guide to overall management of the software documentation process.

Section 4.3 of the plan would describe "project support functions," including the three listed in the table. The corresponding IEEE standards and their accompanying guides are normatively referenced for this portion of the plan. The IEEE standard on quality metrics methodology, 1061, may also be helpful. Some may prefer to view these functions as "project control" and may wish to address them in Section 3.4 of the plan.

Section 6 of the plan prescribed by IEEE Std 1058.1 would contain any "additional components." In appropriate situations, software managers may want to consider including a software safety plan, IEEE Std 1228. If software acquisitions are part of the project, the planning provisions of IEEE 1062 may be helpful.

Obviously, using other IEEE software engineering standards is appropriate in a properly managed software project. This discussion has focused on the particular standards specifically addressing the manager's needs for plans and measurements of the product under development and the processes employed in the development.

Configuration Management Standards

Software professionals may consider configuration management (CM) to be a subject specific to software, but software CM is actually a subset of a far broader discipline. From the viewpoint of project management, it is cited as a "technique" of the "overall change control process" in the PMBOK Guide, and can be used not only to control the software product but also to control the overall management process. CM also has an important relationship to systems engineering processes; particularly for software projects that are a part of the development of an encompassing system, it may be desirable to view software CM as an instance of systems-level CM. Finally, CM can be regarded as an aspect of quality management; ISO 10007 provides guidance from this viewpoint.

EIA/IS-649 is an interim standard addressing the subject from a system-level viewpoint. The interim standard was developed as a replacement for a military standard, Mil-Std 973. It can be expected that further consideration and revision of the interim standard will lead to a follow-on document fully applicable to both defense and commercial systems. That follow-on standard will be submitted for ANSI standardization, probably under the designation EIA-649.

The EIA document does not contain mandatory requirements and is intended for neither compliance nor evaluation. It describes principles that should be observed in the development of enterprise-wide practices for CM in specific areas of application.

It should be noted that ISO/IEC JTC1/SC7 is developing a standard for CM, ISO/IEC CD 12220. Progress, however, has been contentious, hence slow.

CONTEXT OF SOFTWARE ENGINEERING: SYSTEMS ENGINEERING

According to anecdotal accounts, relationships between systems and software engineering functions of the typical organization are contentious enough to confirm their status as sibling disciplines. Nevertheless, modern information technology products, even the software-intensive ones, are complex enough to require application of techniques from both disciplines. Andriole and Freeman write that "we have found that the creation of software-intensive systems demands more than what is traditionally in either of the fields" [Andriole93]. Accordingly, it becomes important to understand the relationships between relevant standards for systems and software engineering.

There are many definitions of systems engineering. The IEEE definition is "the application of the mathematical and physical sciences to develop systems that utilize economically the materials and forces of nature for the benefit of mankind" [IEEE96]. The purposes of this book are better served by a definition emphasizing the activities rather than the results of systems engineering: "An iterative process of top-down synthesis, development, and operation of a real-world system that satisfies, in a near optimal manner, the full range of requirements for the system" [Eisner88].

From this viewpoint, most of the disciplines forming the context of software engineering, though treated separately in Chapters 5-10, are applied by the systems engineering process. Although this book focuses on the software aspects of the contextual disciplines, it must be remembered that the systems engineering process will apply the disciplines in a broader sense to the overall requirements of the product.

Andriole and Freeman make an interesting case for the creation of a new *software systems engineering* discipline, citing the complementary nature of the current fields. Table 55 depicts how Andriole and Freeman compare the relative strengths of the two disciplines in areas regarded as requirements for the development of software-intensive systems.[30] This book will take a more conservative approach and view software engineering as one of several disciplines needed to create the products that are specified and integrated by systems engineers.

Table 55. Relative Strengths of Systems and Software Engineering Disciplines for Developing Software-Intensive Systems (Adapted from [Andriole93])

	Systems Engineering	Software Engineering
Alternative design methods	High	Medium
Multidisciplinary orientation	High	Low
User requirements analysis and prototyping	High	Low
Criteria-based trade-off analysis	High	Low
Detailed software specifications	Medium	High
Optimal software production	Medium	High
Methods integration (re-)planning	Medium	Low
Education and training curricula	Medium	Medium
Artifact profiling	Medium	Medium
Applications range assessment	Medium	Medium
Measurements and standards	Medium	Medium
Processes/metrics introspection	Medium	Medium

Legend: Black = High; Gray = Medium; White = Low.

Table 56 lists systems engineering standards appropriate for usage in software-intensive projects. (Drafts are distinguished by the use of italics.) Work on IEEE 1220 began in 1990 and efforts were coordinated with a parallel effort in the Department of Defense (DoD) to update its systems engineering standard to the document that became Mil-Std 499B. The 1220 document was approved as a Trial Use standard in 1994, at roughly the same time that the DoD decided to shift emphasis from its own standards to commercially available ones. In creating its Interim Standard 632, EIA accomplished the task of converting the defense acquisition jargon of 499B to commercial terminology. So, all of these standards—1220, 499B and IS-632—share a similar model of the systems engineering process. EIA is now in the process of revising IS-632 and promoting it to the status of an ANSI standard with the working title Processes for Engineering a System. Recent events indicate that the EIA group may depart from the previous model

---

[30]If any of the current standards are suitable for the prescription of such a merged discipline, IEEE Std 1220 is probably the closest.

and develop a new one. The motivation for a new model would be a desire for a generalized umbrella under which systems engineering standards for various disciplines (information technology being only a single example) might comfortably fit.

ISO/IEC JTC1 is also developing a systems engineering standard (marked by italics in Table 56). The JTC1 project began in SC7/WG7 in 1996 and will probably complete circa 2000. As of early 1997, the project is proceeding afresh without adopting any of the other standards as a base document. Its primary advantage is an opportunity to concurrently revise the software life cycle processes standard, ISO/IEC 12207, to achieve a good fit between the two.

Table 56. Systems Engineering Standards Relevant to Software

Standard	Title
EIA/IS-632	Systems engineering
EIA Draft 632	Processes for engineering a system
IEEE Std 1220-1994	(Trial Use) Standard for application and management of the systems engineering process
ISO/IEC WD 15288	System life cycle processes

Table 57 lists several standards that can be considered as describing products that are shared between systems and software engineering—products that comprise the "hand-off" from the systems engineers to the software engineers. Two of the IEEE documents are marked with italics to indicate that they are only drafts. It should be noted that both IEEE and AIAA have developed guides for Concept of Operations documents; the AIAA guide might be particularly appropriate for use in aerospace applications.

Table 57. Standards Relevant to Processes Shared by Systems and Software Engineering

Standard	Title
IEEE P1362	Guide for concept of operations document
AIAA G-043-1992	Guide for the preparation of operations concept documents
IEEE P1471	Recommended practice for system design—Architectural description
IEEE Std 1233-1996	Guide for developing system requirements specifications

Finally, Table 58 lists process standards that are strongly related to systems engineering. (The use of italics notes documents that exist only in draft form.) They place requirements on processes that are part of systems engineering, or shared with systems engineering, or that must interface with systems engineering.[31] ISO/IEC 12207 describes software life cycle processes but places requirements on the system architecture and system requirements activities. The other two ISO documents are guides planned to elaborate on the requirements of ISO/IEC 12207. IEEE/EIA 12207.0 is an adaptation of the ISO/IEC standard for use in the United States. The other two parts of the US standard provide guidance regarding life cycle data and detailed implementation of the processes.

Table 58. Software Engineering Standards with a Relationship to Systems Standards

Standard	Title
ISO/IEC 12207:1995	Information technology—Software life cycle processes
ISO/IEC DTR 14759	Software life cycle model tailored for mock-up and prototype
ISO/IEC DTR 15271	Guide to ISO/IEC 12207 (Software life cycle processes)
IEEE/EIA 12207.0-1996	Information technology—Software life cycle processes
IEEE/EIA P12207.1	Guide for information technology—Software life cycle processes—Life cycle data
IEEE/EIA P12207.2	Guide for information technology—Software life cycle processes—Implementation considerations

Systems Engineering Process Standards

The systems engineering road map, shown in Figure 26, is in three layers.[32] (Documents that exist only as drafts are shown in italics.) The top layer depicts the IEEE standard for systems engineering processes, the bottom layer depicts the IEEE standard for software engineering processes, and the middle one shows standards describing the products that form part of the interface between the two disciplines. (The various standards detailing the software life cycle processes are not shown in the figure because their treatment would be identical to that described in Chapter 13.)

---

[31]These distinctions are not strong ones—they largely depend on the point of view that you choose to adopt.

[32]Like the other road maps, this one suppresses second-order relationships to the other contextual disciplines that are provided with their own road maps.

You should not conclude from the diagram that systems engineering and software engineering utilize distinct processes. Software engineering processes are better viewed as specializations of corresponding systems engineering processes. On any given project, the executions of the processes may be largely distinct, but certain activities (listed in Table 59 below) are shared. The interface standards are helpful tools in effecting that sharing.

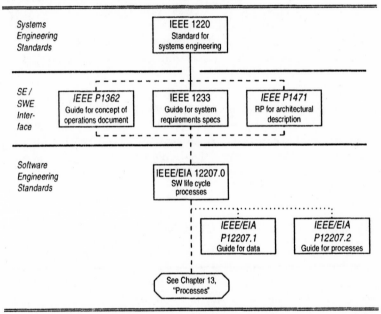

Figure 26. Road map from systems engineering standards to software engineering standards.

IEEE 1220 has the objective of defining the requirements for an enterprise's total technical effort related to development of systems and consumer products (including computers and software) as well as the processes that will provide life cycle support for those products. The integrated technical approach prescribed by the standard requires the application and management of the systems engineering process throughout the product's life cycle. The process is applied recursively to the development of the system, its constituent components and its support processes. The approach is intended neither to provide a mission statement for a systems engineering organization nor a job description for a systems engineer. Instead, it prescribes what must be accomplished across the entire organization to produce the product. The standard is intended to be applicable for incremental enhancements to existing products as well as new products and to one-at-a-time products, like a satellite, as well as mass-produced products. The scope of the standard encompasses all phases of the product's life from initial concept through development, operation and disposal.

The IEEE 1220 document contains normative references to several other standards. In regard to quality management (clause 4.13), it invokes ANSI/ASQC Q91-1987. Today, it would probably be more appropriate to use Q91's replacement, ANSI/ASQC Q9001-1994, the US adoption of ISO 9001. For system requirements specifications (clause 5.1.2), 1220 cites IEEE Std 1233. As a general reference to verification and validation processes, 1220 calls out IEEE Std 1012.

For some applications, the interim standard EIA/IS-632 may be an appropriate alternative to IEEE 1220. When completed, the revised EIA 632 and the planned ISO/IEC 15288 may also provide appropriate alternatives. It is also possible (and the intention of some of the participants) that the completed standards should form a hierarchy proceeding from 15288 (the most general), through 632, to 1220 (sector-specific).

Systems/Software Interface

A system is composed of a hierarchy of component products provided by various suppliers. Each supplier regards its own component product as a system and itself applies the systems engineering process for its development. Most of today's complex systems include a software component. As noted at the beginning of this chapter, the development of a software component requires the application of a different discipline, software engineering. To successfully develop the software, the software engineers need various items from the systems engineers to describe the desired result. History has demonstrated this to be non-trivial.

Concept of Operations

During the past dozen or so years, the development of a Concept of Operations document has become an increasingly popular tool for the transmission of necessary information between systems and software engineers as well as other stake holders. The technique can be traced back to 1980 [Lano80] and the Department of Defense incorporated various descriptions of the document into some of its software development standards—2167, 2167A, and 498. A form of the document now appears in EIA/IEEE J-Std-016. IEEE is preparing a separate standard, IEEE P1362, coordinated with the US adaptation of the 12207 life cycle standard. The document will be a guide, but will contain specific descriptions of desired content and format.

Concept analysis refers to a technique for analyzing a problem and the characteristics of a proposed solution within the context of the operational environment of the solution, so as to view both problem and solution from the vantage point of the intended user. Emphasis is placed on an integrated view of the operational characteristics of the system. The results of the concept analysis are captured in the Concept of Operations document [Fairley95].

A key feature of the IEEE ConOps document is the emphasis on describing the characteristics of both the current system and the proposed system. Furthermore, in long-lived systems, the document can point the way for anticipated evolution, all within the context of the operational environment. A major goal is avoiding the creation of a system which fails to fill a useful role despite the successful technical development of its constituent parts.

AIAA G-043 is a possible alternative to IEEE P1362, especially for aerospace projects. The AIAA standard devotes relatively more attention to the use of the ConOps document and process for preparing it, while the IEEE standard focuses on the contents of the document. The principal drafter of the IEEE document differentiates the two by saying that the AIAA document is more oriented toward the developer's view of the user rather than the user's operational view [Fairley95].

System Requirements

IEEE Std 1233 provides guidance for the document containing the system requirements. Although it cites IEEE 1220 for the process of creating the requirements specification, it does provide additional guidance on that subject. It is important to note that the system requirements specification (SysRS) does more than simply record the desires of the customer. A key function of systems engineering is to capture and articulate additional requirements that have gone unstated by the acquirer of the system.

Of course, the SysRS is the key document relating the needs of the customer to the technical community who will specify and build the system. There is a reason, though, why the SysRS is important as a tool for communication between system and software engineers; during the systems architecture process, requirements from the SysRS are allocated to the various components of the system, including the software components. Therefore, the SysRS not only enumerates the system-level requirements levied on the software component, it also depicts those requirements in relation to those of other components.

Architecture

Perhaps the hottest topic in software engineering today is *architecture*. A planning group of the SESC selected as its definition of the term [SESC96c]:

> An architecture *is the highest-level concept of a system in its environment.*

It should be noted that the definition applies at the "system" level because architecture is perceived as a mechanism for ensuring a harmonious conceptualization of the system at both the systems and software levels of development. The definition refers to the "highest" level in order to prevent diluting the term to describe all of design and reminds us, by emphasis on "environment," that the operational characteristics of the system are to be addressed [Ellis96].

IEEE Project P1471 is intended to develop a recommended practice for architectural description, providing a mechanism for communications of system-level and software-level architectural information among all involved parties.

Systems/Software Process Relationships

ISO/IEC 12207[33] is an important standard, in part because it extends the traditional software life cycle processes to encompass their relationships to systems engineering. Activities and tasks shared with systems level processes are shown in Table 59. The remainder of this section describes those shared functions from the software point of view, using the terminology of 12207. The terminology used for the systems-level processes is generic because the companion effort to create an SC7 systems-level standard has not yet settled on terminology.

The acquisition process of 12207 is initiated by the description of the operational concept for the system. The acquirer is then required to define and analyze requirements for the system.

---

[33]The ISO/IEC version of 12207 is referenced here because the same working group is developing the corresponding standard for systems engineering. The IEEE/EIA version contains identical requirements as well as additional guidance.

Table 59. Relationships of ISO/IEC 12207 Activities and Tasks to
Systems Level Processes

Software process	Clause	Systems level process
Acquisition process	5.1.1.1	Operational concept
	5.1.1.2	System requirements
Supply process	5.2.1.1	System requirements
Development process	5.3.2	System requirements analysis
	5.3.3	System architectural design
	5.3.10	System integration
	5.3.11	System qualification testing
Verification process	6.4.2.3, 6.4.2.6	Requirements and integration verification
Validation process	6.5.2.2, 6.5.2.5	System validation

The supply process is initiated with the supplier's review of the requirements expressed in the request for proposal.

The development process incorporates important relationships with the systems processes. The acquirer's statement of requirements must be validated and expanded. The ISO/IEC 12207 development process prescribes that the system requirements specification must describe:

- Functions and capabilities of the system

- Business, organizational, and user requirements

- Safety, security, ergonomic, interface, operations, and maintenance requirements

- Design constraints

- Qualification requirements

Development of the system architectural design requires identification of hardware, software, and manual components as well as the allocation of the system requirements to those components. System integration requires the integration of those components into the system along with testing of the aggregates. Finally, system qualification is the testing of the integrated systems against the qualification requirements of the requirements specification.

The ISO/IEC 12207 verification process prescribes requirements at both ends of the software development effort. It requires verification that the system requirements assigned to the software parts of the system have been appropriately allocated and are consistent, testable, and feasible. Following development, it requires verification that the software components have been correctly and completely integrated into the system and that the integration tasks have proceeded according to plan.

The ISO/IEC 12207 validation process also prescribes requirements spanning software development. It requires that test requirements, test cases, and test specifications reflect the specific intended use of the system and that the software product be tested in the target environment.

Of course, other software life cycle standards specify interfaces with systems engineering processes and may be useful in appropriate situations. Some alternatives—RTCA DO-178B, ESA PSS-05 and EIA/IEEE J-Std-016—are described in Chapter 15.

CONTEXT OF SOFTWARE ENGINEERING: DEPENDABILITY

IEC TC56 was formed in 1965 to develop standards for reliability and maintainability. Standards focusing on these subjects were appropriate in an era when breakdowns in the field were generally caused by hardware failure. In recent decades, though, hardware reliability has improved dramatically and performance statistics of complex systems, for example, telecommunications equipment, show that failures are dominated by software and procedural problems [Kiang97a].

Motivated by the continuing broadening of their purview due to technological advancement, IEC decided in 1989 to adopt the term *dependability* to replace the more traditional terms [Kiang95]. Because TC56 is a "horizontal committee," its responsibilities cut across those of industry sector committees. It provides broadly applicable, generic standards for dependability. The committee's purview is not confined to the electrotechnical industry but is extended also to the areas of standardization covered by ISO [TC56-95]. The focus of current and future dependability standardization is on system architecture design and software integrity [Kiang97a].

Important Concepts

Dependability is intended as a collective term for product characteristics that encompass all aspects of availability performance and its factors of reliability performance, maintainability performance, and maintenance support processes. The term is deliberately non-quantitative. The responsibility for dependability is shared between the supplier and the customer.

TC56 views dependability as an engineering discipline that builds on a basis of design integrity to develop high-quality, robust products. From this viewpoint, the dependability discipline is intended to improve product performance at smallest life cycle cost. (One of their standards, IEC 300-3-3, addresses the subject of life cycle costing.) Dependability is intended to be a broad-spectrum discipline that achieves its goals by analysis, measurement, and control of design characteristics. Analysis, measurement, and control is performed on the constituent factors of dependability [Kiang95]:

- *Availability* quantifies the product's readiness for use on demand.

- *Reliability* determines the longevity of product performance.

- *Maintainability* guides the ease of maintenance and upgrade.

- *Maintenance support* applies continuing support to achieve availability performance objectives.

To quantify the factors of dependability, you must be able to characterize the system's responses to changes in the environment or in the system itself that might affect dependable operation. Additional terms are needed to make this characterization. A *threat* is a state of the system or its environment that can have adverse effects. A *risk* is a combination of the probability of a threat and the adverse consequences of its occurrence. An important step in developing dependable systems is to perform a *risk analysis* that considers the threats, their frequency, and their consequences.

Using the risk analysis, one must consider *risk control* measures during the system design in order to achieve a dependable system. However, dependability is a characteristic manifested by the system as a whole; that is, one cannot isolate any particular component of the system and say, "that's the part that makes it dependable." Nevertheless, the system's developers need some concept that they can use to manage the development of the system so that the desired dependability will emerge as a result. That concept is called *integrity*.

Integrity refers to the capability of system or software to contain risk. It is to be regarded as a inherent design attribute [Kiang95]. According to DIS 15026:

> A software integrity level *denotes a software property necessary to maintain system risks within acceptable limits. For software that performs a [risk] mitigating function, the property is the reliability with which the software must perform the mitigating function. For software whose failure can lead to a system threat, the property is the frequency or probability of that failure.*

An integrity level is a negotiated expression of the requirement for containing risk within the software, and is best applied in situations where either an acquirer and a supplier must reach agreement or when a supplier must deal with a regulator. In short, an integrity level is one of a predefined set of labels that can be applied to a system or software component to summarize its required risk containment properties. Standards prescribing development practices can apply the label to recommend techniques appropriate for achieving the desired level of integrity.

So, the connection between the discipline of dependability and the corresponding software engineering disciplines is made via the concept of integrity. This connection is reflected in the organization of the standards bodies as well as the organization of the standards that they create. To address the software-specific aspects of dependability, ISO TC56 formed WG10, which operates jointly with ISO/IEC JTC1/SC7/WG9, the working group with responsibility for the software engineering standards related to integrity. The results of the collaboration are apparent in the remainder of this chapter.

Dependability Standards for Software

Because dependability encompasses a broad collection of engineering and management considerations, the achievement of dependability requires the implementation of a dependability programme.[34] The various parts of IEC 300 prescribe such a programme; the parts directly relevant to software engineering are listed in Table 60. (Draft documents are noted by the use of italics.) TC56 is also developing six documents numbered in the range from 1700 through 1720 to directly explain the relationships of the dependability programme to software; except for 1720, they are omitted from the remainder of this chapter because, in their current incomplete state, the precise relationships are unclear.

Applying the dependability discipline to a system depends crucially on analyzing the risks.[35] Two important TC56 standards for risk analysis are listed in Table 61.

---

[34]The TC56 dependability standards use the English spelling of the word.

[35]The dependability discipline applies the term "risk" narrowly, to refer to the possibility of designated adverse consequences of operation, rather than the more typical, broad sense of anything that might go wrong in a development effort.

Table 60. Dependability Programme Standards Relevant to Software

Standard	Title
IEC 50-191 (1990)	Vocabulary—Chapter 191: Dependability and quality of service
IEC 300-1 (1993)	Dependability management—Part 1: Dependability programme management
IEC 300-2 (1995)	Dependability management—Part 2: Dependability programme elements and tasks
IEC FDIS 300-3-6	Dependability management—Part 3: Application guide—Section 6: Software aspects of dependability
IEC 300-3-9 (1995)	Dependability management—Part 3: Application guide—Section 9: Risk analysis of technological systems
IEC NP 1720	Guide to techniques and tools for achieving confidence in software

Table 61. Standards for Risk Analysis Techniques

Standard	Title
IEC 812 (1985)	Analysis techniques for system reliability—Procedure for failure mode and effects analysis (FMEA)
IEC 1025 (1990)	Fault tree analysis

Table 62. Standards that Define the Relationship between Dependability and Software Engineering

Standard	Title
ISO/IEC DIS 15026	System and software integrity levels

Table 63. Software Engineering Standards that Contribute to Dependability

Standard	Title
IEEE/EIA 12207.0-1996	Information technology—Software life cycle processes
AIAA R-013-1992	Recommended practice for software reliability
IEEE Std 982.1-1988	Standard dictionary of measures to produce reliable software
IEEE Std 982.2-1988	Guide for the use of standard dictionary of measures to produce reliable software
IEEE Std 1012-1986	Software verification and validation plans
IEEE Std 1044-1993	Standard classification for software anomalies
IEEE Std 1044.1-1995	Guide to classification for software anomalies
IEEE Std 1061-1992	Standard for a software quality metrics methodology

The connection between dependability and software engineering is made through a concept called integrity. The crucial standard, under development in ISO/IEC JTC1/SC7/WG9, is listed in Table 62.

Many of the good practices prescribed by software engineering standards can assist in achieving the goals of the dependability analysis of the system. The ones most directly relevant are listed in Table 63.

The dependability road map is shown in Figure 27. To focus on the direct relationship between dependability and software engineering, many secondary relationships have been omitted from the map:

- IEC 300-1 is the same document as ISO 9000-4, the quality management standard dealing with dependability. This clearly establishes a relationship between dependability and quality management, a relationship that is suppressed in this diagram.

- As will be described below, the operational relationship among the responsibilities for risk analysis, risk control and achieving confidence is mediated by systems engineering. Since the software engineering's relationship to systems engineering is treated in Chapter 8, the relationship is omitted here.

- The development of dependable software would require the use of many practices described in various software engineering standards. Most have been omitted in favor of the ones directly related to reliability.

As usual, draft standards are noted in the diagram by the use of italics.

Dependability Programme Standards

The policy-level document in this collection is IEC 300-1. It explains that a dependability programme is "the organizational structure, responsibilities, procedures, processes and resources used for managing dependability." It states a clear relationship to the overall system life cycle by saying that the dependability programme covers all phases of the product life cycle, from conception, to final disposal. However, a dependability standard is not the appropriate place to prescribe a system life cycle; instead it must describe how a relationship may be established to an existing life cycle standard. This is accomplished by decomposing the overall programme into programme elements and then, further, into tasks. The programme elements and tasks are then associated with the relevant life cycle processes. The decomposition into programme elements and tasks is prescribed in IEC 300-2.

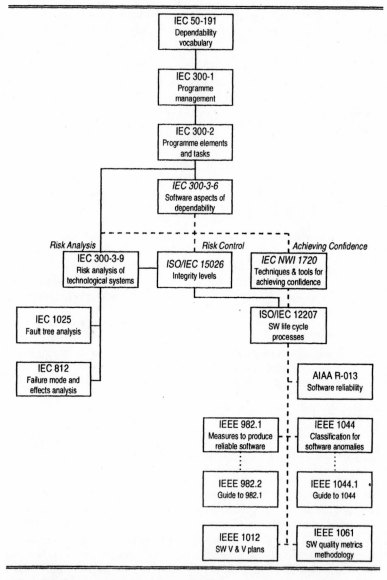

Figure 27. Road map from dependability standards to software engineering standards.

IEC 300-2 is applicable to hardware products and systems, including those containing software. It primarily addresses a two-party relationship and explains how acquirer and supplier should cooperate in assessing "the conditions of the market, the requirements and expectations of users, the contractual situation and the overall requirements for the product and it support." As a result, programme elements and tasks are selected and associated with the life cycle processes.

IEC 300-3 is a collection of application guides elaborating various portions of the reliability discipline. From the viewpoint of this book, the key one will be the draft standard IEC 300-3-6, Software Aspects of Dependability.

IEC 300-3-6 describes the relationships of software dependability to system level dependability, quality management, and the dependability programme prescribed by the IEC 300-2 standard. The document provides guidance on the software application of the elements and tasks of the 300-2 dependability programme and reconciles them with the software life cycle processes of ISO/IEC 12207. Recommendations for time-phasing within a product life cycle are also provided.

IEC 300-3-9 provides guidelines for the selection and implementation of risk analysis techniques for the assessment of technological systems. The analysis can be used in subsequent risk control activities.

Risk Analysis

Some of the traditional techniques useful for risk analysis can be applied in the context of software dependability. Two standards describe suitable techniques.

Fault tree analysis traces the conditions and factors that contribute to the occurrence of an undesirable event affecting the satisfactory performance of the system. This technique is often applied in safety analysis. IEC 1025 describes fault tree analysis and provides guidance on its use.

Failure mode and effects analysis (FMEA) is intended to identify failures that have significant consequences affecting system performance of the application. It is a qualitative method typically limited to failure modes of hardware, but capable of broadening to human and software errors. When the method is extended to consider the severity of the consequences of failure, it is called *failure mode effects and criticality analysis* (FMECA). IEC 812 specifies both techniques and provides guidance on their application.

Risk Control

The key documents achieving the connection between dependability and software engineering are all incomplete. ISO/IEC 15026 has achieved the status of a Draft International Standard, though, and provides important information regarding the intentions of the joint working group. DIS 15026 defines integrity level as a fundamental unifying concept. It closely intertwines the disciplines of dependability, systems engineering, and software engineering as shown in Figure 28.

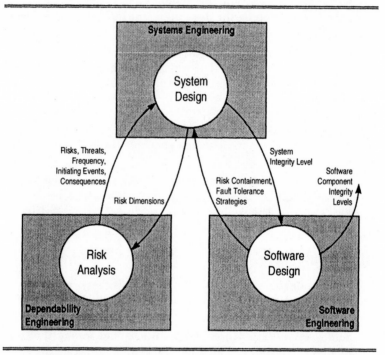

Figure 28. Software integrity-level determination.

The software aspects of dependability address the performance of the software as a part of a system functioning in its operational environment. The software, system, and operational aspects are inseparably related. The concept of integrity is intended to achieve the relationship.

Integrity is regarded as the attribute of the design with the unique ability to contain risk. Despite being a holistic property, it must, nevertheless, be built into the system when it is developed and will affect the performance of the system during its operation.

The integrity level is used to establish benchmarks intended to balance the consequences of the risk against the consequences of mitigating the risk. Due to the importance of this trade-off, determination of the desired integrity level is best considered as a negotiation between two parties, the developer and the buyer, user or regulator [Tripp96].

As shown in Figure 28, determination of software integrity levels inherently involves an iteration among the disciplines of dependability, systems engineering, and software engineering. The risk analysis techniques of dependability engineering are used to analyze threats, their frequency, and their consequences. This analysis is used to determine an integrity level for the system, and based on its design, to assign integrity levels for software components. Based on this analysis, software risk containment requirements can be postulated and provided to the systems engineering process for consideration in modifying the system concept and design. These results, in turn, lead to a revised risk analysis, continuing the iteration.

Referring to Figure 27, DIS 15026 references IEC 300-3-9 to explain the *risk analysis* activity. To add details to the *risk control* activity, ISO/IEC 15026 describes the concept of software integrity. Finally, 15026 refers to the 12207 life cycle processes and lists exemplar techniques that might be employed within the context of those processes to *achieve confidence* in the attainment of determined integrity levels. (The planned IEC 1720 document will treat the subject in greater detail.) The next section will consider some of those techniques.

Achieving Confidence

In describing techniques that may be appropriate to achieving confidence in a system's dependability, DIS 15026 presumes a simple development cycle model and refers to ISO/IEC 12207 for a more complete description of life cycle processes. ISO/IEC 12207, and its US adaptation, IEEE/EIA 12207.0, include appropriate provisions for the risk management and risk control activities noted above:

- Clause 5.1.1.2 places on the acquirer the responsibility for defining and analyzing system "criticality requirements," such as dependability. In a complementary fashion, clause 5.3.2.1 requires the developer to analyze the requirements with reference to the "specific intended use of the system."

- Clauses 5.2.4.2 and 5.3.1.1 place requirements on the supplier and the developer, respectively, to select an appropriate life cycle model and map required activities and tasks into that model, thus accommodating the process requirements of 15026.

- Clause 5.2.4.5(e) requires that the supplier include provisions for managing "critical requirements" in project management plans.

- Clause 5.3.1.4 requires the developer to make plans for the development process that include specific "standards, methods, tools, actions and responsibility" for "safety and security."

- Clause 5.3.4.1 requires establishing and documenting software requirements, specifically including those related to safety and security.

DIS 15026 describes the risk analysis and risk control activities in substantial detail. The mechanisms for achieving a given integrity level, however, are briefly described as "achieving confidence." Of course, it is not the role of DIS 15026 to prescribe appropriate methods. Other software engineering standards do that job.

We can expect that the planned IEC 1720 document will provide guidance for achieving varying degrees of confidence in the correct implementation of certain desired software attributes. It will do this by nominating tools and techniques that are appropriate for attaining the designated integrity level and for the achievement of risk containment and risk mitigation strategies.

Absent current guidance for achieving particular integrity levels, the remainder of this chapter will describe IEEE and AIAA standards specifically relevant to *software reliability*, a term that TC56 regards as problematic. The relationship to the IEEE standard for software verification and validation will also be discussed.

AIAA R-013 is a recommended practice for software reliability, particularly within the context of aerospace systems. The document defines software reliability engineering as "the application of statistical techniques to data collected during system development and operation to specify, predict, estimate, and assess the reliability of software-based systems." The document specifies an 11-step generic procedure for estimating software reliability, provides guidance in selecting a model, and recommends three particular models along with providing information on others. Appendices describe approaches to determining the reliability of hardware/software systems and for using reliability models to develop test strategies.

Based in part on this document, IBM Federal Systems[36] developed a process for onboard space shuttle systems that has achieved a level 5 rating for maturity in the SEI Capability Maturity Model [Schneidewind96]. On the other hand, the document has been criticized for placing undue emphasis on modeling rather than field-tested approaches [Knafl95].

IEEE Std 982.1 is called a dictionary of measures for the production of reliable software. It provides a brief taxonomy of the measures and then reference material describing the applicability and implementation of the various measures. The measures are intentionally low-level because they are intended as a foundation on which methods can be built.

IEEE Std 982.2 provides overall guidance on how the measures defined in 982.1 can be applied as a part of a software reliability engineering program. It includes guidance for measure selection and application. After providing functional and life-cycle taxonomies of the measures, it develops an overall nine-stage measurement process that can be integrated into a selected life cycle.

IEEE Std 1044 provides an approach to the classification of anomalies found in software. Its companion guide, IEEE Std 1044.1, provides supporting information for the implementation of the standard. Information gained from the careful treatment of anomaly reports can be very helpful in supporting a measurement program.

IEEE Std 1061 describes a hierarchical approach to a metrics framework. Starting at the top, desired attributes of the system are represented by the assignment of quality factors. Associated with each factor is a direct metric that could be measured in the completed system, but which probably cannot be measured during development. Each factor is decomposed into sub-factors representing concrete attributes of software meaningful to the developers. The sub-factors are decomposed into metrics that are used to make measurements during development. These permit estimating of the top-level desired attributes of the system.

Norman Schneidewind provides an interesting framework for integrating the application of these standards [Schneidewind95]:

- IEEE 982.1 is used to provide overall terms.

- IEEE 982.2 and AIAA R-013 provide process guidelines.

---

[36]Briefly part of Loral Corporation and now part of Lockheed-Martin.

- IEEE 1044 [and, presumably 1044.1] are used to classify faults and failures observed in the product.

- AIAA R-013 provides the methodology for making reliability predictions.

- IEEE 1061 provides the methodology for identifying and validating metrics that can be used as early indicators during development.

SESC has made plans for a revision of the 982 standards. In addition to the expected review and update (to add, for example, metrics suitable for object-oriented development), SESC plans to add specific criteria for inclusion of a metric in the dictionary and a set of generic metric classes suitable for categorizing the metrics.

The primary mechanism for ensuring that the derived software requirements for dependability are properly implemented would be the careful application of a validation and verification (V & V) program. IEEE Std 1012 prescribes the requirements for such a program. The standard makes a distinction between critical and non-critical software and prescribes a certain minimum set of V & V tasks for use in developing critical software. IEEE Std 1012 was reaffirmed in 1992 and is currently undergoing revision. Plans for the revision include incorporating a concept for levels of integrity similar to that of DIS 15026.

CONTEXT OF SOFTWARE ENGINEERING: SAFETY

Traditionally safety standards are written for application to specific industrial sectors by standards groups representing those sectors. In fact, there is some debate on the issue of whether it is appropriate to attempt to develop generic systems safety standards and, furthermore, whether the term "software safety" makes any sense at all. The custom of writing sector-specific standards has caused a large number of them to be written. A Software Safety Planning Group of the IEEE SESC [SESC96b] examined 44 completed or in-process standards under the auspices of the organizations shown in the list of Table 64—a list that is certainly incomplete.

Table 64. Some of the Organizations Responsible for Standards Related to Software Safety

American Nuclear Society
American Society of Mechanical Engineers
Canadian Standards Association
Department of Defense (US)
Electronic Industries Association (US)
European Space Agency
IEC SC45A, TC56 and SC65A
Institution of Electrical Engineers (UK)
IEEE Power Engineering Society
IEEE Computer Society
Instrument Society of America
Japanese Electric Association
Ministry of Defense (UK)
National Aeronautics and Space Administration (US)
North Atlantic Treaty Organization
Ontario Hydro (Canada)
Professional Engineers of Ontario (Canada)
RTCA, Inc. (US)—working jointly with EUROCAE (Europe)

It would be impossible for this book to examine all of these approaches to safety in software-intensive systems. The book will instead focus on a few notable collections, selected primarily because the organizations that are developing them are attempting to form relationships with other collections:

- The functional safety standards, from IEC SC65A—an example of a safety collection which began as sector-specific and is now evolving toward generality

- The standards for software in safety systems of nuclear reactors, from IEC SC45A—an example of a sector-specific collection forming a relationship with a more general one

- Standards for software in safety systems of nuclear reactor from the IEEE Power Engineering Society—an example of a sector-specific national collection harmonizing with other national and international collections and citing normative relationships to software engineering standards

The text will also briefly discuss the role of standards in regulation using examples from the United States and Canada.

Of course, other industries have a compelling interest in software safety. One of them, the avionics industry, has chosen to centralize its requirements for software development practices in a single document, RTCA DO-178B, described as an important alternative in Chapter 15.

Two characteristics of these collections make it a challenge to draw connections to relevant software engineering standards. First, there has been a tendency within each of the safety communities to write their own standards, even for software. Second, even when relationships to existing software engineering standards have been made, there has been a tendency for the writers of the safety standards to themselves select individual software engineering standards rather than to negotiate a shared concept forming a more general and enduring relationship, such as the integrity concept that was discussed in Chapter 9 on dependability. Achieving an interface through a general relationship would have the benefit of permitting continued evolution of the software engineering standards without suffering the inevitable obsolescence of specifically cited relationships.

Faced with these circumstances, this chapter will generally refrain from recommending standards that might fill the intent of requirements of other standards and, instead, observe the recommendations made by those who wrote the standards, except for those cases where the cited standard has been renumbered in a subsequent revision.

Table 65. Functional Safety and Related Standards of IEC SC65A

Standard	Title
IEC 1069-1 (1991)	Industrial-process measurement and control—Evaluation of system properties for the purpose of system assessment—Part 1: General considerations and methodology
IEC 1069-2 (1993)	Industrial-process measurement and control—Evaluation of system properties for the purpose of system assessment—Part 2: Assessment methodology
IEC CD 1069-7	Industrial-process measurement and control—Evaluation of system properties for the purpose of system assessment—Part 7: Assessment of system safety
IEC CDV 1508-1	Functional safety—Safety-related systems—Part 1: General requirements
IEC CD 1508-2	Functional safety—Safety-related systems—Part 2: Requirements for electrical/electronic/programmable electronic systems
IEC CDV 1508-3	Functional safety—Safety-related systems—Part 3: Software requirements
IEC CDV 1508-4	Functional safety—Safety-related systems—Part 4: Definitions and abbreviations of terms
IEC CDV 1508-5	Functional safety—Safety-related systems—Part 5: Guidelines on the application of part 1
IEC CD 1508-6	Functional safety—Safety-related systems—Part 6: Guidelines on the application of parts 2 and 3
IEC CD 1508-7	Functional safety—Safety-related systems—Part 7: Bibliography of techniques and measures

Hazard Analysis

Software safety is a discipline different from reliability, or even the more general discipline of dependability described in the previous chapter. Reliability deals with all possible software errors while the safety discipline concerns itself with those errors that cause or fail to mitigate system hazards. Dependability concerns the ability of the system to perform its required functions; safety concerns the ability of the system to avoid hazard conditions regardless of whether the intended function is executed [Ippolito95][37]. Hazard analysis begins at the earliest conceptualization of a safety-critical system and continues throughout its development [Wallace94].

---

[37]Ippolito actually uses the term "reliability." In context, though, the remark is relevant to the term "dependability" as it is used in this book.

Functional Safety Standards

IEC SC65A is assigned the responsibility for the system aspects of industrial process measurement and control systems. It takes a particular interest in programmable electronic systems, a category into which computer-based systems can be placed. In pursuing its work, it has initiated a work program for "functional safety" standards that have relevance beyond the scope of the subcommittee. The relevant standards are listed in Table 65. Most are incomplete; they are marked by italics.

Figure 29 shows the functional safety standards in the context of the industrial process measurement and control (IPMC) standards that are the primary business of SC65A. (As indicated by the italics, most of the documents exist only in draft form.) IEC 1069 is intended to provide methods and procedures for the assessment of IPMC systems, where assessment is regarded as evidence-based judgment of a system's suitability for its mission. Part 1 of the standard outlines the general methodology for performing such assessments. The scope of an assessment can be depicted by a matrix where system properties are shown on one axis and conditions

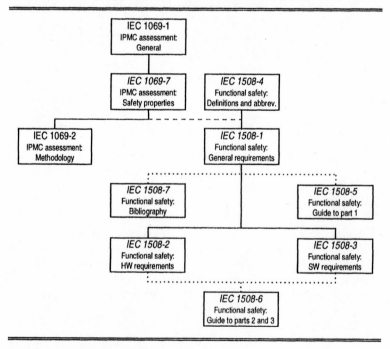

Figure 29. Functional safety standards.

which affect those properties are shown on the other. Parts 3-8 of the standards provide guidance in treating the various categories of system properties[38]; Part 7 deals with safety properties. Part 2 provides a detailed methodology for the assessment of the properties described in the other parts.

The functional safety standard exists only in draft form and information regarding its content comes from planning documents and articles by participants in its development. IEC 1508 will be a seven-part document with Part 1 describing the general requirements using the terminology of Part 4. Parts 2 and 3 will partition and detail the hardware (programmable electronic systems) and software requirements of Part 1. Parts 5 and 6 will provide additional guidance in applying the other parts. The standard will describe an overall safety life cycle as well as specific safety-related activities triggered by the risk-based assignment of Safety Integrity Levels. It is hoped that IEC 1508 will become a baseline—in effect, a set of principles—for future standards dedicated to particular application sectors [Leret95].

The objective of IEC 1508 is to provide a basis for treating safety in the automation of process plants, machinery, and other industrial equipment. It is concerned with preventing two types of safety incidents: failures of control systems that trigger unsafe conditions; and covert failures in protection systems making them unavailable when needed. Recognizing that safety cannot be "tested into" a system, the document deals with all phases of development with an emphasis on preventing errors. Three basic elements are treated:

- Safety management—Because most incidents are caused by a combination of managerial and technical failures, reliance solely on technical criteria is inadequate.

- Safety life cycle—Because assessment of control system functionality is relative to the design of which it is a part, this is a systems-like life cycle beginning with the device being controlled.

- Assessment[39]—This is intended as a "second opinion" in addition to normal verification activities.

---

[38]Part 5 of the standard deals with dependability and includes normative references to IEC 300-3-2 and IEC 1025.

[39]In some fields of application, notably regulated ones, assessment may be subsumed by a "certification" activity.

IEC 1508 takes a risk-based approach, treating risk as a combination of probability and consequences of occurrence. Risk represents forces external to the system. Safety integrity levels represent measures internal to the system intended to deal with the risk. For example, safety integrity level 4 requires, in part, that the component shall be able to perform the safety function in the presence of two faults and that the faults must be detected with on-line diagnostics. A risk analysis is performed to designate a safety integrity level for the system. The three elements previously described are applied to ensure that the designated level is achieved in the system. The document recommends specific architectural and design techniques as suitable for contributing to the achievement of the various integrity levels [Brazendale95].

Table 66. Nuclear software safety standards of IEC SC45A

Standard	Title
IEC 557 (1982)	IEC terminology in the nuclear reactor field
IEC 643 (1979)	Application of digital computers to nuclear reactor instrumentation and control
IEC 880 (1986)	Software for computers in the safety systems of nuclear power stations
IEC CDV 880-1	Supplement 1 to IEC 880, Software for computers important to safety for nuclear power plants
IEC NWI 880-2	Supplement 2 to IEC 880, Software for computers important to safety for nuclear power plants
IEC 987 (1989)	Programmed digital computers important to safety for nuclear power stations
IEC 1226 (1993)	Nuclear power plants—Instrumentation and control systems important for safety—Classification
IEC CD 1513	General requirements for computer-based systems important to safety in nuclear power plants
IEC NP 1838	Supplement to IEC 1226, Risk-based classification

IEC Nuclear Software Safety Standards

Changing technology, differing regulatory climates, and varying national and professional interests have resulted in a large number of standards regarding safety-related systems of nuclear power plants. This section will focus on one important and well-integrated collection—that of IEC SC45A. Relevant standards from that collection[40] are listed in Table 66. Some are unfinished (and shown in italics), including two that are important to this discussion. IEC 1513, the so-called "chapeau" document, is intended to provide a unifying systems-level treatment of the same issues as the software-oriented IEC 880 and the hardware-oriented IEC 987. IEC 880 itself is being augmented with two supplements addressing a set of issues whose omission caused some criticism of the original standard.

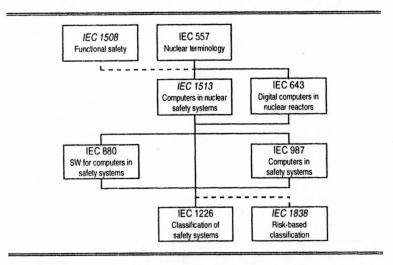

Figure 30. Road map of IEC standards for software safety in nuclear plants.

The road map for these standards is shown in Figure 30 with incomplete standards projects shown in italics. Although the standards refer to IEC 50 for general vocabulary, SC45A controls its own specific terminology in the IEC 557 document. This standard defines a *safety system* as:

> *All those systems important to safety provided to ensure, in any condition, the safe shutdown of the reactor and the heat removal from the core and/or to limit the consequences of [undesirable conditions]. Note: The Safety system consists of the pro-*

---

[40]Not described is the close relationship of the SC45A standards with the safety guides of the International Atomic Energy Agency; the standards are used to implement the regulatory requirements of those guides.

*tection system, the safety actuation systems, and
the safety system support features.*

In many of the documents, the term "system important to safety" is
used in a sense that is more general than that of "safety system".

IEC 643 is a relatively old document (1979) that remains important because it describes the "principles which should be followed in the use of digital computers for alarm, instrumentation,
record, control, and equipment protection purposes on nuclear reactor units." Use of computers for reactor protection is explicitly excluded, though. The document includes a few requirements on
software design, such as modularity and "self-monitoring."

A frequently referenced document from this collection is IEC
1226 which provides a consequence-based method for the classification of functions, systems, and equipment (FSE) important to
safety. The three-level scheme, which has largely supplanted that
of 643, assigns Category A to FSE which play a principal role in the
achievement or maintenance of nuclear plant safety, Category B to
those playing a complementary role, and Category C to those playing an auxiliary or indirect role [Leret95].

The standard prescribes some general requirements for dealing
with systems in each of the categories. Furthermore, the assignment of category is important in determining the application of the
other standards in the collection. The full requirements of IEC 880
and 987 are to be applied to Category A systems while Category B
systems can be developing according to the "intent" of these standards.

The categorization method is based on qualitative criteria, although it is promised that a future revision will incorporate quantitative criteria. A new work item, 1838, has been approved to complement 1226 with a risk-based approach, but work has proceeded
slowly waiting for input on national practices in this area and, possibly, to determine the applicability of the TC56 standard on risk
analysis of technological systems, IEC 300-3-9 [Leret95].

At this point, the existing SC45A collection designates separate
standards, 880 and 987, to deal with software and hardware concerns, respectively. Believing that there is a need for a systems-level approach, though, the subcommittee is drafting the
"chapeau" document, 1513, to provide the unifying description.

One of the most important motivations of 1513 is to integrate
the existing nuclear safety documents with the functional safety
approach taken by IEC 1508, discussed in the previous section. Accordingly, 1513 takes a systems-level view of the safety FSE, view-

ing its requirements in relation to the requirements of the overall plant. The document provides a view of a systems life cycle intended to be complementary with the software and hardware life cycles of 880 and 987, and maps that life cycle, as well as other important material, to the provisions of 1508.

The IEC 987 standard applies the principles of IEC 643 to the "utilization of digital...hardware for systems important to safety." It is intended to be a complement to the IEC 880 software standard.

IEC 880 describes software system principles and requirements to be applied in the development of safety systems of nuclear power plants. Although it disclaims any intention of prescribing new requirements, its recommendations are detailed. The standard includes recommendations related to:

- Hardware criteria as they affect the software

- An approach to software development

- An approach to software verification and computer system validation

- Procedures for software maintenance, modification, and configuration control

In addition, appendices are devoted to several more detailed subjects:

- Software requirements specification

- Design and coding of safety-related software

- Software performance specification

- Language processors

- Testing

- Documentation

In short, it appears that the standard was intended as a comprehensive interpretation of nuclear safety principles as applied to software development.

Nevertheless, there are some shortcomings. The original IEC 880 standard was intended for application to Category A systems; the user would be responsible for appropriately relaxing its provisions for application to FSE of other categories. Furthermore, 880 has been criticized as inadequately treating common mode failures, use of pre-developed software, the application of formal methods, use of support tools, security and maintenance, as well as general evolution in computing technology. Two supplements to the standard are being developed to address these needs [Leret95]. Furthermore, the high level of detail in IEC 880, approximately 500 requirements and recommendations, makes the standard more useful for developing new systems than for assessing existing ones [Tate95].

US Nuclear Software Safety Standards

Table 67 shows a selection of important US standards related to software in the safety systems of nuclear plants. They are created by three different standards development organizations, the American Nuclear Society (ANS), the American Society of Mechanical Engineers (ASME), and the IEEE Power Engineering Society.

Table 67. US Standards Relevant to Software in Safety Systems of Nuclear Plants

Standard	Title
ANS 51.1-1983	Nuclear safety criteria for the design of stationary pressurized water reactor plants
ANS 52.1-1983	Nuclear safety criteria for the design of stationary boiling water reactor plants
ASME NQA-1-1989	Quality assurance program requirements for nuclear facilities
ASME NQA-2a-1990	Part 2.7, Quality assurance requirements of computer software for nuclear facility applications
IEEE Std 7-4.3.2-1993	Standard criteria for digital computers in safety systems of nuclear power generating stations
IEEE Std 603-1991	Standard criteria for safety systems for nuclear power generating stations

The road map for these standards, shown in Figure 31, begins with IEEE Std 603. That document establishes "minimum functional design criteria for the power, instrumentation, and control portions of nuclear power generating station safety systems." The criteria are regarded as promoting safety but not guaranteeing it. The document's foreword describes the criteria as "general in nature" and says that additional standards prescribing detailed criteria are also needed for meaningful application. It specifically mentions the two ANS standards that prescribe design characteristics for two commonly used reactor types.

As the lines in the map suggest, IEEE Std 7-4.3.2 is the conceptually central document of this group. It is intended to amplify the safety systems criteria of IEEE 603 for application to computers in such systems. In so doing, it correlates the requirements of several documents for nuclear safety:

- ANS 51.1 and 52.1 for design criteria of two common reactor types

- IEEE Std 603 for safety system criteria

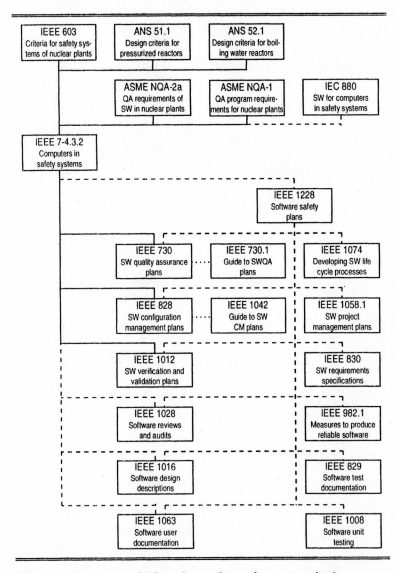

Figure 31. Road map of US nuclear safety software standards.

- ASME NQA-1 and NQA-2a for quality assurance requirements

- IEC 880 for additional guidance

Therefore, IEEE 7-4.3.2 serves as the integrator of the requirements and guidance from all of these standards, both national and

Table 68. Standards Referenced by IEEE Std 7-4.3.2

Selected sections of IEEE Std 7-4.3.2	Nuclear standards referenced	SESC standards referenced
4. Safety system design basis	IEEE 603, ANS 51.1, ANS 52.1	
5 and subclauses—Safety system criteria	IEEE 603	
5.3 Quality	ASME NQA-1	
5.3.1 Software development	ASME NQA-2a, IEC 880	IEEE 730
5.3.2 Qualification of existing commercial computers	ASME NQA-1	
5.3.3 Software tools		
5.3.4 Verification and validation	ASME NQA-1, ASME NQA-2a, IEC 880	IEEE 1012
5.3.5 Software configuration management	ASME NQA-1, ASME NQA-2a	IEEE 828
Annex E—Verification and validation (informative)		
E.1 Background		IEEE 1028
E.2 Discussion		
E.2.1 and subclauses. Independent V & V activities	ASME NQA-1	
E.2.2 V & V for development activities	IEC 880	IEEE 1012
E.2.2.4 Software requirements V & V	IEC 880	IEEE 830, IEEE 1012
E.2.2.8 Software design and implementation V & V	IEC 880	
E.2.2.8.1 Software design		IEEE 1016, IEEE 1063
E.2.2.9 Computer integration V & V	IEC 880	
E.2.2.10 System testing V & V	IEC 880	
E.2.2.12 Operation and maintenance	IEC 880	
E.2.3 Documentation		IEEE 1012
Annex F—Identification and resolution of abnormal conditions and events		IEEE 1228
Annex H—Computer reliability		IEEE 1012

Table 69. IEEE SESC Standards Supporting Development of
Safety-Critical Systems

Standard	Title
IEEE Std 730-1989	Standard for software quality assurance plans
IEEE Std 730.1-1995	Guide to software quality assurance planning
IEEE Std 828-1990	Standard for software configuration management plans
IEEE Std 829-1983	Standard for software test documentation
IEEE Std 830-1993	Recommended practice for software requirements specifications
IEEE Std 982.1-1988	Standard dictionary of measures to produce reliable software
IEEE Std 982.2-1988	Guide for the use of standard dictionary of measures to produce reliable software
IEEE Std 1008-1987	Standard for software unit testing
IEEE Std 1012-1986	Standard for software verification and validation plans
IEEE Std 1016-1987	Recommended practice for software design descriptions
IEEE Std 1028-1988	Standard for software reviews and audits
IEEE Std 1042-1987	Guide to software configuration management
IEEE Std 1058.1-1987	Standard for software project management plans
IEEE Std 1063-1987	Standard for software user documentation
IEEE Std 1074-1995	Standard for developing software life cycle processes
IEEE Std 1228-1994	Standard for software safety plans

international. As the requirements are integrated, the standard suggests specific software engineering standards that may be applied to satisfy the requirements, either normatively or as guidance. The correlations among all of these standards are summarized in Table 68.

The mention of IEEE Std 1228, Standard for software safety plans, deserves some particular attention. The 1228 standard existed only in draft form when IEEE Std 7-4.3.2 was finished. Unsure of its ultimate content, the writers of 7-4.3.2 did not rely on 1228 as a summary and a gateway to appropriate software engineering standards; instead they did that job themselves. They did cite 1228, though, for techniques intended to minimize the introduction of Abnormal Conditions and Events (ACE) during the design process of the system, techniques considered to be alternatives to the more usual Failure Modes and Effects Analysis (FMEA) and Fault Tree Analysis (FTA). More information regarding ACE analysis can be found in [Matras95].

Software Standards Supporting Safety

Although the writers of IEEE Std 7-4.3.2 elected to select appropriate software engineering standards themselves, others concerned with safety-critical systems might prefer to cite a single umbrella software engineering standard that would, in turn, describe appropriate roles for other software engineering standards. An appropriate standard for the role would be IEEE Std 1228. It and the standards to which it refers are listed in Table 69.

IEEE Std 1228 establishes "minimum acceptable requirements for the content of a Software Safety Plan." It provides more than a format, though. Because the plan is required to address "processes activities intended to improve the safety of safety-critical software," the standard levies implicit requirements on the activities applied to the development of the software. Other IEEE standards are cited as appropriate to achieving those requirements. Table 70 shows the outline of the safety plan required by IEEE Std 1228 along with the standards cited as supporting execution of the plan.

It should be noted that IEEE 1228 requires that the software safety plan be prepared within the context of a more general system safety program; it recognizes that software safety must be considered in the context of its associated hardware, environment, and operators.

Standards Supporting Regulation

Of course, the construction and operation of nuclear power plants is a regulated business and the selection and application of voluntary standards must be reconciled with the requirements of the regulatory process and rules. It is helpful when the two coincide. To that end, the US Nuclear Regulatory Commission has issued, for public comment, drafts of six regulatory guides that would have the effect of endorsing eight of the IEEE SESC standards, listed in Table 71, for use in the development of nuclear reactor software. The regulatory guides provide information on methods deemed acceptable to NRC staff for complying with their regulations for promoting reliability and design quality in software used in the safety systems of nuclear power plants [FedReg96].

Experience in Canada, however, illustrates some of the difficulties in applying voluntary standards in a regulatory environment. In 1990, Ontario Hydro and Atomic Energy Canada, Ltd. (AECL) undertook a collaborative effort to develop appropriate standards in response to earlier licensing problems encountered with their regulator, the Atomic Energy Control Board (AECB).

Table 70. Outline of the IEEE 1228 Safety Plan and Standards that
Support Execution of the Plan

Section of Plan	IEEE Standards Referenced
1 Purpose	
2 Definitions, acronyms and abbreviations, and references	610.12
3 Software safety management	
3.1 Organization and responsibilities	
3.2 Resources	
3.3 Staff qualifications and training	
3.4 Software life cycle	1074
3.5 Documentation requirements	
(a) Software project management	1058.1
(b) Software configuration management	828, 1042
(c) Software quality assurance	730, 730.1
(d) Software safety requirements	830
(e) Software safety design	1016
(f) Software development, methodology, standards, practices, metrics and conventions	730, 982.1
(g) Test documentation	829, 1008
(h) Software V & V	1012
(i) Reporting safety V & V	1012
(j) Software user documentation	1063
(k) - (o) Safety analysis results	
3.6 Software safety program records	
3.7 Software configuration management activities	828, 1042
3.8 Software quality assurance activities	730, 730.1
3.9 Software V & V activities	1012
3.10 Tool support and approval	
3.11 Previously developed or purchased software	
3.12 Subcontract management	
3.13 Process certification	
4 Software safety analyses	
4.1 Software safety analyses preparation	
4.2 Software safety requirements analysis	1028
4.3 Software safety design analysis	1028, 982.1
4.4 Software safety code analysis	1028
4.5 Software safety test analysis	1028
4.6 Software safety change analysis	
5 Post development	
6 Approval	

Table 71. SESC Standards listed in the NRC Regulatory Guides

Standard	Title
IEEE Std-828-1990	Standard for software configuration management plans
IEEE Std-829-1983	Standard for software test documentation
IEEE Std-830-1993	Recommended practice for software requirements specifications
IEEE Std-1008-1987	Standard for software unit testing
IEEE Std-1012-1986	Standard for software verification and validation plans
IEEE Std-1028-1988	Standard for software reviews and audits
IEEE Std-1042-1987	Guide to software configuration management
IEEE Std-1074-1995	Standard for developing software life cycle processes

To license the Darlington plant in the late 1980s, Ontario Hydro and their regulator wrestled with the problem of finding software standards satisfactory for regulatory application in determining if software embedded in critical applications was good enough for acceptance. They assessed existing quality management standards for suitability including ISO 9000-3 and the Canadian Q396 series, both described in Chapter 6. Both were judged to provide requirements insufficiently specific for the development of nuclear safety-critical software. IEC 880 was also considered; it was judged as an insufficient basis for achieving regulatory concurrence because of its reliance on recommendations, ranging in nature from overly general to overly prescriptive, rather than precisely specified mandatory requirements [Joannou95]. (This result is an instance of a broader characteristic of standards. The desire for broad applicability in a voluntary standard may conflict with the regulator's need for a clear binary discrimination between compliance and non-compliance in all possible situations. Often a single document cannot fill both roles satisfactorily.)

To license the system, Ontario Hydro, at substantial expense, applied the following techniques:

- Mathematically based software specifications
- Formal verification of code to design and design to specifications
- Coding guidelines
- Software architecture analysis
- Detailed design, unit testing and integration testing procedures

- Fault-tree analysis of code

- Statistically random trajectory-based testing

No single standard or integrated collection describes all of these techniques. Satisfied with the safety of the software but concerned about maintenance in the absence of a standard, the regulator ultimately granted a temporary license with the proviso that the software be redesigned in accordance with a standard to be developed [Harauz97].

Since existing standards were regarded as inadequate, the two companies, with comment from their regulator, jointly developed a suitable standard themselves. Their framework is intended to be in three levels: categorization and high-level requirements; methodology-specific standards, procedures, and guidelines to be applied as appropriate; and additional guidelines on special topics. Standards at the top level define different degrees of engineering rigor—the one suitable for nuclear safety is shown in Table 72.

Table 72. Canadian Standard for Nuclear Safety Software

Standard	Title
CANDU CE-1001-STD	Standard for software engineering of safety critical systems

The standard is specifically written to address regulatory concurrence by carefully distinguishing requirements from advice and carefully mapping those requirements to deliverable documents. The standard has been successfully applied both in Canada and elsewhere [Harauz96].

Objects of Software Engineering: Resources

In the SESC model of the objects of software engineering, resources are used in the execution of processes to develop products on behalf of customers. The SC7 model differs slightly in using the term "technology" in place of "resources."[41]

This chapter will briefly describe the resource standards of both collections. For convenience, standards relating to the terminology and techniques levels of the layered model have also been included in this chapter.

Terminology and Taxonomy

The most fundamental standards for software engineering provide terminology to be used in the other standards as well as taxonomies for classifying standards and their subjects. Important examples are listed in Table 73. Unfinished projects are shown in italics.

IEEE Std 610.12—Software Engineering Terminology

IEEE Std 610.12 is the 12th chapter of the IEEE standard vocabulary for the entire field of computing.[42] It defines terms in the field of software engineering and contains about 1,300 entries. Although the vocabulary is intended to be comprehensive, terms are

---

[41]The distinction pursued by some principals in SC7 is that resources are generally consumed in use whereas technologies are not.

[42]Other relevant chapters of IEEE Std 610 include: 2, computer applications; 3 modeling and simulation; 4, image processing and pattern recognition; 5, data management; 6, computer graphics; 7, computer networking; 10, computer hardware; and 13, computer languages.

excluded if they are trademarked or otherwise specific to a group or organization. Multi-word terms following from the definition of their constituent words and words whose meaning in the computer field can be inferred from the standard English meaning are also excluded. The vocabulary also notes synonyms, contrasting terms, and related terms.

The 610.12 standard was approved in 1990 and is currently undergoing revision. It is managed by the Standards Coordinating Committee of the IEEE Computer Society.

Table 73. Standards Providing Terminology and Taxonomy

Standard	Title
IEEE 610.12-1990	Standard glossary of software engineering terminology
IEEE P729	Standard for software engineering—Fundamental terms
IEEE Std 1002-1987	Standard taxonomy for software engineering standards
ISO/IEC 2382-1:1993	Information technology—Vocabulary—Part 1: Fundamental terms
ISO/IEC 2382-7:1989	Information technology—Vocabulary—Part 7: Computer programming
ISO/IEC 2382-20:1990	Information technology—Vocabulary—Part 20: System development
ISO/IEC TR 12382:1992	Permuted index of the vocabulary of information technology
ISO/IEC DTR 12182	Categorization of software
ISO/IEC DTR 14399	Mapping of relevant software engineering standards

IEEE P729—Fundamental Terms of Software Engineering

Those involved with software engineering standardization for many years will recall that 729 was the number of the original 1983 IEEE vocabulary on the subject. Circa 1990, the IEEE Computer Dictionary product gathered all of the glossaries of the computing field into a single document, IEEE Std 610. The successor of IEEE 729 was chapter 12 of the 610 standard. In a recent policy change, IEEE has decided to centrally manage revisions to the 610 standard. SESC has decided that such a process may result in a standard insufficiently responsive to their needs to manage the terminology of their collection. Accordingly, they have initiated a project, using the familiar old number, for a vocabulary under their direct control. The 729 standard will gather key terms used by one or more standards in the SESC collection. Presumably, as IEEE 610 is periodically updated, terms from IEEE Std 729 will be swept into the more comprehensive vocabulary.

IEEE Std 1002—Taxonomy for Software Engineering Standards

IEEE Std 1002, approved in 1986 and reaffirmed in 1992, is a standard about standards. It provides a taxonomy for software engineering standards that permits such a standard to be classified in a two-dimensional framework. The first dimension characterizes the role of the standard by providing four categories—process standard, product standard, notation standard, and professional standard. The second dimension provides categories based on job functions and life cycle phases. If the two dimensions are considered as rows and columns of a table, any particular standard can be categorized as occupying one or more cells of the table. IEEE Std 1002 could be utilized for organizing and comparing collections of standards.

ISO/IEC 2382 and ISO/IEC TR 12382—Information Technology Vocabulary

ISO/IEC 2382 is the international standard for information technology vocabulary. It is composed of 28 parts (with another 3 under development) providing definitions for a total of more than 5,000 terms. The parts are updated periodically and individually and carry a range of dates going back to 1976. Some parts are labeled as ISO standards because they predate the creation of JTC1. The parts of most interest for the purposes of this book include: 1, fundamental terms; 7, computer programming; and 20, system development.[43] Part 7 is currently (spring 1997) under revision at the DIS stage. Technical Report 12382, dated 1992, is a permuted index of the contents of the 2382 standard.

The ISO/IEC vocabularies are centrally managed by Subcommittee 1 of JTC1.

---

[43]Other relevant parts include: 8, controls, integrity, and security; 13, computer graphics; 14, reliability, maintenance, and availability; 16, information theory; 17, databases; 18, distributed data processing; 24, computer integrated manufacturing; and 28, artificial intelligence.

ISO/IEC DTR 12182—Categorization of Software

This document describes a scheme for the categorization of software in accordance with different viewpoints. The intention is to provide an aid for the positioning of software engineering standards and work items within the scope of SC7. By providing a uniform framework of viewpoints, readers of the document will be better able to express relationships among standards. The technical report describes 16 views and a set of categories appropriate for each view. The document is a draft technical report prepared by WG9 of JTC1/SC7.

ISO/IEC DTR 14399—Mapping of Software Engineering Standards

This document is a Type 3 Technical Report, meaning that it is never intended to be a standard, merely useful information. It is intended as a single listing of all standards relevant to the scope and work program of JTC1/SC7 and is maintained by WG9. The report lists 550 standards documents, either completed or in progress, from 76 different organizations. The citations are listed both by organization and by subject area.[44]

Notations

The SESC and SC7 collections include a number of standards prescribing notations that may be employed in various situations. The SESC standards are presently under development (hence, shown in italics in Table 74) and tackle current problems; on the other hand, the SC7 standards predate the formation of JTC1 and deal with issues generally regarded as dated.

IEEE P1320—IDEF

IDEF is a modeling language, combining graphics and text, used to analyze and define functions and requirements of a system. A model consists of a hierarchical series of diagrams, with accompanying explanation, depicting functions as well as the data and objects that relate the functions.

---

[44]Because the document will require continual maintenance, it is likely that JTC1 will ultimately decide to remove the designation as a Technical Report and instead label it as some sort of standing document governing the operations of SC7 itself.

The IDEF notation was born in the 1970s Air Force program for Integrated Computer Aided Manufacturing (ICAM). (In fact, the "I" in "IDEF" originally stood for ICAM, Now, the acronym is usually decoded as "Integrated DEFinition.") Three notations were originally developed:

- IDEF0 for function models

- IDEF1 for information models

- IDEF2 for dynamics models

In 1991, a collaboration between the National Institute of Standards and Technology (NIST) and the DoD Office of Corporate Information Management (CIM) produced Federal Information Processing Standard Publication 183 (FIPS Pub. 183), as a specification for IDEF0. Two years later, SESC initiated commercial standardization of IDEF0 using FIPS Pub. 183 as the base document. P1320.1.1 describes the syntax and semantics of the IDEF0 language that are required to draw physical diagrams. Unlike earlier specifications, this standard views the abstract structure of IDEF0 as distinct from its physical representation. The abstract formalization is described in P1320.1 of the standard. IDEF0 is generally viewed as encompassing both a modeling language and a methodology for developing models. This standard does not address the methodology—only the syntax and semantics of the modeling

Table 74. Standards Describing Notations

Standard	Title
IEEE P1320.1	Standard syntax and semantics for IDEF0
IEEE P1320.1.1	Standard users manual for IDEF0
IEEE P1320.2	Standard syntax and semantics for IDEF1X97
IEEE P1320.2.1	Standard users manual for IDEF1X97
IEEE P1471	Recommended practice for system design—Architectural description
ISO 5806:1984	Specification of single-hit decision tables
ISO 5807:1985	Documentation symbols and conventions for data, program and system flowcharts, program network charts and system resources charts
ISO 8790:1987	Computer system configuration diagram symbols and conventions
ISO/IEC 8631:1989	Program constructs and conventions for their representation
ISO/IEC 11411:1995	Representation for human communication of state transition of software

language. Methodology is treated in several available textbooks and may be the subject of a future project.

A 1983 Air Force project extended IDEF1 to perform semantic modeling, calling the resulting notation IDEF1X. Recently, object-oriented extensions to IDEF1X have been proposed; they go under the name IDEF1X97 or sometimes IDEFObject, and are also the subject of SESC standardization. This project will also produce both a user's manual, P1320.2.1, and a formal description, P1320.2.

It is expected that both parts of the IDEF0 standard will be approved in 1997, and that the IDEFObject standard will be approved shortly thereafter.

IEEE P1471—Architectural Description

The SESC project P1471 is intended to deal with one of software engineering's hot topics, the description of software architecture. In recent years, many practitioners have come to believe that successful development of modern distributed and client/server systems requires a description of the system that is more abstract than its design and which provides a focused and selective treatment of strategic issues crucial to the operation of the system while suppressing less important issues. Although there is much disagreement regarding the precise definition, most refer to the general concept as *architecture*.

The project is intended to produce a Recommended Practice document defining a conceptual framework for software systems architectures, their construction and usage throughout the full life cycle. The framework will include terminology, concepts, and principles presented as a meta-model [AWG97].

ISO 5806—Single-Hit Decision Tables

This standard specifies the format for documentation of single-hit decision tables. Approved in 1984, the standard is part of the legacy inherited by JTC1 at its formation.

ISO 5807, Charting Symbols

ISO 5807 superseded two older standards in describing charts useful for documenting information systems. The charts include data flowcharts, program flowcharts, system flowcharts, program network charts, and system resources charts. Although these notations were once widely used, it is unusual to see them in modern documentation. Another JTC1/SC7 legacy document, this standard was approved in 1985.

ISO 8790—Computer Configuration Diagrams

ISO 8790 establishes graphical symbols that can be used to represent the physical structure of computer systems and their connection cables. The standard is probably most useful for mainframe systems. It was approved in 1987.

ISO/IEC 8631—Program Constructs

Approved in 1989, this document can be viewed as the standard for *structured programming*. It defines a set of program constructs, specifies how they are combined, and describes how they may be depicted in various forms of charts. The specified constructs include imperative, serial, parallel, iterative, and selective choice.

ISO/IEC 11411—State Transition Diagrams

This standard prescribes two ways to draw state transition diagrams—one with nodes and arcs and the other using a table. It is intended for the specification of interactive software, data communication software, and command languages. The standard was approved in 1995.

Techniques

The SESC model of standardization uses the word "technique" to describe a practice that can be used in the pursuit of a variety of objectives. A standard prescribing a technique is conceptually like a subroutine that is invoked to satisfy one or more requirements of a variety of other standards. Standards prescribing techniques are listed in Table 75. In addition, IEEE Std 1028, described from the process viewpoint in Chapter 13, prescribes techniques for various forms of review and audits.

Table 75. Standards Describing Techniques

Standard	Title
IEEE Std 1044-1993	Standard classification for software anomalies
IEEE Std 1044.1-1995	Guide to classification for software anomalies
ISO 6593:1985	Program flow for processing sequential files in terms of record groups

IEEE Std 1044 and 1044.1—Classification of Anomalies

IEEE Std 1044, maintained by SESC and approved in 1993, provides a uniform approach to the classification of anomalies found in software and its documentation. An *anomaly* is any condition that departs from the expected; the term is used in preference to terms such as error, fault, failure, incident, flaw, bug, etc. The standard provides a sequence of steps from the initial recognition of the anomaly to its final disposition as well as suggestions for classifications into which anomalies may be classified. Conformance to the standard requires the use of a specified minimal set of classifications. Some guidance is provided in the standard itself and additional guidance is supplied in its guide, IEEE Std 1044.1. The documents may be employed to a number of ends, including software product measurements, quality records, and process improvement.

ISO 6593—Processing Sequential Files of Record Groups

This standard is a codification of a programming technique. It describes two alternative methods for processing sequential files where the individual records have been organized into hierarchical groups based on control fields that affect the processing of the records. Although the techniques were common in the days of mainframe processing of sequential files, more modern systems usually provide for online updating of randomly accessed databases. The standard was approved in 1985 and is assigned to JTC1/SC7 for maintenance.

Process Information Products

The pretentious-sounding term *process information product* (PIP) is motivated by a desire to differentiate from other more common terms. First, a PIP is not necessarily a *document*—at least, it's not necessarily a paper document—although it might be. Instead, it might, for example, be some entries in a database or some electronic data managed by a CASE tool. Second, a PIP is not necessarily an *end-product* of software development—although it might be. For example, a software product must include some sort of user manual or on-line help—they would be part of the software product. PIPs, on the other hand, include many documents that are not provided to the end user, but are instead passed from one software process to another. Finally, a PIP is not necessarily a *deliverable* of a contract—although it might be. It's true that a contract might call for the delivery of one or more PIPs, but even if the contract does not call for delivery, the developer may consider it sensible to create the PIP anyway.

The concept of a PIP is intended to capture the idea that in a well-managed software program, it is appropriate to capture data from each process for the use of other related processes, even if the data is not a product of the development, does not have to be delivered, and is not on paper. The standards listed in Table 76 can be applied to specify the sort of information that should be recorded in a PIP.[45] (The SC7 standard is unfinished and shown in italics.)

Table 76. Standards for Process Information Products

Standard	Title
IEEE Std 829-1983	Standard for software test documentation
IEEE Std 830-1993	Recommended practice for software requirements specifications
IEEE Std 1016-1987	Recommended practice for software design descriptions
IEEE Std 1016.1-1993	Guide to software design descriptions
ISO/IEC WD 15289	Guidelines for the content of software life cycle process information products

IEEE Std 829—Software Test Documentation

The SESC standard for software test documentation, IEEE Std 829, was approved in 1983 and most recently reaffirmed in 1991. It specifies the form and content of a set of basic PIPs (it calls them "documents") that may be used to carry out a software testing program. It does not specify a minimum acceptable set of such PIPs, instead assuming that the project plans will designate the appropriate set. The standard prescribes one PIP for test planning, three for test specification, and four for test reporting. Annexes provide examples of application.

---

[45]It should be noted that some more general standards also include PIPs. An annex of EIA/IEEE J-Std-016 specifies a large number of PIPs that would be useful in implementing the requirements of that standard. IEEE/EIA 12207.1 provides PIPs useful in implementing Part 0 of 12207.

IEEE Std 830—Software Requirements Specifications

This SESC standard is a Recommended Practice originally approved in 1984 and revised in 1993. The standard is based on the premise that the software requirements specification is intended to be a complete and unambiguous specification of the characteristics required of the completed system. Although the standard makes some provision for evolution, it is apparently inapplicable to situations where the requirements document provides merely a first approximation as a baseline for further refinement. The standard is written in the form of guidance, providing many recommendations of good practice but no requirements. The guidance includes qualities desired in a specification, as well as recommendations for the format and content of the PIP.

IEEE Std 1016 and 1016.1—Software Design Descriptions

IEEE Std 1016 is a Recommended Practice (RP) for the description of software design. It is not intended to represent the results of any specific design methodology or descriptive technique; instead, it is intended to be broadly applicable. So, at a suitably general level, the standard describes the sort of information that should be recorded for a software *design entity*. Although a table of contents is provided as an example, a particular format for the design description is not a requirement of the standard. This SESC standard was first approved in 1987 and was reaffirmed in 1993.

The guide—IEEE Std 1016.1—explains how the information requirements of 1016 may be met by any of several well-known design methods, including Jackson Structured Programming, Ward-Mellor, Layered Virtual Machines, etc. The guide was approved in 1993.

ISO/IEC WD 15289—Process Information Products

This project is in an early stage of development in JTC1/SC7/WG2. The intent is to describe nearly two dozen PIPs applicable to various stages of software development. The initial draft was derived from the Data Item Descriptions contained in Mil-Std 498.

Reuse Libraries

Effective software reuse is generally regarded as a desirable, if not completely achievable, characteristic of a mature software development process. Lack of evidence of repeatable effectiveness of specific techniques has inhibited the codification of standards for reuse [SESC96d]. The IEEE standards are narrowly based, dealing only with reuse libraries, and then only with the interchange of reusable components among them. All are listed in Table 77 along with a broader AIAA document. Draft standards are listed in italics. IEEE plans additional work in the area of reuse life cycle processes and domain analysis.

Table 77. Standards for Reuse Libraries

Standard	Title
AIAA G-010-1993	Guide for reusable software: Assessment criteria for aerospace application
IEEE Std 1420.1-1995	Standard for software reuse—Data model for reuse library interoperability: Basic Interoperability Data Model (BIDM)
IEEE Std 1420.1a-1996	Standard for software reuse—Data model for reuse library interoperability: Asset certification framework
IEEE P1420.1b	Standard for software reuse—Data model for reuse library interoperability: Intellectual property rights framework
IEEE P1420.2	Standard for software reuse—Data model for reuse library interoperability: Bindings to HTML and SGML
IEEE P1420.3	Standard for software reuse—Data model for reuse library interoperability: Model extensions
IEEE Std 1430-1996	Guide for software reuse—Concept of operations for interoperating reuse libraries

AIAA G-010—Reusable Software: Assessment Criteria for Aerospace Applications

This 22-page AIAA standard grew out work done in the early 1990's by the DoD's Defense Advanced Projects Research Agency (DARPA), notably the Software Technology for Adaptable, Reliable Systems (STARS) program. It was completed in 1993 by the AIAA's Software Systems Committee. The document provides guidance on "performing domain analysis as the basis for developing criteria for assessing potentially reusable software and establishing a software reuse library." Although the scope is stated as aerospace applications, the guidance seems more broadly applicable. Appendices suggest possible criteria for use in domain analysis, component assessment, and reuse library selection. The component assessment criteria are mostly Ada coding guidelines.

IEEE Std 1420—Data Model for Reuse Library Interoperability

SESC's standards for reuse library interoperability grew out of a situation in the late 1980s and early 1990s when it became clear that various organizations within the federal government were each interested in establishing themselves as the sole software reuse library for all government users. Taking a contrary approach, the Reuse Library Interoperability Group (RIG) asserted that no single library could meet the needs of all communities of users and that libraries should instead promote interoperability [Moore91, Moore94]. This would permit each library to focus on the needs of its own community while still being able to access other components by obtaining them from other libraries.

To promote interoperability among libraries, the RIG specified an abstract data model for the description of assets. Following an approach of specifying in small, incremental pieces, the RIG has produced a series of standards, parts and supplements gradually elaborating the model. The various specifications have been adopted by the SESC. IEEE Std 1420.1 is the basic data model. A supplement, 1420.1a, elaborates the model by adding descriptions of certifications of quality and fitness.[46] Another planned supplement, 1420.1b, will further elaborate the model by adding intellectual property rights information. The planned Part 2 of the standard will be a binding,[47] explaining how the model may be expressed in terms of HyperText Markup Language (HTML) and

---

[46]The manner in which vendors have implemented the RIG data model illustrates an interesting characteristic of interchange standards. One of the premises of the RIG was that individual libraries should store and describe their components in the manner best suited to their users; that the interchange format was useful only as an interface to other libraries. Without exception, though, vendors who implement the RIG specifications apply them to the internal organization of the library. The general principle is that external interchange gradually, but inevitably, drives the internal characteristics of the entities that they bound.

[47]A "binding" is a particular type of standard that explains how the interface prescribed by a standard may be achieved in a particular language.

Standard Generalized Markup Language (SGML) tagging. Finally, the planned Part 3 will provide rules for extending the model.

IEEE Std 1430—Concept of Operations for Interoperating Reuse Libraries

This is a curious document in the SESC collection of standards. Reluctant to provide normative guidance for the organization of reuse library networks, the RIG instead decided to write a document describing its assumptions. Users could decide for themselves whether the assumptions fit their own situation. IEEE Std 1430 is a guide describing the RIG's assumptions.

Tools

Much of the work performed by ISO/IEC JTC1/SC7 and by IEEE SESC in the area of tools has dealt with processes for evaluating, selecting and adopting CASE tools. The two organizations have a history of close cooperation in the development of the standards shown in Table 78. (Two of the SC7 projects are shown in italics because they are incomplete.) IEEE SESC has also developed a trial use standard reference model for the interconnection of CASE tools.

Table 78. Standards for CASE tools

Standard	Title
IEEE Std 1175-1992	Standard reference model for computing system tool interconnections
IEEE Std 1209-1992	Recommended practice for the evaluation and selection of CASE tools
IEEE Std 1348-1995	Recommended practice for the adoption of CASE tools
ISO/IEC NWI	Reference model for software engineering environments
ISO/IEC DTR 14471	Adoption of CASE tools
ISO/IEC 14102:1995	Guideline for the evaluation and selection of CASE tools

In addition to the standards described below, SC7/WG4 has submitted a new work item proposal for the development of a reference model for software engineering environment services. The project will address the problem of a lack of common understanding of the meaning of the term "software engineering environment." It will deal with the situation by describing a comprehensive set of services that would be considered to comprise an environment. The

WG is also considering work on a compliance standard for configuration management tools.

IEEE Std 1175—Reference Model for Tool Interconnections

Originally approved for trial use in 1992, this standard was not sponsored by SESC but rather the Standards Coordinating Committee of the IEEE Computer Society, a sponsor that deals with standards cutting across the concerns of various committees within the Computer Society. The motivation of the standard is to help users of computer-based tools to interconnect those tools and to integrate them into "families." It pursues this desire by providing reference models for interconnecting tools to organizations, interconnecting tools to computing platforms, and transferring information among tools. To facilitate these interconnections, the standard specifies a Semantic Transfer Language (STL) providing for the exchange, but not the representation, of information to be shared by tools. Conformance to the reference models is achieved by completing "tool profiles" that identify the context for tool interconnection. Conformance to the STL is achieved by completing other profiles that serve to identify which portions of the STL are used by a particular tool. Profiles can be compared to learn if tools share semantics and can transfer information without conversion. The 151-page document is accompanied by a diskette containing the STL profiles.

IEEE Std 1209 and ISO/IEC 14102—Evaluation and Selection of CASE Tools

These two standards provide an excellent example of cooperation among national and international standards bodies. The IEEE SESC standard was approved in 1992 and submitted for consideration by the relevant international committee, JTC1/SC7/WG2. Three years later, after appropriate revision to deal with international interests, JTC1 approved the resulting ISO/IEC standard. IEEE is now conducting a ballot to adopt the international version as a US standard replacing the original 1209, possibly with an annex containing provisions specific to the United States. (The new IEEE standard may have a different number—1462.)

The IEEE 1209 standard is a recommended practice for evaluating tools for Computer-Aided Software Engineering (CASE) and selecting them for deployment. The document describes processes for selection and evaluation, processes that include the determination of relevant selection criteria. All criteria are based on the viewpoint of a CASE tool user; hence they deal with externally visible characteristics. The standard recognizes that the evaluation and selection process is complex and has organizational implications; therefore it does not generalize the processes beyond tools specifically applicable to software engineering. Furthermore, the standard does not advocate any specific development standards, design methods, or life cycle models. The document applies the framework of product characteristics provided by ISO/IEC 9126:1991.

In comparison, the ISO/IEC 14102 standard places relatively less emphasis on describing the processes for evaluation and selection and relatively greater emphasis on describing candidate criteria that may be applied during the processes. The criteria are based on the model provided by the ISO/IEC 12119 standard on quality requirements for software packages, which, in turn, is an elaboration of the 9126 model.

In academic settings, the evaluation process of 14102 has been successfully expanded to a generic process for dealing with new technologies [Abran96].

IEEE Std 1348 and ISO/IEC DTR 14471—Adoption of CASE Tools

IEEE Std 1348 is a 1995 recommended practice for the *adoption* of CASE tools in an organization. Adoption is an activity with a wider scope than selection and evaluation and, accordingly, the 1348 standard references the 1209 standard as useful for accomplishing the appropriate portions of the larger process. The document describes four steps in the adoption process: defining CASE needs; evaluating and selecting tools; conducting a pilot project; and fostering routine use of the tool. It is recognized that CASE tool adoption is challenging; hence the document refrains from "cookbook" solutions in favor of more general advice for developing a process suiting the needs of the organization.

IEEE SESC and JTC1/SC7 benefit from close collaboration on CASE tool standards. The IEEE standard is being applied as a source for a JTC1 document on the same subject. This planned Technical Report has reached the DTR stage.

SEDDI

ISO/IEC JTC1/SC7/WG11 is devoted to projects for Software Engineering Data Definition and Representation (SEDDI). The basic intent is to take a large number of EIA standards on CASE Data

Table 79. Standards for Software Engineering Data Interchange
      (SEDDI)

Standard	Title
ISO/IEC 14568:1997	Diagram eXchange Language for tree-structured charts
ISO/IEC CD 15474-1	Software engineering data definition and interchange—Part 1: Overview
ISO/IEC CD 15474-2	Software engineering data definition and interchange—Part 2: Framework for modeling and extensibility
ISO/IEC WD 15474-3	Software engineering data definition and interchange—Part 3: Framework for mapping PCTE to CDIF
ISO/IEC WD 15474-4	Software engineering data definition and interchange—Part 4: Framework for mapping IRDS to CDIF
ISO/IEC CD 15475-x	Software engineering data definition and interchange—Transfer format [three parts]
ISO/IEC CD 15476-x	Software engineering data definition and interchange—Integrated meta-model [nine parts]
ISO/IEC CD 15477-x	Software engineering data definition and interchange—Presentation meta-model [three parts]
ISO/IEC WD 15478-x	Software engineering data definition and interchange—PCTE schema definition sets [six parts]
ISO/IEC WD 15479-x	Software engineering data definition and interchange—IRDS content modules [six parts]

Interchange Format (CDIF) and promote them to the level of inter-national standards. These standards will provide a means for users of software engineering tools to consistently access and interpret descriptive data used for software engineering because the design-ers of file and repository storage formats have applied the data de-scriptions contained in the documents. The project is huge, involv-ing at least six standards totaling at least 31 parts as shown in Table 79. Most are in preliminary stages, Committee Draft or ear-lier (hence, listed in italics), and all require appropriate coordina-tion between EIA and SC7.

ISO/IEC 14568—DXL for Tree-Structured Charts

One WG11 project has been completed. Published in 1997, the Diagram eXchange Language (DXL) permits CASE tools to inter-change information regarding tree-structured charts, such as the program constructs of ISO 8631 or the structured program flow-charts of ISO 5807. The standard does not specify how charts are visually represented for the use of humans.

OBJECTS OF SOFTWARE ENGINEERING: PRODUCTS

It should be obvious that the purpose of software engineering is to produce software products, but you could be forgiven for failing to grasp that truth from viewing the corpus of software engineering standards. The desirable characteristics of software products are so difficult to precisely specify that standardization efforts have generally avoided confronting them. Nevertheless, there are a few standards dealing with product characteristics; this chapter will describe them.

The overall organization of this chapter is provided by the SC7 standards for software product evaluation—a collection that is currently growing from one document to nine. The collection has been criticized by some as lacking substantive content. Others suggest that the model is an appropriate complement to the usual process-centric bias because performance of process requirements is evaluated by examination of the products produced by the processes. Readers may judge the value of the SC7 product standards for themselves.

Table 80 lists the product evaluation standards that are the responsibility of IEEE and of ISO/IEC JTC1/SC7, with the draft standards shown in italics. Only one of the SC7 standards, the 9126 model for quality characteristics, exists in finished form, and it is being revised into a three part document. To that collection will be added a six-part standard describing how product evaluations should be performed.

The model provided by the ISO/IEC 9126 standard lists six product characteristics that are then refined into sub-characteristics. A number of standards, listed in Table 81, are available to aid in the evaluation of those characteristics. The ISO/IEC standards, shown in italics, are still being developed.

A software product is incomplete without certain items that help to "package" the product and make it marketable. Standards dealing with those items are listed in Table 82. The ISO/IEC standard for evaluation of CASE tools, 14102, will be described in Chap-

Table 80. Software Product Evaluation Standards

Standard	Title
IEEE Std 1061-1992	Standard for a software quality metrics methodology
ISO/IEC 9126:1991	Software product evaluation—Quality characteristics and guidelines for their use
ISO/IEC CD 9126-1	Software quality characteristics and metrics—Part 1: Quality characteristics and subcharacteristics
ISO/IEC pDTR 9126-2	Software quality characteristics and metrics—Part 2: External metrics
ISO/IEC pDTR 9126-3	Software quality characteristics and metrics—Part 3: Internal metrics
ISO/IEC DIS 14598-1	Software product evaluation—Part 1: General overview
ISO/IEC CD 14598-2	Software product evaluation—Part 2: Planning and management
ISO/IEC CD 14598-3	Software product evaluation—Part 3: Process for developers
ISO/IEC CD 14598-4	Software product evaluation—Part 4: Process for acquirers
ISO/IEC DIS 14598-5	Software product evaluation—Part 5: Process for evaluators
ISO/IEC CD 14598-6	Software product evaluation—Part 6: Documentation of evaluation modules

Table 81. Standards Supporting Evaluation of Product Characteristics

Standard	Title
IEEE Std 982.1-1988	Standard dictionary of measures to produce reliable software
IEEE Std 982.2-1988	Guide for the use of standard dictionary of measures to produce reliable software
ISO/IEC DIS 14143-1	Software measurement—Functional size measurement—Part 1: Definition of concepts
ISO/IEC CD 14756	Measurement and rating of performance of computer-based software systems

ter 11 but is listed in the table because it applies the general software packaging requirements of ISO/IEC 12119.

Although the ISO/IEC 9126 model deals with the quality aspects of functionality (including sub-characteristics of suitability, accuracy, interoperability, compliance and security), it does not deal with function per se. Standards dealing with that subject are described elsewhere in this book but are listed in Table 83, with chapter references for convenient reference. (Draft standards are shown in italics.) They are not further treated in this chapter.

Table 82. Standards for "Packaging" Software Products

Standard	Title	Chapter
IEEE Std 1063-1987	Standard for software user documentation	
ISO 9127:1988	User documentation and cover information for consumer software packages	
ISO/IEC 12119:1994	Software packages—Quality requirements and testing	
ISO/IEC 14102:1995	Guideline for the evaluation and selection of CASE tools	11

Table 83. Standards Dealing with Software Functionality

Standard	Title	Chapter
AIAA G-043-1992	Guide for the preparation of operations concept documents	14
IEEE Std 830-1993	Recommended practice for software requirements specification	11
IEEE Std 1233-1996	Guide for developing system requirements specifications	14
IEEE P1362	Guide for concept of operations document	14

Also excluded from discussion in this chapter are the standards for software development processes and plans supporting the achievement of product quality. For convenient reference, they are listed in Table 84.

Table 84. Plans and Processes Supporting Product Quality

Standard	Title	Chapter
IEEE Std 730-1989	Standard for software quality assurance plans	13
IEEE Std 730.1-1995	Guide to software quality assurance planning	13
IEEE Std 1012-1986	Standard for software verification and validation plans	13
IEEE Std 1059-1993	Guide for software verification and validation plans	13
IEEE Std 1228-1994	Standard for software safety plans	14

The relationships among the product quality standards are summarized in the road map diagram of Figure 32. (As usual, draft standards are shown in italics.) The mostly unfinished standard ISO 9241 is shown because several parts are referenced in ISO/IEC 12119; they prescribe ergonomic requirements for various products

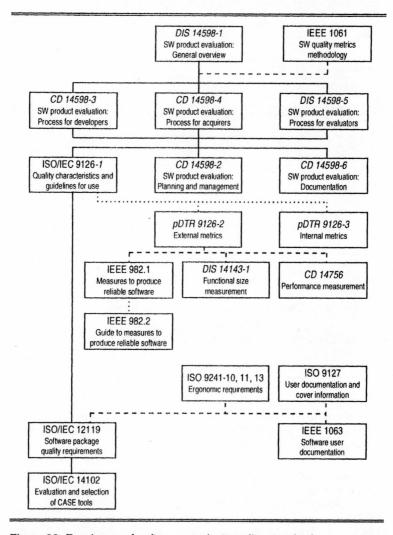

Figure 32. Road map of software product quality standards.

including software. ISO/IEC 14102 is shown on this road map diagram because it applies the packaging requirements of 12119; it is described in Chapter 11. The other standards are described in the remainder of this chapter.

Product Evaluation Standards

ISO 8402 defines quality as "the totality of characteristics of an entity that bear on its ability to satisfy stated or implied needs."

The ISO 9000 series, though, addresses only the quality management systems for developing a product rather than the product's own characteristics. There are software standards, however, intended to directly address the quality of the products themselves.

There are two major choices in this area. The IEEE collection is represented by a single, comprehensive standard. The current SC7 collection consists of a single standard, ISO/IEC 9126 (as well as two applications of it, ISO/IEC 12119 and ISO/IEC 14102). The plans for the collection, however, are much larger. Therefore much of this section will describe planned SC7 standards rather than current ones.

In JTC1, software product quality standards are the primary responsibility of SC7/WG6 but relate to the work of other groups within SC7. For example, ISO/IEC 9127 is maintained by WG2, the working group for documentation, and 14102 is maintained by WG4, whose work is CASE tools. The ISO 9241 standard is the responsibility of ISO TC159.

IEEE Std 1061—Software Quality Metrics Methodology

The IEEE standard in this niche is 1061. Completed by SESC in 1992, this 88-page standard provides a methodology for establishing quality requirements and developing the supporting metrics. (Some may believe that the word "quality" is misapplied in the title of this standard and is another example of the term being stretched to include everything. The standard seems to be suitable for measuring any characteristic of a software product.) It may be applied by acquirers, developers, maintainers, users, or independent assessors.

Although the standard does not prescribe metrics, the annexes provide exemplar metrics along with two fully worked examples of application. The basic approach is to establish a metrics framework that is a three-level hierarchy. The framework begins with the establishment of quality requirements and an agreed set of attributes defining the requirements. Factors representing user and management views are associated with the attributes. "Direct metrics" are selected to quantitatively represent the factors. For example, mean time to failure might serve as the direct metric for a factor of reliability. At the second level of the hierarchy, the factors are decomposed into sub-factors representing software-oriented attributes that are more directly measurable and more meaningful to the developers. For example, a sub-factor of reliability might be a measure of the system's ability to continue to operate in the presence of hardware failure. Finally, at the third level is found a decomposition of sub-factors into metrics to be used to measure system products and processes during development. These third-level metrics, that are to be validated against the direct metrics, are used to estimate factor values during the development process.

Although there are disagreements in terminology, IEEE Std 1061 can be viewed as providing an outline of the methodology to be specified by the ISO/IEC 9126 and 14598 standards.

ISO/IEC 9126—Software Product Quality Characteristics

So far, the primary contribution of ISO/IEC JTC1/SC7/WG6 has been this 13-page standard, published in 1991, defining a framework of software product quality characteristics and sub-characteristics based on the terminology in the quality vocabulary of ISO 8402. As Figure 32 shows, however, more is intended.

ISO/IEC 9126 is the key existing standard in the group. It defines, with minimal overlap, six characteristics of software quality that are intended to cover all of the aspects of software quality resulting from the ISO definition of quality. The standard also recommends a set of sub-characteristics applicable to each:

- Functionality: suitability, accuracy, interoperability, compliance, security

- Reliability: maturity, fault tolerance, recoverability

- Usability: understandability, learnability, operability

- Efficiency: time behavior, resource behavior

- Maintainability: analyzability, changeability, stability, testability

- Portability: adaptability, installability, conformance, replaceability

Finally, the standard introduces the concept of evaluating quality from each of several viewpoints: those of the user, the developer and the manager.

SC7/WG6 plans to elaborate on the basic model provided by ISO/IEC 9126 in future revisions. The material formerly covered in the single-part 9126 document will now be elaborated in greater detail in a three-part 9126 document plus a six-part document to be designated 14598.

ISO/IEC 9126-1 will describe the quality characteristics and sub-characteristics (with some changes from the model in the existing 9126) not only for evaluating product quality, but also for the purposes of specifying quality requirements and designing checklists for design reviews and product testing. Parts 2 and 3 of the 9126 standard will specify, respectively, external and internal metrics useful for measuring quality characteristics and sub-characteristics. The distinction between external and internal is analogous to the distinction between an acquirer and a developer: internal metrics are intended as direct measurements of items such as source code or specifications; external metrics are intended to deal with externally manifested characteristics of the product. Parts 2 and 3 of 9126 will be technical reports because it is believed that the area of quality metrics is still immature.

ISO/IEC CD 14598—Software Product Evaluation

The material regarding evaluation process will be moved from ISO/IEC 9126 into a new six-part guide, 14598, Software Product Evaluation. Part 1 will provide a general overview of the series. Parts 3, 4, and 5 will prescribe software product evaluation activities for developers, acquirers, and evaluators, respectively. Part 2 will provide overall direction to the management of a product evaluation function as well as the preparation and implementation of product quality measurement plans. Finally, Part 6 will describe the documentation of an "evaluation module" [Bøegh95], a structured set of instructions and data used for evaluation. The documents are at various stages of progress—Parts 1 and 5 are Draft International Standards while the others are only CDs.

All of this work is governed by the usual vocabulary standards as well as the overall approach of the ISO 9000 series of quality management standards. In addition, the documents may make normative references to the software process framework provided by ISO/IEC 12207 and the system and software integrity level definitions to be provided by DIS 15026.

Product Characteristic Standards

Several of the SESC and JTC1 standards are useful for specifying or elaborating material useful in dealing with the quality characteristics and sub-characteristics specified by ISO/IEC 9126.

IEEE Std 982.1 and 982.2—Measures to Produce Reliable Software

The IEEE 982.1 standard is a dictionary, providing definitions and a taxonomy of measures that can be applied in the development of reliable software. This 36-page SESC document was approved in 1988 and is currently being reviewed for possible revision. Emphasis is placed on measures that can be made early in the development process as indicators of the eventual reliability of the software product. Six categories of product measures and three categories of process measures are described along with the proper conditions for the use of a measure and its method of computation. Measures of errors, faults, and failures serve as primitives for many of the remaining measures.

The 96-page SESC guide for this standard—IEEE Std 982.2— was approved in 1988 and corrected in 1989. It is currently the subject of a revision effort. The document provides underlying concepts and motivation for establishing a measurement activity for reliable software using the measures described in IEEE Std 982.1. It includes guidance for applying product and process measures throughout the life cycle, optimizing the development of reliable software with respect to cost and schedule, maximizing the reliability of software during its operational phase, and developing the means to manage reliability. The application of 982.1 and 982.2 for dependability is discussed in Chapter 9.

ISO/IEC DIS 14143-1—Functional Size Measurement

Document 14143 is under development by WG12 of SC7 to define functional size measurements (FSM) of software, usually known simply as "function points." Delegates to the Working Group include representatives of the International Function Point Users Group and other interested organizations.

Functional size measurement is intended to measure the size of software in a manner independent of its implementation, by examining the functions required by the user. One such method, known as function point analysis, was proposed by Alan Albrecht of IBM [Albrecht83]. Since his paper, various other methods have been proposed, lessening the value of the technique as inconsistencies accumulate.

The current document, Part 1 of a planned five-part set, is at the DIS stage of development. It defines the fundamental concepts of FSM with the intention of promoting consistent interpretations. It does not endorse any specific method for measurement.

ISO/IEC CD 14756—Measurement and Rating of Performance

SC7/WG6 is itself developing a document detailing one of the external metrics, *time behavior*, to be listed in the planned 9126-1. The 14756 document, based on a´German national standard and now at the CD stage, explains how user-oriented performance of computer-based software systems may be objectively measured and rated using a "remote terminal emulator" to interact with the system. A variety of metrics are described in this document.

Software Product Packaging Standards

WG6 has built on the quality model of ISO/IEC 9126 to prescribe requirements for software *packages*, that is, end item software, like a spreadsheet program or a word processor, intended for off-the-shelf purchase. Standards useful for that purpose are discussed in this section.

ISO 9127—Consumer Software Documentation and Cover Information

ISO 9127, approved by ISO in 1988 and assumed by JTC1/SC7, prescribes requirements for user documentation and cover information (i.e., the information visible through the shrink wrap in which software is packaged). Its scope includes requirements for the content of user documentation and cover information supplied with consumer software packages sold off-the-shelf for business, scientific, education, and home usage. Its provisions cover the information needed to install and run the software and the extent of information needed on external packaging to allow the potential customer to evaluate its applicability. The standard references ISO 6592, Guidelines for Documentation, for general documentation provisions. Users of ISO 9127 should also consider the use of ISO/IEC 12119, Software Package Quality Requirements, described below.

ISO/IEC 12119, Software Package Quality Requirements and Testing

ISO/IEC 12119, produced by SC7/WG6, is an application of the quality framework described by ISO/IEC 9126. The 16-page standard, approved in 1994, provides quality requirements for software packages, such as spreadsheets, word processors, utilities, etc. (The term "package" is intended to suggest a bundle of documentation, programs, and data.) Packages are required to include user documentation and a product description that enables prospective buyers to determine if the package is suitable for the intended use. General quality requirements are placed on the programs and data as well as specific requirements for the content of the user documentation and the product description. The standard also provides instructions for testing the product for compliance with quality requirements including the claims made in the product description.

In some cases, the requirements of ISO/IEC 12119 are explicitly related to two other documents, ISO 9127 and ISO 9241. The text of 12119 includes specific comparisons of its provisions and the recommendations of 9127 covering consumer software documentation. Some users of ISO/IEC 12119 may find it appropriate to also apply the stricter requirements for user documentation found in ISO 9127.

ISO 9241, a multi-part standard prepared by ISO TC159, contains ergonomic requirements for many computer system components, including hardware, software, and the environment for usage. ISO 12119 references Parts 10, 11, and 13 for considerations of software ergonomics on dialogue, specifying and measuring usability, and user guidance, respectively [Billingsley93].

The IEEE standard on software user documentation, 1063, may also be useful to some users of ISO/IEC 12119.

ISO/IEC 12119 is being considered for adoption by the IEEE as IEEE 1465. Additional material describing ISO/IEC 12119 can be found in [Wegner95].

IEEE Std 1063—Software User Documentation

This 15-page document, approved in 1987 and reaffirmed in 1993, is SESC's standard for traditional printed user manuals; on-line documentation is excluded from its scope. It provides minimum requirements on the structure and information content of such manuals. The provisions of this standard may also be useful in conjunction with the requirements of the other standards described in this section.

Objects of Software Engineering: Processes

13

Of all of the objects of software engineering, process is the one receiving the most attention today. It is commonly believed that the implementation of a sound software development process is strongly correlated with the production of high-quality software products. Of course, this attitude is not unique to software development—the ISO 9000 standards apply the same premise to the manufacturing of systems.

Even in the early days of the software discipline, it was recognized that some crucial aspects of the software development, such as configuration management, had to be rigorously defined and enforced. Since Winston Royce's seminal presentation in 1970 [Royce70], emphasis has been broadened and placed on a disciplined, procedural approach to the overall processes for software development, and more recently, maintenance and operation. The body of available standards represents both viewpoints—singular processes and life cycle frameworks. An important challenge for the standards organizations is to rationalize their collections, merging the viewpoints by harmonizing the standards. An additional dimension is the interest during the last decade in the assessment and improvement of the processes themselves. Both IEEE SESC and SC7 are pursuing the goals of integrating individual processes into life-cycle frameworks, frameworks that include approaches for self-improvement.

The treatment in this book anticipates that ongoing rationalization, taking advantage of planning information available from the two organizations to fit the standards prescribing individual processes into an overall life cycle framework.

This chapter will provide a brief history of software life cycle process standards and a framework intended to clarify the relationships among various kinds of process standards. This framework will be applied to differentiate some of the available alternatives and will be used to explain the relationship to the organizational adoption of process standards. Following a discussion of the process standards themselves, the final section will review available standards for assessing organizational software process capability.

Background

One of the difficult questions in selecting a software life cycle process standard is to understand why so many of them are available at all. This section provides historical and technological background to help you select from the alternatives.

History

The Royce paper was presented at a time when even the concept of "software engineering" was in its infancy—the term itself had been coined only two years previously. The paper suggested that it was possible to organize software development as a series of phases with staged objectives rather than following the simple-minded "code and fix" cycle typically practiced at the time, a process that today we would call "hacking." Largely because of the appearance of his diagrams, the Royce model was dubbed the "waterfall," a term that he did not use.[48]

The decades of the 1970s and 1980s saw a proliferation of life cycle definitions and standards, mostly adding details to the waterfall concept. Inspired by the Royce paper, numerous military, regulatory, commercial, and standards organizations wrote life cycle standards that, although boringly similar in concept, were mad-

---

[48]This historical example provides an important lesson—names *are* important. As managers put the waterfall model into practice, they were persuaded by the name that, just as water never goes up the waterfall, a particular piece of software should never move backward in the life cycle. In practice, the prototyping and cyclical activities that Royce built into his model were systematically ignored on the premise that each of the staged activities should and could "get it right the first time." Ironically, many of the reforms that modern models introduce were, in fact, present in Royce's original model. The persistence of unenlightened application of the waterfall model, despite repeated failure, is remarkable and is perhaps explained by its convenience to the manager. Applying the unenlightened waterfall model, a manager can summarize the status of even a large software development project on a single sheet of paper, an important advantage. Reformers must demonstrate that their proposed models are capable of similarly succinct summarization before they will make much headway in displacing the waterfall model.

deningly different in the details. Some of those standards are still in use and are pertinent to the current discussion.

Defense Life Cycle Standards

All of the current major life cycle (and development cycle) process standards have an ancestry that includes important Department of Defense (DoD) development standards. In 1974, the US Navy initiated the project to write Mil-Std 1679, Weapons System Software Development, one of the first standards treating the usage, control and management of embedded computer resources [SESC93]. (Figure 33.) It was followed, in the early 1980s, by DoD-Std 2167, intended as applicable to all mission-critical defense computing systems. A subsequent revision, DoD-Std 2167A, corrected some technical characteristics that complicated use with modern programming languages and techniques and created a link between the software and its encompassing system. In the late 1980s, the DoD decided to consolidate DoD-Std 2167A and DoD-Std 7935 standard (for information systems) to produce a single standard, Mil-Std 498, that unified the requirements of its predecessors. After seeing the result, the National Security Agency also dropped its own standard, 1703, in favor of the new one.

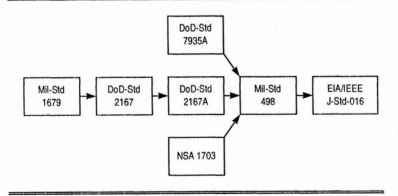

Figure 33. Family tree of DoD life cycle standards. (Adapted from [Moore95].)

Just as Mil-Std 498 was completed, the DoD announced a policy emphasizing the use of commercial standards and canceled many of its own standards, including the predecessors of 498. Because no equivalent commercial standard was in place, 498 was approved for an interim period while a suitable commercial standard was developed. The IEEE and the EIA formed a joint committee to develop the replacement, largely similar to Mil-Std 498 with some of the defense-specific jargon removed. The result was issued under a number suggesting the collaborative nature of the project, EIA/IEEE J-Std-016, where the J stands for "Joint."[49] Despite the commercial designation, the result still very much represents three decades of DoD experience in the development of very large, complex software systems. Although new defense software development projects should probably apply the new IEEE/EIA 12207 standard, the J-Std-016 document is still useful to projects where it is desirable to retain the documentation structure of previous defense efforts or to organizations that have existing organization-level processes conforming with those military standards.

Commercial Life Cycle Standards

Many of the early commercial standards on the software life cycle were either proprietary, regarded as trade secrets bestowing competitive advantage, or specific to an industry sector. Some industry sectors still employ their own standards; modern examples include RTCA DO-178B, used in the avionics industry, and IEC 880, used in the nuclear industry.

IEEE Std 1074 was developed with the goal of being independent of any particular industry sector and independent of any specific life cycle model. It specified life-cycle process fragments and how they could be connected to create life-cycle processes. Meanwhile, there was growing interest in the international community in developing a life-cycle framework, primarily as an aid to an anticipated international market for software development services. SC7 initiated the ISO/IEC 12207 project to develop a high-level life cycle framework suitable primarily for use in two-party acquisition situations but also appropriate for internal use within an enterprise. Both Mil-Std 498 and IEEE 1074 were used as base documents for this development, even though the result, which was approved in 1995, is quite different from either. (See Figure 34.)

Completion of ISO/IEC 12207 put the IEEE SESC in an awkward position. It now had two national standards, IEEE 1074 and EIA/IEEE J-Std-016, already quite different in nature, and perceived that the ability of the United States to compete in the international software marketplace might depend on the adoption of a third, very different standard, ISO/IEC 12207. Its response was threefold: first, an effort to incorporate the best of US industrial practices and experience into a US adaptation of the international

---

[49]The "J" nomenclature is used by ANSI for standards developed jointly by two or more standards organizations.

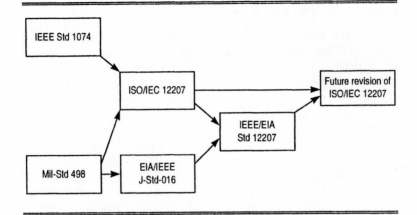

Figure 34. Family tree of ISO/IEC 12207. (Source: Adapted from [Moore95].)

standard (called IEEE/EIA 12207); second, recommendations for harmonization of the three standards to remove capricious differences; and third, an explanation of the relative positioning and utility of the three standards. The positioning of IEEE 1074 and the two versions of 12207 will be described in this chapter. EIA/IEEE J-Std-016 will be described as an important alternative in Chapter 15.

As of this writing, in the summer of 1997, these standards have the following status:

- EIA/IEEE J-Std-016 is about to undergo final revision to incorporate the harmonization recommendations and trial use experience and to promote it from its current status as an EIA Interim Standard to the status of a full-use standard.

- IEEE 1074 is undergoing a revision intended to update it and incorporate the harmonization recommendations.

- Part 0 of IEEE/EIA 12207 has been approved and two additional parts are being completed.

- ISO/IEC 12207 is completed but, in accordance with normal procedures, will be revised circa 2001, probably in concert with the systems life cycle process standard, 15288, currently under development in the same working group.

The US adaptation of the 12207 standard will be forwarded to SC7 for consideration during the revision of ISO/IEC 12207.

Levels of Process Abstraction

Process standards provide a representation of ideal processes intended to be implemented by the users of the standards. Part of the difficulty in applying the documents is that different standards present their views of the desired processes at different levels of abstraction. To relate the process standards, it is helpful to have an overall architecture for process abstraction. For this we use a framework developed by Basili for his *component factory* [Basili92] and applied by Heineman to general process modeling [Heineman94]. In this discussion, their terminology will be modified slightly to conform with that used by 12207. The framework provides for three levels of abstraction in representing processes:

- The *reference* level, representing agents that carry out the processes. Decisions represented at this level are the selection of a coherent and cohesive set of activities that may be sensibly performed by a single agent. Such a set of activities is a process.

- The *conceptual* level, representing the flow of control and data among the agents. Decisions at this level include the logical relationships among the agents both for control and for the communication of data.

- The *implementation* level, representing the implementation, both technical and organizational, of the agents and their interfaces. Decisions at this level include mapping the agents to the management organization of the particular project or enterprise and the selection of policies, procedures, and tools to enable the agents to perform their tasks.

These levels are not to be regarded as successive functional decompositions. In fact, any one of them can be independently refined into greater details. The distinction between the former two levels permits discussion of the objectives of the processes independently of their fine-grained relationships. The distinction between the latter two levels permits discussion of specific processes independently of the structure of the organization that will implement them.

The 12207 standard is an example of specifying software life cycle processes at the reference level. The writers of the standard identified processes, in part, by applying the criterion that it should be possible to assign the responsibility for a process to a single organization or party, the "agent" in the framework described above. The requirements of 12207 are, then, the specified responsibilities placed upon the agents executing the processes. From this viewpoint, one can view 12207 as a list of agents and their minimum responsibilities.

In applying the process standards, the next step would be to move to the conceptual level. The generic processes of ISO/IEC 12207 must be instantiated in terms of specific processes with specific flows of control and data. IEEE Std 1074 is useful at this level. It provides "activity groups," collections of related activities each with specified inputs and outputs. These activities can be assembled into processes. A process architect could apply IEEE Std 1074 to specify conceptual-level processes implementing the requirements of 12207, or any other reference-level process standard.

The final step is at the implementation level, where the processes of the conceptual level are mapped to the specific characteristics of the organization that is implementing the processes. The agent roles must be assigned to organizational units and various policies and procedures implemented to ensure that the agents execute their assigned responsibilities.

Another distinction—the difference between *process* and *procedure*—is crucial to understanding the role of the 12207 and 1074 standards. The processes described in the standards are not to be understood as a series of steps (procedures) to be performed; instead the processes are assignments of continuing responsibilities to agents. Those assignments of responsibility persist for the duration of the life cycle. For example, when 12207 states that the developer should evaluate the software architecture, that does not necessarily mean that a single review should be conducted, or even that a sequence of reviews should be conducted. Instead, it means that for the duration of the development activity, the developer is assigned the responsibility for evaluating the architecture for the specified characteristics. To derive a time-phased sequence of activities to be performed, one must first select a life cycle model and then implement procedures describing the steps to be performed. Neither 12207 nor 1074 provides a life cycle model and neither provides procedures for implementation.

Traditionally, process standards have been targeted for implementation at the project level. In recent years, though, there has been increasing emphasis on organizational process capability, and the Basili model supports this emphasis. ISO/IEC 12207 viewed some project processes as instances of enterprise-level processes but still evaluated compliance at the project level. The US adaptation of 12207 shifted emphasis from project-level compliance to compliance by entire enterprises via implementation of conforming organizational policies and procedures.

To briefly recap this discussion, both the international and the US versions of 12207 are examples of reference-level process descriptions. IEEE Std 1074 is a tool that can be applied by a process architect to create conceptual-level process descriptions implementing the requirements of the 12207 standard. Organizations— or, less desirably, projects—develop policies and procedures that provide the implementation-level descriptions of the processes complying with the standards.

Most of the other software process standards of IEEE SESC straddle the reference and conceptual level of abstraction. Written when process description tools were not in general usage, the authors of these standards generally resorted to the artifice of specifying a plan, the contents of which implicitly impose process requirements. Flows of data were generally unspecified except for the flows to and from the plan's manager.

IEEE/EIA 12207 and ISO/IEC 12207

The discussion of software process standards will be organized around the set of software life cycle processes specified by the 12207 standards listed in Table 85. The two guides still being developed by SC7 are suitable for use with the international version of the standard. The US version of 12207 includes two additional guidance parts that are still being completed under the indicated IEEE project numbers.

Table 85. The 12207 Software Life Cycle Process Standards

Standard	Title
ISO/IEC 12207:1995	Information technology—Software life cycle processes
ISO/IEC DTR 14759	Software life cycle model tailored for mock-up and prototype
ISO/IEC DTR 15271	Guide to ISO/IEC 12207 (Software life cycle processes)
IEEE/EIA Std 12207.0-1996	Information technology—Software life cycle processes
IEEE/EIA (P1448.1) 12207.1	Guide for information technology—Software life cycle processes—Life cycle data
IEEE/EIA (P1448.2) 12207.2	Guide for information technology—Software life cycle processes—Implementation considerations

Alternative life cycle standards that one might consider in appropriate circumstances are listed in Table 86. Each is described elsewhere in this book, in the chapter indicated.

Table 86. Alternative Life Cycle Process Standards

Title	Standards	Chapter
CANDU CE-1001-STD	Standard for software engineering of safety critical systems	10
EIA/IEEE J-Std-016-1995	Software development—Software life cycle processes—Acquirer-supplier agreement*	15
ESA PSS-05-0	Software engineering standards	15
IEC 880 (1986)	Software for computers in the safety systems of nuclear power stations	10
IEEE Std 7-4.3.2-1993	Standard criteria for digital computers in safety systems of nuclear power generating stations	10
RTCA DO-178B-1992	Software considerations in airborne systems and equipment certification	15
*The title of this standard may be changed when it is promoted to full use status.		

In addition, system-level life cycle process standards are described in Chapter 8.

ISO/IEC 12207 occupies an important role in software process standardization for reasons in addition to its content. It is the first software process standard in recent history that has been widely viewed as a framework with which other standards should be unified.[50] IEEE SESC has adopted a policy that its other standards will be harmonized with 12207. Oddly, SC7 itself seems unwilling to take a similar step.

Overview of 12207

The 12207 standard specifies three classes of processes: *primary*, *organizational*,[51] and *supporting*.[52] (There is also a special

---

[50]IEEE Std 730 on Software Quality Assurance may have briefly occupied a similar role when there were few other software engineering process standards and when the ISO 9000 series had yet to be developed.

[51]It would have been more convenient if the writers of 12207 had used the word "enterprise" instead of "organizational." Used as the name of a specific class of processes, the term is easily confused with the concept of implementing a process at the organizational (as opposed to the project) level.

[52]Most of the material in this section is based on Annex E of IEEE/EIA 12207.0. The principal drafter of the annex is Raghu Singh, the project editor of ISO/IEC 12207.

tailoring process, constrained in the US version of the standard, that is applied to adapt the requirements of the other processes to deal with project-specific circumstances.) The primary processes identify five major roles played by an organization in the life cycle of software: *acquisition, supply, development, maintenance,* and *operation.* In the model chosen by the standard, an acquirer and a supplier enter into an agreement for the completion of a particular product or service. The supplier then executes one of the other three primary processes to perform the development, maintenance, or operations appropriate to the performance of the agreement. It is important to understand that, since 12207 is at the reference level of abstraction, the agents performing the processes are roles to be assumed rather than permanent organizational entities. For example, a developer choosing to purchase a component of the software system would additionally execute the acquirer role. Or, a maintainer electing to rewrite a portion of the system could execute the developer role to do that job or could execute the acquirer role to arrange for some other organization to perform the development.

Any of the primary processes can invoke one or more of the supporting processes to accomplish appropriate objectives. (The supporting processes can be regarded as process subroutines.) The eight supporting processes are: *documentation, configuration management, quality assurance, verification, validation, joint review, audit,* and *problem resolution.*

Finally, four processes are regarded as inherent to an organization at the enterprise level: *management, infrastructure, improvement,* and *training.* Initiating any of the primary processes has the effect of instantiating the management process and the other appropriate organizational processes.

The life cycle processes of 12207 are deliberately broad and are intended to cover the entire life of software from conception through retirement—not just the development effort. Each of the processes of 12207 is hierarchically decomposed into a set of *activities* and then *tasks*—although, in some cases, the tasks are better regarded as simply individual requirements on the activities.

Evaluation is built into each of the processes rather than segregated. There are processes for verification, validation, and quality assurance, but these are all in addition to the fundamental requirements for evaluation incorporated in each process. The integral nature of evaluation is a consequence of a more general principle of total quality management—each of the primary processes incorporates its own "plan-do-check-act" cycle inherited from its instantiation of the organizational management process. For this reason, 12207 may be a better choice than IEEE Std 730 for implementing software processes intended to comply with the requirements of ISO 9001 and its guide, ISO 9000-3.

Although 12207 does not prescribe systems engineering life cycle processes, it does prescribe the minimum systems engineering context necessary for the successful execution of the software processes. The systems engineering context is specified as a set of tasks intended to be shared with systems engineering activities. These tasks include system requirements, system architecture, system integration, and system qualification testing. (To make the connection even clearer, the same ISO/IEC JTC1 working group has initiated the development of a systems life cycle process standard, ISO/IEC15288.)

The standard is intended to be independent of development technologies and methodologies and useful for any form of life cycle model, for example, waterfall, incremental, spiral, etc. In fact, one of the specified responsibilities of the supplier's role is to select a life cycle[53] model and map the requirements of the standard to that model. Furthermore, the developer is specifically tasked to detail the development portion of the model. Using the Basili reference architecture [Basili92], we can understand those responsibilities as moving from the reference to the conceptual level of process implementation.

The 12207 standard is written in language appropriate for a contractual agreement between the acquirer and the supplier. It is a premise that even within a single organization, some form of agreement must be reached between the party desiring the software and the party supplying the software.

Although 12207 requires that certain information be documented, it does not prescribe any recording medium, format or detailed content requirements. The *documentation* process is intended to plan and implement such requirements.

IEEE Guides: IEEE/EIA 12207.1 and 12207.2

The US project to adapt 12207 has added two additional informative parts to the standard. Part 1 is a guidance document providing recommendations expanding on the data objectives that were added as an annex of Part 0. For those desiring guidance on how

---

[53]It is intentional that the supplier must describe the entire life cycle rather than merely the process being contracted. The motivation is to force contractors to take a broader view of the life cycle impact of their decisions.

specific documents or electronic data should be associated with specific processes, this part provides recommendations on the content of various possible documents. In all, IEEE/EIA 12207 offers four different levels of detail regarding data recording:

1. The two-page Annex H of 12207.0 lists general objectives for the recording of life cycle data, including purpose, operations, characteristics, types, and presentation form.

2. The normative descriptions of processes in the main body of 12207.0 provide requirements for specific data that must be recorded in some manner.

3. Clause 5 (clause numbering is still subject to change) of Part 1 lists seven "kinds" of generic information items (for example, plan, procedure, specification) and summarizes in a few hundred words the purpose and contents of each one. Clause 4 lists specific information items appropriate to the clauses of part 0, shows which "kind" of document is appropriate, and references other standards that may be helpful detailing them.

4. Clause 6 selects 29 of the most significant specific information items from Clause 4 and provides further details regarding recommended content.

It should be noted that Part 1 can be used as a compliance document even though it is labeled as a guide. Acquirers should refrain from using it to mandate documentation requirements, however, because it specifies requirements for the recording of data rather than the production of documents. Means for the appropriate and economical production of data are to be regarded as inherent to the deployment of the organization-level processes promoted by IEEE/EIA 12207.

Part 2 of IEEE/EIA 12207 is a guide providing advice on the implementation of the processes prescribed by Part 0 in the context of US industrial and professional practices. The normative text of Part 0 is quoted and typographically enclosed in boxes. At appropriate intervals, guidance notes provide explanatory material and recommendations. In addition, several annexes have been added:

- A brief annex on the use of reusable software products. (IEEE plans additional standards development projects on this subject.)

- A list of 11 candidates for joint management reviews along with the purposes to which each might be applied.

- A brief discussion of software measurement categories.[54]

- Guidance on development strategies.

- Guidance on categorization and prioritization of problem reports, along with a reference to IEEE Std 1044.

- A discussion of software product evaluation with references to ISO/IEC 9126, ISO/IEC 12119, and ISO/IEC 9127.

- A discussion of risk management.

- A summary matrix of IEEE and ISO/IEC standards that may usefully be applied in the implementation of the processes of 12207.

Parts 1 and 2 of IEEE/EIA 12207, as well as the material added in Part 0, will probably become part of a US position for the revision of ISO/IEC 12207. In the normal routine of JTC1 business, that revision would occur circa 2000.

ISO/IEC Guides: ISO/IEC 14759 and 15271

ISO/IEC JTC1/SC7/WG7 has itself drafted two Technical Reports (guides) for the application of ISO/IEC 12207. The general guide, DTR 15271, elaborates on the factors to be considered in application of the standard. Although it disclaims the intention to provide a rationale for the standard, it does provide useful insight into the criteria for identification and selection of the particular processes chosen for 12207. Information provided by the guide includes:

- Basic concepts of the standard

- Approaches to implementing the standard, including examples of tailoring

- Application at the project level

- Application at the organizational level

- Relationship to system life cycle

- A summary of the quality processes and evaluation requirements that appear in various parts of the standard

- Guidance (less extensive than that of IEEE/EIA 12207.1) concerning the data output from the various processes

---

[54]For defense and other large-scale programs, an extensive treatment of measurement can be found in [JLC96].

- Application to three different life cycle models—waterfall, spiral, and evolutionary

Although the material of DTR 15271 overlaps with the IEEE/EIA additions, US organizations interested in international trade in software may find knowledge of this document to be advisable.

The second WG7 guide, 14759 (now a Draft Technical Report), is more limited in scope, applying 12207 to "mock-up and prototype" efforts. A key objective of the report is to discriminate between three pairs of terms:

- Mock-up (throw-away) versus prototype (usable)

- Illustrative (non-functional) versus functional

- Demonstrative versus operational

Those pairs of terms are applied in various sensible combinations to enumerate eight different types of products. The report is intended to explain the appropriate role of 12207 in an incremental life-cycle utilizing various of the eight types of products.

Primary Processes of 12207

The five *primary* processes include *acquisition, supply, development, maintenance,* and *operation.* The standards related to the acquisition and supply processes are listed in Table 87, but since they are inherent to the customer relationship, they will be described in Chapter 14, along with other standards dealing with system-level concerns.

As shown in Table 88, IEEE has a standard elaborating on the software maintenance process. ISO/IEC JTC1/SC7 recently commenced a project to develop a standard with a similar scope.

Standards related to the development process are listed in Table 89. Several of them are more completely described in other chapters as indicated; the others will be described later in this chapter.[55]

With these building blocks, a road map for the primary processes of 12207 can be depicted as shown in Figure 35.

The road map begins with a reminder that any significant software project is initiated in the broader context of a set of sys-

---

[55]AIAA R-013 on software reliability is listed here while IEEE Std 982 is listed below under the management process because of the former's emphasis on modeling and the latter's emphasis on metrics.

Table 87. Standards Related to the 12207 Acquisition and Supply
Processes

Standard	Title	Chapter
Acquisition Process		
IEEE Std 1062-1993	Recommended practice for software acquisition	14
Supply Process		
none		
System-level Concerns		
AIAA G-043-1992	Guide for the preparation of operations concept documents	14
EIA/IS-632	Systems engineering	14
IEEE Std 1220-1994	(Trial Use) Standard for application and management of the systems engineering process	14
IEEE Std 1228-1994	Software safety plans	14
IEEE Std 1233-1996	Guide for developing system requirements specifications	14
IEEE P1362	Guide for concept of operations document	14
ISO/IEC DIS 15026	System and software integrity levels	14

tem-level considerations. Some of those contexts are described in
Chapters 5 through 10 of this book. It must be understood that they
may levy process requirements in addition to those of the 12207
standard.

Those wishing to apply the standard have their choice of the international version and the US version. Although the differences
between the two will be explained in more detail on page 220, it can
be noted now that the US version is fully compliant with the international version. Nevertheless, in international trade situations, it
may be preferable to use the international version simply because
one or more of the agreeing parties may be unfamiliar with the U. S
adaptation.

The paragraphs to follow will look more closely at three of the
primary processes—development, operation and maintenance. The

Table 88. Standards Related to the 12207 Maintenance Process

Standard	Title
IEEE Std 1219-1992	Standard for software maintenance
ISO/IEC WD 14764	Software maintenance

Table 89. Standards Related to the 12207 Development Process

Standard	Title	Chapter
AIAA G-010-1993	Guide for reusable software: Assessment criteria for aerospace application	11
AIAA R-013-1992	Recommended practice for software reliability	11
IEEE Std 829-1983	Standard for software test documentation	11
IEEE Std 830-1993	Recommended practice for software requirements specifications	11
IEEE Std 1008-1987	Standard for software unit testing	
IEEE Std 1016-1987	Recommended practice for software design descriptions	11
IEEE Std 1016.1-1993	Guide to software design descriptions	11
IEEE Std 1028-1988	Standard for software reviews and audits	
IEEE Std 1074-1995	Standard for developing software life cycle processes	
IEEE Std 1074.1-1995	Guide for developing software life cycle processes	
IEEE Std 1228-1994	Software safety plans	14
IEEE Std 1233-1996	Guide for developing system requirements specifications	14
IEEE P1471	Recommended practice for system design— Architectural description	11
ISO/IEC 9126-1991	Software product evaluation—Quality characteristics and guidelines for their use	12

acquisition and supply processes, inherent to customer interaction, are discussed in Chapter 14.

Development Process

The development process of 12207 is subdivided into 13 activities involving various types of analysis, design, coding, testing, integration and acceptance. Virtually all of the activities have evaluation and review requirements. Rather than being separately cited for each process, the appropriate SESC standard for review and audit, IEEE Std 1028, will be described in the section "Supporting Processes of 12207," below. Table 90 lists the activities of the development process and suggests where other standards may be helpful.

The development process begins with the process implementation activity. A major requirement of this activity is to define or select a software life cycle process model appropriate to the project. The activities and tasks of the development process are then to be mapped onto the life cycle model. The activity also requires that detailed plans for conducting the activities of the development process be formulated and documented, including the selection of organizational procedures and methods. As mentioned previously, IEEE Std 1074, and its guide, IEEE Std 1074.1, both described later in this chapter, can be useful in performing this activity.

The system requirements analysis and the system architec-

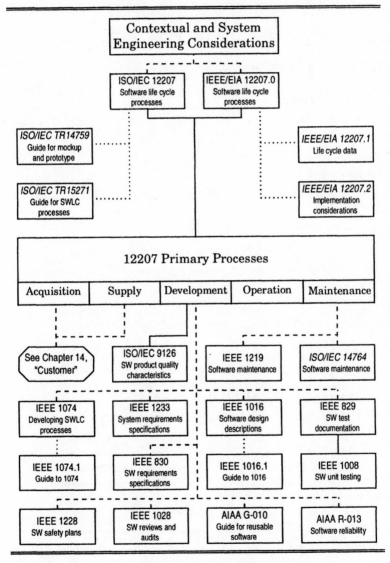

Figure 35. Road map for the primary processes of 12207.

Table 90. Other Standards Useful in Implementing the 12207
Development Processes

Activity	Standard	Title
Process implementation	IEEE 1074 IEEE 1074.1	Developing SWLC processes
System requirements analysis	IEEE 1233	System requirements specifications
System architectural design	*IEEE P1471*	Architectural description
SW requirements analysis	ISO/IEC 9126	SW product quality characteristics
	IEEE 830	Software requirements specifications
SW architectural design	*IEEE P1471*	Architectural description
	AIAA R-013	SW reliability
SW detailed design	IEEE 1016 IEEE 1016.1	SW design descriptions
SW coding and testing*	IEEE 1008	SW unit testing
SW integration		
SW qualification testing	IEEE 829	SW test documentation
System integration		
System qualification testing	IEEE 829	SW test documentation •
SW installation		
SW acceptance support		
Overall	AIAA G-010	Software reuse
	IEEE 1228	Software safety plans
*Of course, standards for programming languages and application program interfaces are also useful for this activity; they are beyond the scope of this book.		

tural design activities form the minimum necessary front-end interfaces to the systems engineering effort that is the context for the
software development. The IEEE 1233 guide for system requirements specifications is described in Chapter 14, and the planned
IEEE 1471 practice for architectural description is described in
Chapter 11.

The software requirements analysis is performed by the developer to establish and document the requirements and specifications[56] for the software product to be produced. The 12207 document prescribes that ISO/IEC 9126, described in Chapter 12, is a
suitable framework for defining the required quality characteristics

---

[56]Specifications are viewed as quantitative; requirements are
not. Thus, specifications are requirements that have been refined or
elaborated in quantitative terms.

of the products to be developed. IEEE Std 830, described in Chapter 11, may be useful in writing software requirements specifications.

No specific methodology or technique is specified for the software (nor for the system) architectural design. The specific requirements focus upon the identification of components and their interfaces. If reliability is a specific concern, the modeling techniques of AIAA R-013, described in Chapter 11, may be helpful, as may many other standard and non-standard mechanisms dealing with disciplines or technologies that are important to the operation of the system. In fact, the essential step in architecture is probably the identification of the crucial drivers for the design of the system and the selection of the standards and techniques for dealing with them. The planned IEEE practice for architectural description, 1471, described in Chapter 11, may be useful in describing the selected architectural viewpoints.

The software detailed design activity is intended to refine the architectural description of the software components into successively finer levels of detail, while maintaining traceability of requirements, until software units appropriate for coding are specified. IEEE Std 1016, described in Chapter 11, and its guide, 1016.1, may be useful in organizing the design activity and its documentation, perhaps even at the architectural level.

The next activity, software coding and testing, also includes requirements for evaluating the results and providing appropriate documentation. IEEE Std 1008 provides a standard approach to unit testing and is well integrated with the IEEE 829 standard for software test documentation. (IEEE 1008 is described later in this chapter and 829 is described in Chapter 11.)

The software integration and software qualification testing activities complete the integration and testing of the software components of the system, and the system integration and system qualification testing activities form the project's back-end interface with the systems engineering activities for developing the system. The final two activities, software installation and acceptance support, complete the work of turning the software component of the system over to its operator and its maintainer.

As a final item in the discussion of the development process, note that the 12207 standard recognizes the concept of software reuse although it does not levy any specific requirements for it. An annex of the draft for IEEE/EIA 12207.2 offers some general advice. We would hope for a supplementary standard explaining how software reuse activities could be integrated into the 12207 process framework. Indeed, such a standard is planned by SESC, but is probably a few years in the future. In the mean time, AIAA G-010 is the best available standard for general guidance on software reuse.

Finally, you should note that software critical to system safety should be developed in accordance with the provisions of IEEE Std 1228, Software Safety Plans. The provisions of this standard touch all aspects of the development process. The 1228 standard is described in Chapter 14.

IEEE STD 1008—SOFTWARE UNIT TESTING

The primary objective of IEEE Std 1008 is to provide a standard approach to the software unit testing. Completed by SESC in 1987 and reaffirmed in 1993, this 24-page standard is intended to be applied as a basis for comparison of current practices, a source of ideas to modify those practices, and a replacement for current practices.

The document provides an integrated approach to systematic unit testing based on requirements, design, and implementation information to determine the completeness of testing. The required testing process is a hierarchy of phases, activities, and tasks. Performance of each activity is required; each of the activity's required tasks must be performed or the results of their prior performance must be available for reverification. The 1008 standard is consistent with IEEE Std 829 on software test documentation and requires the use of the test design specification and the test summary report specified in 829.

The specified unit testing process is applicable to either new or modified code. The standard does not address software debugging, other aspects of comprehensive software verification, or related processes like configuration management and quality assurance.

Appendixes of the standard include usage guidelines, concepts and assumptions, and references for additional information.

IEEE STD 1074 AND 1074.1—DEVELOPING SOFTWARE LIFE CYCLE PROCESSES

SESC originally developed IEEE Std 1074 in 1991, performed minor revisions in 1995, and is now engaged in a major revision to "harmonize" the document with ISO/IEC 12207 and make other changes. The 176-page guide document, IEEE Std 1074.1, is consistent with the first version of the standard and the 1995 revision. (The current revision effort, however, may render it obsolescent.) Because of the importance of the current revision, this description describes a draft of that revision, a draft which will probably be approved in late 1997 or early 1998.

The document is a standard for *generating* processes for software development and maintenance. It does not itself provide life cycle processes nor does it provide a life cycle model. The user, a *process architect*, must define the intended life cycle of the software, select a life cycle model and then apply the standard to define processes suiting those needs.

As explained above, the 1074 standard is best understood at the contextual level of the Basili model. The resource that it provides to the architect is a set of 17 predefined and interrelated activity groups, composed from 65 activities, along with specified inputs and outputs, and entry and exit criteria. The architect composes the activity groups to create appropriate processes. (Requirements for those processes may be provided by other standards, notably 12207.) Finally, the processes may be augmented with *organizational process assets*, such as policies, standards, procedures, etc., to create implementable processes. (This last step may be regarded as leading into the implementation level of the Basili model.)

The purpose of the 1074.1 guide is to describe approaches for implementing IEEE Std 1074-1995. by providing examples and tutorials. It is intended to be suitable for use by any organization or individual responsible for the implementation of the 1074 standard. It is not intended to be a detailed procedures manual for developing or maintaining software or software life cycles.

Operation Process

The operation process places requirements on the party that will operate the system of which the software is a part. Neither SESC nor SC7 have standards specifically applicable to implementing this process.

Maintenance Process

The maintenance process places requirements on the party responsible for maintaining the software after it has been completed and delivered. Of course, in some cases, the maintainer is the same organization that developed the software; nevertheless, the two roles are distinct.

IEEE STD 1219 AND ISO/IEC WD 14764—SOFTWARE MAINTENANCE

SESC has a standard suitable for use in implementing the maintenance process, the 39-page IEEE Std 1219, approved in

1992. The standard describes an iterative process for managing and executing the maintenance activity for software regardless of size, complexity, criticality, or application. It has its own "process model" of "phases" which differ slightly from the activities prescribed by the maintenance process of 12207. For each phase, inputs, outputs and controls are specified. Metrics for each phase are also provided. Finally, the standard suggests other SESC standards that may be applied in detailing its phase requirements. (Those standards are not detailed here because they duplicate, in an obvious manner, the standards cited in support of the other 12207 processes.)

Although the current 1219 standard is not completely reconciled with the 12207 standard, it should be a useful tool in implementing a maintenance process complying with the requirements of 12207. The most troublesome misfit of the two is in a basic premise. The 12207 maintenance process would execute the development

Table 91. Standards Related to the 12207 Supporting Processes

Standard	Title	Chapter
IEEE Std 730-1989	Standard for software quality assurance plans	
IEEE Std 730.1-1995	Guide to software quality assurance planning	
IEEE Std 828-1990	Standard for software configuration management plans	
IEEE Std 1012-1986	Standard for software verification and validation plans	
IEEE Std 1028-1988	Standard for software reviews and audits	
IEEE Std 1042-1987	Guide to software configuration management	
IEEE Std 1044-1993	Standard classification for software anomalies	11
IEEE Std 1044.1-1995	Guide to classification for software anomalies	11
IEEE Std 1059-1993	Guide for software verification and validation plans	
IEEE Std 1061-1992	Standard for a software quality metrics methodology	12
IEEE Std 1298-1992	Software quality management system—Part 1: Requirements	
ISO 9001:1994	Quality systems—Model for quality assurance in design, development, production, installation, and servicing	6
ISO 9000-3:1991	Quality management and quality assurance standards—Part 3: Guidelines for the application of 9001 to the development, supply, installation and maintenance of computer software	6
ISO 10005:1995	Quality management—Guidelines for quality plans	6
ISO 10007:1995	Quality management—Guidelines for configuration management	6
ISO/IEC TR 9294:1990	Guidelines for the management of software documentation	

process in order to create a software change and then return to the maintenance process for the remaining work, for example, assuring that the untouched code still works. In the 1219 standard, required development activities are simply subsumed into the maintenance process. This difference is more legalistic than substantive and simply introduces a degree of awkwardness in the explanation of compliance.

SC7 is developing its own maintenance standard, ISO/IEC 14764, which can be expected to fit neatly with 12207. Work on that standard began only in 1996 and it is still in the Working Draft stage.

Supporting Processes of 12207

The eight supporting processes of 12207 are *documentation, configuration management, quality assurance, verification, validation, joint review, audit,* and *problem resolution.* Standards related to those processes are shown in Table 91. Although some are discussed more completely in other chapters, several will be described in this one.

A road map for the supporting processes of 12207 is shown in Figure 36.

The supporting processes of 12207, like subroutines, may be invoked by any of the other processes to execute the desired function. In one of the marvelous subtleties of 12207, ultimate responsibility for the requirements of any supporting process can be made to roll up to any party depending on who invoked the supporting process. For example, the development manager (more precisely, the party executing the development process) could choose to invoke the verification process to ensure traceability of requirements. On the other hand, if this responsibility is assigned to a separate department within the organization, then the verification process could be invoked by the supplier. Finally, if independent verification is desired, the acquirer could make an agreement with another supplier to execute the process.

In the 12207 standard, the objective of the *quality assurance* process is specified as "providing adequate assurance that the software products and processes in the project life cycle conform to their specified requirements and adhere to their established plans." Two IEEE standards are applicable, IEEE Std 730 and IEEE Std 1298. Of these, 730 is probably preferable because the original motivation for IEEE's adoption of the 1298 standard was the murky correspondence between 9001 and its software guide 9000-3, a

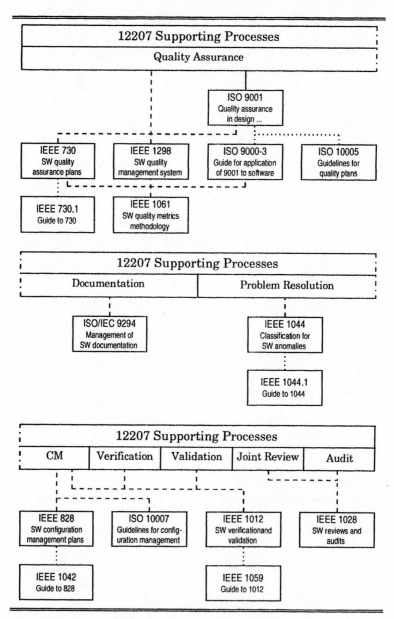

Figure 36. Road map of the supporting processes of 12207.

problem that is about to be fixed, presumably obviating 1298. (IEEE 730, its 730.1 guide, and 1298 are described below.)

The 12207 standard includes a single sentence making a normative reference to ISO 9001 for the activity of assuring quality systems. This, of course, is a grand requirement and its implementation is probably doomed to failure if considered as simply a detail of the 12207 quality assurance process. Organizations stand a far greater chance of success if they view 12207 as part of the implementation of an overall ISO 9000 quality management system rather than the other way around. Of course, the ISO 9000-3 and 10005 guides, both described in Chapter 6, are helpful in applying the requirements of ISO 9001 to software. Any of the quality assurance standards could be supported by the quality metrics methodology provided by IEEE Std 1061, described in Chapter 12.

The *documentation* process contains the activities needed to "plan, design, develop, produce, edit, distribute, and maintain" all of the documents needed by all of the parties to the project. A standard that may be helpful in implementing this process is ISO/IEC TR 9294, described below.

The *problem resolution* process is used to analyze and resolve all problems that are discovered during the execution of the other processes. A specific requirement is that problems should be categorized. IEEE Std 1044 and its guide, 1044.1, may be useful in implementing procedures for categorization of the problems. Both are described in Chapter 11.

Responsibility for configuration management in 12207 is delegated to the *configuration management* process which incorporates activities for the identification, control, accounting, and evaluation of configurations as well as release management and delivery. IEEE Std 828 is suitable for implementing a detailed configuration management process. IEEE 828 and its guide, 1042, are described below. Some organizations may prefer to view configuration management as an integral part of their overall quality assurance program; in this case, ISO 10007, described in Chapter 6, may be helpful in detailing the configuration management activity.

The 12207 standard separates *verification* and *validation* into two distinct processes. Of course, idiomatic usage so closely merges the two that some software engineers manage to pronounce the "V & V" acronym in not much more than a single syllable. The appropriate IEEE standard for implementing both of these activities is IEEE Std 1012. That standard and its guide, 1059, are described below.

The *joint review* process provides for both technical and management reviews so that one party may evaluate the status of the products produced and the activities performed by another party.

On the other hand, the *audit* process is specifically intended for one party to audit another party's compliance with requirements and plans as well as the agreement between the two parties. Both of these activities, as well as reviews required by other supporting processes, may be detailed by applying IEEE Std 1028, described below.

IEEE Std 730 and 730.1—Software Quality Assurance Plans

IEEE Std 730 has a distinguished history, being the first standard to be approved (in 1979) by the predecessor organization of today's SESC. The current 12 page revision was approved in 1989. Consideration of its future has been delayed pending resolution of related developments in the ISO 9000 series. The 52 page guide document, 730.1, was completed in 1995.

(Referring to back-level versions, always risky, is particularly confusing in the case of this document. The current standard was once numbered 730.1, the number now used by the guide, which was itself renumbered from a previous designation as IEEE Std 983.)

This standard provides minimum requirements for the content and preparation of a Software Quality Assurance Plan (SQAP) for the development and maintenance of critical software. Although the standard describes the SQAP itself, the requirements for the content of the various sections induce implicit requirements for various SQA activities.

The 730 standard is most directly applicable to detailing the Quality Assurance Process of 12207. It should be noted, though, that the efforts described in the SQAP could be appropriately applied to any of the other standards prescribing life cycle processes.

730 is also appropriate for providing the link between the quality management requirements of ISO 9001 and the software engineering standards of the SESC as a part of an overall program for conformance with the ISO 9000 series standards. Completion of an SQAP in accordance with 730 would satisfy many of the requirements of 9001 as interpreted by 9000-3. (This usage is explained in Chapter 6.)

The future of the 730 standard is unclear. Current plans for the revision of ISO 9000-3 may cause it to become more directly applicable to the needs of software engineers. If so, IEEE Std 730 will represent little additional value and may be withdrawn, or it may be revised to directly focus on the planning rather than the processes of quality assurance.

The purpose of the 730.1 guide is to identify approaches to good Software Quality Assurance practices in support of IEEE 730. If 730 is withdrawn, it is possible that this document will be revised to provide a mapping from ISO 9001/9000-3 to the collection of the SESC standards.

IEEE Std 828 and 1042—Software Configuration Management Plans

The SESC standard for software CM plans, IEEE Std 828, was originally written in 1983. The 1990 revision is a complete rewrite that, among other changes, reconciles the 16-page standard with the separately written guide, IEEE Std 1042. The 92-page guide, approved in 1987, was reaffirmed in 1993.

The concerns of the document are described in its foreword: "Software configuration management (SCM) is a formal engineering discipline that, as part of the overall system configuration management, provides the methods and tools to identify and control the software throughout its development and use. SCM activities include the identification and establishment of baselines; the review, approval, and control of changes; the tracking and reporting of such changes; the audits and reviews of the evolving software product; and the control of interface documentation and project supplier SCM."

The standard is based on the premise that configuration management, at some level of formality, occurs in all software projects. Proper planning of the activity and effective communication of the plan increases its effectiveness. Hence, the standard prescribes the minimum required contents of an SCM plan. Developing the required plan will implicitly induce process requirements on the conduct of the project. Those requirements are intended to be consistent with those of IEEE Std 730 on software quality assurance plans.

The 1042 guide takes a broader view than the standard and provides a "technical and philosophical overview of the SCM planning process." The main body describes principles, issues for consideration, and lessons learned, all organized around the outline of the plan prescribed by IEEE Std 828. Four appendices provide examples for the application of 828 and a fifth appendix suggests additional references.

IEEE Std 1012 and 1059—Software Verification and Validation Plans

IEEE Std 1012 was approved in 1986 and reaffirmed in 1992. The 27-page document has three purposes: to define minimum requirements for the contents of a Software Verification and Validation Plan; for critical software, to define the minimum set of V & V tasks and their required inputs and outputs; and to suggest optional V & V tasks. The writers of the document intend for it to be applicable to all phases of a software life cycle from conception through operation and maintenance; V & V activities are viewed as performed in parallel with software development.

The standard is designed to fit well with several other SESC standards. It derives its scope from the 1984 version of IEEE Std 730 on software quality assurance plans and contains configuration analysis tasks from the 1983 version of IEEE Std 828 on software configuration management plans. Prescribed test documentation is compatible with IEEE Std 829.

A project is currently under way to revise IEEE Std 1012. Important objectives include reconciling the standard with the separate verification and validation processes of ISO/IEC 12207 and listing V & V tasks appropriate to multiple levels of software criticality. [Fujii95] is an overview of software V & V written by two of the officers of the original and current working groups of the 1012 project.

The 87-page IEEE Std 1059 provides extensive guidance for the preparation of the Software V & V Plan prescribed by IEEE Std 1012; it does not provide guidance for the verification and validation processes themselves. An appendix of the guide approaches the subject of criticality analysis, an important subject of the current effort to revise 1012.

IEEE Std 1028—Software Reviews and Audits

This SESC standard was originally approved in 1988, corrected in 1989, and reaffirmed in 1993. It is currently under revision to achieve goals including improved compatibility with 12207. This description considers the current draft revision, expected to be approved in late 1997 or early 1998.

The standard provides direction to the reviewer or auditor on the conduct of management and technical evaluations. Included are activities applicable to both critical and non-critical software and the procedures required for the execution of reviews and audits. The standard specifies the characteristics of five different types of reviews and audits (management review, technical review, inspection, walk-through, audit).

The 12207 standard specifies evaluations intrinsic to the primary processes and specifies Joint Review and Audit processes fundamental to a two-party relationship. IEEE 1028 could be applied to implement the intrinsic reviews and could satisfy some of the substantive requirements of the Joint Review and Audit processes.

The standard is intended to support review and audit requirements of several other IEEE standards including 730, 838, 1012, 1058.1, 1074, 1219, 1220, 1228, 1298, and 12207.

IEEE Std 1298—Software Quality Management System Requirements

This SESC standard has an unusual history; being an adoption of another standard rather than a product of the usual SESC drafting process. It has been mentioned elsewhere in this text that ISO 9000-3, which interprets the requirements of ISO 9001 for application to software, is organized substantially differently from 9001. This mismatch caused many ISO 9000 auditors, who may not have been software experts, to inappropriately rely on the *recommendations* of 9000-3 rather than the *requirements* of 9001. In the early 1990s, SESC was interested in a standard that would properly restate the provisions of ISO 9001 as requirements. Rather than having to write one, they found an existing document, AS 3563.1-1991, written by Standards Australia, for a similar purpose. With minor changes and clarifications (listed in the foreword), the document was adopted as IEEE Std 1298.

The document is designed to be used as either a supplement or a replacement for ISO 9001. Since its 12-page size precludes extensive detail, it is designed to be supplemented by additional listed standards. In the IEEE version, these are selected from the SESC collection. The provisions of the standard are applied to the developer's quality management system for the objective of ensuring that the software will meet the requirements of a contract or other agreement. It is applicable in contractual situations where the contract specifically requires design and the product requirements are stated in performance terms or remain to be formulated.

With the planned reorganization of ISO 9000-3, the confusing mismatch of its structure will be resolved and IEEE may decide to withdraw the 1298 standard.

ISO/IEC TR 9294—Management of Software Documentation

This Type 3 Technical Report[57] was approved by ISO/IEC JTC1 in 1990 and is the responsibility of SC7/WG2. It offers guidance on the management of the software documentation process. It addresses policies, standards, procedures, resources, and plans needed for the process but refrains from advice concerning the content and layout of the documents to be produced.

Predating ISO/IEC 12207, the seven page report is not specifically coordinated with that standard. Nevertheless, the advice is general enough that there is probably no inconsistency.

Although the report makes general reference to ISO 6592 and ISO 9127, no specific dependencies are apparent.

Organizational Processes of 12207

The four organizational processes of 12207 are *management, infrastructure, improvement,* and *training.* The organizational processes of 12207 are expected to be inherent in the responsible organization; instances of those processes are instantiated for the execution of the specific project. It is the instantiation of the management process that provides the "Plan-Do-Check-Act" (PDCA) cycle[58] inherited by the primary processes for the purpose of implementing general quality management principles.

Table 92. Standards Related to the 12207 Management Process

Standard	Title	Chapter
IEEE Std 982.1-1988	Standard dictionary of measures to produce reliable software	12
IEEE Std 982.2-1988	Guide for the use of standard dictionary of measures to produce reliable software	12
IEEE Std 1045-1992	Standard for software productivity metrics	
IEEE Std 1058.1-1987	Standard for software project management plans	

Relevant standards are available for two of these processes: management (shown in Table 92) and infrastructure (shown in Table 93).

---

[57]A type 3 TR provides material not suitable for a standard but otherwise of interest, for example, models, frameworks, guidance.

[58]PDCA is a basic quality management concept on which ISO 9000 is based [Ling96].

Table 93. Standards Related to the ISO/IEC 12207 Infrastructure
Process

Standard	Title	Chapter
CASE Tool Standards		
IEEE Std 1209-1992	Recommended practice for the evaluation and selection of CASE tools	11
IEEE Std 1348-1995	Recommended practice for the adoption of CASE tools	11
ISO/IEC 14102:1995	Guideline for the evaluation and selection of CASE tools	11
ISO/IEC DTR 14471	Guidelines for the adoption of CASE tools	11
Reuse Library Standards		
IEEE Std 1420.1-1995	Standard for software reuse—Data model for reuse library interoperability: Basic Interoperability Data Model (BIDM)	11
IEEE Std 1420.1a-1996	Standard for software reuse—Data model for reuse library interoperability: Asset certification framework	11
IEEE P1420.1b	Standard for software reuse—Data model for reuse library interoperability: Intellectual property rights framework	11
IEEE P1420.2	Standard for software reuse—Data model for reuse library interoperability: Bindings to HTML and SGML	11
IEEE P1420.3	Standard for software reuse—Data model for reuse library interoperability: Model extensions	11
IEEE Std 1430-1996	Guide for software reuse—Concept of operations for interoperating reuse libraries	11

The standards for measures to produce reliable software deal
with both the software product and the development processes;
they are discussed in Chapter 12. The standards related to the
infrastructure process fall into two areas: CASE tools and software
reuse libraries. All are described in Chapter 11.

Both IEEE and ISO/IEC JTC1 have standards related to CASE
tools. IEEE is currently conducting a ballot (P1462) to adopt 14102
as a replacement for IEEE Std 1209. The two standards are already
very similar, as 1209 was the original base document on which
14102 was based. IEEE may choose to either adopt the international document as is, or may write an annex specifying additions,
interpretations and changes.

The current and planned software reuse library standards are
all results of submissions to the IEEE SESC from the Reuse Library Interoperability Group (RIG). They all concern the capability

for reuse libraries to exchange information regarding their contents.

Figure 37 provides a road map from the organizational processes of 12207 to IEEE standards that may be useful in implementing the processes.

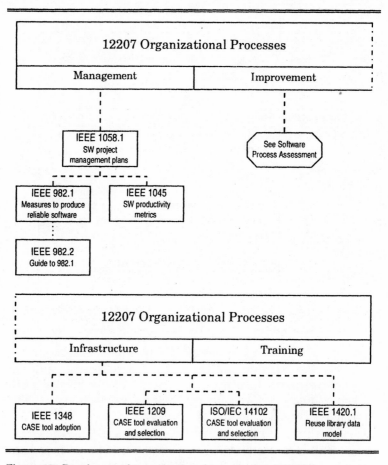

Figure 37. Road map of organizational processes of 12207.

The *management* process is intended to provide management of all of the other processes of the project, including "product management, project management, and task management." Of course, the appropriate IEEE standard is 1058.1. Other standards helpful in meeting the particular requirements of 12207 include 982.1 and 982.2, reliability measures, and IEEE 1045, productivity metrics.

The 982 documents are described in the chapter on software product standards, Chapter 12; the others are described below.

The *infrastructure* process establishes and maintains the "hardware, software, tools, techniques, standards and facilities" required for the execution of the other processes. Trivially, of course, any standard utilized on a project or by an organization becomes part of the infrastructure. More to the point, IEEE and international standards are available to provide guidance on the selection and adoption of CASE tools, on the implementation of software reuse libraries, and on the application of other software engineering resources. All of these standards are described in Chapter 11.

The *improvement* process is intended for "establishing, assessing, measuring, controlling and improving" the software life cycle processes at the level of the enterprise. One aspect of improvement, process assessment, will be described thoroughly at the end of this chapter.

The final process of 12207 is *training*—activities for "providing and maintaining trained personnel." There seem to be no software engineering standards specific to this subject; more general references, like the Project Management Institute guide, are described in Chapter 7.

IEEE Std 1045—Software Productivity Metrics

The SESC standard for software productivity metrics, 1045, was completed in 1992. Its introduction describes its premise:

> *Although there is more than 20 years of data, consistent productivity indicators for software development have not emerged from this information. The problem is not as much the fault of the metrics being used as it is the inaccuracy and incompleteness of the data being collected...Interpreting productivity based on a single number leaves much unknown about the process being measured. Without knowing the scope and characteristics of the process measured, or the precision of the data used in the calculations, the resulting productivity values are inconclusive.*

To deal with this situation, the 32-page standard is intended to structure the productivity data so that it becomes useful for process improvement. Therefore, it defines a framework for measuring and reporting that data. Separate clauses prescribes data collection for input, data collection for output, and measures that can be obtained from them. Another clause prescribes capturing characteristics of the development process to improve comparability of the data.

IEEE Std 1058.1—Software Project Management Plans

SESC completed this 15-page standard in 1987 and reaffirmed it 6 years later. A revision effort is under way and the result will probably be renumbered as 1058.

This is the key standard in the IEEE SESC collection for project management requirements focusing specifically on software. It specifies the format and content of a software project management plan but does not prescribe the techniques used in developing the plan nor the techniques for managing the project. The standard is addressed to software project managers and personnel who prepare and update plans and control adherence to those plans. It is intended to be applicable to all forms of software projects, not merely those concerned with new product development. Projects of all sizes can make use of this standard although smaller ones may require less formality.

The document could be useful in a variety of contexts, including implementing software project management practices conforming to the Project Management Institute standard, implementing the management requirements of the ISO 9001 standard, or implementing the management process of the 12207 standard.

The relationship of IEEE Std 1058.1 to other IEEE standards and to more general project management standards is described in Chapter 7. A notable relationship is that the software development plan specified in IEEE 730 is incorporated and subsumed by the plan in IEEE 1058.1.

Differences Between ISO/IEC 12207 and IEEE/EIA 12207

IEEE/EIA 12207[59] is packaged into three parts designated 12207.0, 12207.1 and 12207.2. Part 0 is a "sandwich" that wraps US material around the full text of ISO/IEC 12207. The US additions include:

- An informative annex describing basic concepts of 12207.

- An annex listing a few errors that have been discovered in the text of the international standard.

---

[59]The material in this section is adapted from [Moore97].

- A set of process objectives and data objectives that assist in determining the intent of the process requirements specified in the standard as well as the data (paper or electronic) produced by those processes.

- A replacement compliance clause that shifts emphasis toward compliance at the organizational level and that requires documentation of the means of compliance.

Part 1 of IEEE/EIA 12207 is a guidance document providing recommendations expanding on the data objectives of Part 0. For those desiring guidance on how specific documents or electronic data should be associated with specific processes, this part provides recommendations on the content of various possible documents. However, Part 1 also contains compliance provisions allowing it to be used as a standard rather than a guide when so desired.

Part 2 of IEEE/EIA 12207 is a guidance document providing recommendations on the implementation of the 12207 processes in the context of US best practices. The normative text of Part 0 is quoted and typographically enclosed in boxes. At appropriate intervals, guidance notes provide explanatory material and recommendations regarding the implementation of the processes.

The US adaptation of the standard, IEEE/EIA 12207, has shifted its focus toward compliance at the organizational level rather than at the level of the individual project.[60] The preferred usage is that an enterprise would develop its own set of processes and procedures that comply with the requirements of IEEE/EIA 12207 and which would be applied across the enterprise. Any individual project conducted by the enterprise would select the appropriate enterprise processes and procedures and parameterize them for application to the individual project.

The material provided in the US adaptation has the effect of constraining the use of *tailoring*. The writers of the original 12207 standard understood that not all of the requirements of the standard might be applicable to every project. Therefore, they adopted a concept of tailoring, which allows the deletion of specified processes, activities and tasks from the standard for application to a

---

[60]Although the international standard has a provision for organizational compliance, that provision is intended for use by an organization to specify "conditions of trade," that is, requirements on the processes of its suppliers rather than on its own processes.

specific project.[61] With the shift toward organization-level compliance in the US version, a refined approach is needed. Complying enterprises should implement organization-level processes capable of executing any requirement of 12207 when so tasked by a particular contract. Therefore, the concept of tailoring in the US version is better understood as a parameterization of the organization-level processes to the contracted scope of work for a particular project.

IEEE/EIA 12207 offers some important advantages over the international version of the standard:

- It provides a set of process and data objectives that guide adaptation of the requirements of the standard in unusual situations.

- It incorporates specific references to other US standards that may be helpful in the detailed implementation of life cycle processes.

- It incorporates guidance based on US "best practices" in the development of complex computer-based systems.

- It incorporates a set of recommended contents of data items produced by the execution of 12207 processes.

It remains, however, fully compliant with the international version of the standard, permitting US companies to develop a single set of enterprise processes applicable to both global and domestic business.

Part 0 has already been completed and has been approved by the IEEE Standards Board. Parts 1 and 2 are in their final stages and probably will be approved in December 1997. The Electronic Industries Association (EIA) will complete its approval process concurrently and the document will be submitted to ANSI for what is expected to be routine approval as an American National Standard. The US representatives to the international group responsible for ISO/IEC 12207 will offer the US material as suggestions for any revision of 12207. That international group is currently working on systems life cycle processes; it is expected that any revision of

---

[61]The ISO/IEC 12207 concept of tailoring should not be confused with the traditional usage of the DoD software process standards, in which tailoring means "change anything." ISO/IEC 12207 limits tailoring to simple deletion. Any additions to process requirements desired by the acquirer would have to be specified in the contract or the statement of work.

12207 will have the effect of positioning the software life cycle processes in the context of the overall system life cycle.

Compliance with 12207

ISO/IEC 12207 provides two types of compliance. The most typical type of conformance is appropriate to a project. In this case, compliance is achieved by completing the performance of the processes, activities and tasks selected by the tailoring process. The tailoring process permits the deletion of any process, activity, or task.

An additional provision permits any organization (ranging from individual companies to national standards bodies) "imposing [the] standard as a condition of trade" to comply by "making public the minimum set of required processes, activities and tasks." IEEE/EIA 12207 is a public statement corresponding to this form of compliance. So the US standard is a complying adaptation of ISO/IEC 12207.

The drafters of the US adaptation had several objectives concerning its provisions for compliance:

- They wanted to encourage organizational-level implementation of processes (as opposed to project-level implementation), hence they wanted to permit (nay, encourage) organizational-level compliance with the standard.

- They wanted to constrain the apparently free scope for tailoring provided by the international standard—in short, they wanted to standard to provide a meaningful minimum set of requirements.

- They wanted the standard to be usable in regulatory situations.

In tightening the provisions for compliance, one must deal with two difficult characteristics of the international standard: its dependence on tailoring to delimit the scope of work for a contract; and its inclusion of clauses containing phrases such as "in accordance with the requirements of the contract." The first characteristic implies that tailoring is "built into" the standard, that is, the standard cannot be applied without allowing some tailoring. The second characteristic implies that the full text of the standard cannot be applied in the absence of a contract, for example, at the organizational level. Both of these problems had to be solved to meet the objectives of the joint IEEE/EIA working group.

An annex of IEEE/EIA 12207 provides the definition of compliance with the US standard. It describes two levels of compliance: *tailored*, similar to the compliance provisions of the international 12207 standard; and *absolute*, whereby adherence to all of the mandatory clauses of the standard is required. The annex permits absolute conformance to be separately claimed for specific processes. For example, absolute conformance could be claimed individually for the verification process. It is hoped that the absolute level of conformance will be commonly used. Throughout the IEEE/EIA adaptation, guidance is provided indicating that the proper use of tailoring is to delimit the scope of work (for example, development but not maintenance) rather than the elimination of inconvenient provisions.

The provisions of the annex describes four "compliance situations":

1. *Organization-level.* The organization claiming compliance asserts that it has implemented procedures and methods to meet all of the requirements of the standard. The organization is required to prepare a public document describing any tailoring of the standard and describing how it deals with the clauses of the standard that reference the "contract." The annex invites the organization to state that such clauses are to be detailed in the plans of specific projects.

2. *Project-level.* The project claiming compliance documents its tailoring of the standard and the clauses that reference the contract. The most highly desired situation for project compliance is within a complying organization. In this case, the project simply cites the organizational documents describing compliance, explains any tailoring necessary for the specific project, and explains the interpretation to be place on clauses of the standard that reference the "contract."

3. *Multiple supplier programs.* In this case, responsibility for the execution of some of the processes have been subdivided among one or more suppliers in a manner that does not allow any of them to sensibly claim compliance for their individual scope of work. However, the acquirer may claim compliance for the program as a whole by explaining how each of the provisions of the standard are accomplished.

4. *Regulatory.* This provision permits the regulator, in effect, to give the desired tailoring to the developer. It permits tailoring to be constrained by regulatory requirements, supplemental standards, legal regulations, or sector-specific requirements.

One final provision is intended to deal with unusual situations. Sometimes, because of very special requirements of the job, the usual requirements of 12207 (or any standard for that matter) just do not make sense. Rather than encouraging free tailoring in such a case, the annex permits compliance by an alternative method. Two other annexes of the US adaptation specify objectives for each of the processes of 12207 as well as data objectives. One is allowed to claim conformance with a process by implementing procedures that directly achieve those objectives rather than the specific requirements stated in the main body of 12207.

Software Process Assessment Methods

The decade beginning circa 1985 saw increasing interest in both software process improvement (for example, the Software Engineering Institute's Capability Maturity Model) and quality process improvement (for example, the development of the ISO 9000 series of standards with their provisions for the certification of quality management processes). Although US interest has tended to focus on the former, interest in other countries has focused on the latter. We are now seeing the emergence of software process assessment approaches which converge the two interests. This section will discuss a few of the major assessment models and methods used in major countries and a new international standards effort that may serve to unify them.

TickIT

TickIT grew out of an initiative in the late 1980s by the United Kingdom's Department of Trade and Industry, with the close cooperation of the British Computer Society, and is now published as [DTI92]. The purpose of TickIT is to provide guidance on the construction and assessment of software development and maintenance processes that meet the requirements for certification under ISO 9001 and the ISO 9000-3 guide.

Part 1 is an overall guide. Part 2 provides an authoritative interpretation of the requirements of ISO 9001 in the production of information technology products. Parts 3 and 4 are guides to 9000-3 for acquirers and suppliers of software. Part 5 provides guidance to assessors and auditors [Magee97, Peach94].

SEI CMM

Probably the best known software process assessment approach in the US is the Software Engineering Institute's (SEI) Software Capability Maturity Model[62] (SW-CMM) [Paulk93]. The model characterizes five successive levels of maturity in the software process capability of the assessed organization. The model, along with an appropriate assessment method, may be applied to evaluate a developer's maturity either as an assessment (for purposes of self-improvement) or as an evaluation (for purposes of supplier qualification). The Department of Defense is particularly interested in the latter usage because its rules regarding open competition require objective evidence for vendor qualification (or, more pointedly, disqualification).

Unfortunately, the CMM has only coincidental correlation with ISO 9001. A study done at the SEI suggests that while some level 1 organizations might qualify for ISO 9001 registration, some (presumably more capable) level 3 organizations might not [Paulk95].

Trillium

Trillium was developed by Bell Canada and its partners to assess the development and support capabilities of prospective suppliers of telecommunications and related information technology products. *Capability*, in this context, is regarded as "the ability of a development organization to consistently deliver a product...that meets customer expectations, with minimal defects, for the lowest life-cycle cost, and in the shortest time." The model is being extended to address management information systems and Bell is considering further extensions to deal with hardware development as well as manufacturing and service capabilities. Trillium may be used for organizational self-assessment and improvement or for assistance in selecting suppliers. The model was developed through a benchmarking study of various standards describing key industry practices. Although the model was largely based on Version 1.1 of the SEI CMM, additional practices were added from ISO 9001 and 9000-3, IEC 300, eight IEEE software engineering standards, the Malcolm Baldrige Quality Awards criteria, two internal

---

[62]Capability Maturity Model and CMM are service marks of Carnegie Mellon University.

corporate standards and various other sources. Achieving the third-level rating on Trillium's five level scale indicates that the organization's practices conform to the intent, but not necessarily the detailed requirements, of the standards listed previously [Bell94].

Version 3.0 of the Trillium model is hierarchically organized around eight capability areas that span 28 road maps composed of 508 individual practices. An organization gains maturity in a particular road map by incrementally implementing practices of increasing effectiveness [April95].

Bootstrap

Bootstrap was developed by the European Esprit consortium in 1993 to provide a mutually satisfactory method for software process and improvement. Version 1.0 of the SEI CMM was enhanced and refined for the particular characteristics of the European software industry, including non-defense sectors. Material was added to address the quality guidelines of ISO 9000 and the ESA PSS-05 software engineering standard [Bootstrap93]. Bootstrap is intended for application to both software developers and their projects.

Although Bootstrap was based on the original CMM, the added material has effected important differences. Bootstrap defines a quality-attribute hierarchy based on 31 quality factors abstracted from ISO 9000-3 and ESA PSS-05. The hierarchy is organized to consider three dimensions regarded as important to process definition: organization, methodology and technology. Questions were added to address process modeling requirements and risk management. The intent is to encourage organizations to create a software life-cycle model, with detailed standards and methods, prior to setting up the quality system intended to check if the standards and methods actually succeed in promoting high-quality results.

Rather than being oriented toward discrete levels of maturity, Bootstrap provides a process quality profile indicating strengths and weaknesses in various areas. As a result, Bootstrap results provide a finer-grained analysis of the capabilities of an organization or a project than does CMM, and provide better correspondence to the requirements and guidelines of the ISO 9000 series. It is estimated that Bootstrap can assess conformance to 85 percent of the ISO 9000 attributes [Haase94].

ISO/IEC DTR 15504—Software Process Assessment

A unification of the surfeit of software process assessment approaches may come from an effort to develop an international standard under the auspices of ISO/IEC JTC1/SC7/WG10. A companion effort—commonly known as SPICE (Software Process Improvement and Capability dEtermination)—developed the initial document baseline, is conducting field trials for the purpose of empirical validation, and will continue to promote awareness, understanding, and adoption of the ultimate standard.

The project was born in the 1991 ImproveIT study [DEF91] conducted by the British Ministry of Defence into methods for assessing the software development capability of suppliers. The study considered two dozen existing methods and concluded that there was a need to supplement the reliance of software procurers on ISO 9001 with a standardized, widely accepted, public domain software capability assessment scheme directed toward continuous process and quality improvement positioned within the context of business needs. Based on the study's conclusion, the British Standards Institution proposed the initiation of a three-part standardization effort within ISO/IEC JTC1/SC7: a study period; development of a Type 2 Technical Report[63]; and, finally, development of a full international standard. The planned standard is broader in scope than the CMM, dealing with all of the processes of ISO/IEC 12207—acquisition, supply, maintenance, operation, and supporting processes, in addition to development. It is intended that the standard may be used for organizational process assessment and improvement as well as supplier capability determination [Kitson96].

The planned standard is intended to define a framework for assessment methods and models, not to provide a single method or model for universal application. The architecture of the standard is structured to encourage the development of methods specifically tailored to particular domains or markets. On the other hand, the standard does include an example assessment model which, some critics claim, might itself become a de facto standard. Aside from differences in the breadth of scope, the most noticeable difference between CMM and 15504 is the contrast between a staged and a

---

[63]In ISO/IEC JTC1, a Type 2 Technical Report is a mechanism for provisionally publishing a standard that remains under development. It is the closest JTC1 equivalent to an IEEE Trial Use Standard.

continuous model. CMM constrains process ratings to discrete maturity levels, while 15504 rates processes along a continuous capability dimension on a process by process basis.

The SEI is striving to offer a revised CMM and accompanying methods which will comply with 15504; this goal has not yet been achieved [Kitson97].

Running in parallel with the development of the standard are the SPICE trials, intended to gather early experience data that will provide a basis for revision of the Technical Reports prior to final standardization. The so-called Phase 2 trials will continue until the document set reaches the stage of Draft Technical Report. The current set of documents planned for the 15504 standard is listed in Table 94.

Table 94. Plan and Status of ISO/IEC JTC1/SC7 Standards Related to Software Process Assessment

ISO/IEC Std	Title
DTR 15504-1	Software process assessment—Part 1: Concepts and introductory guide [Informative]
DTR 15504-2	Software process assessment—Part 2: Reference model for processes and process capability [Normative]
DTR 15504-3	Software process assessment—Part 3: Performing an assessment [Normative]
DTR 15504-4	Software process assessment—Part 4: Guide to performing assessments [Informative]
DTR 15504-5	Software process assessment—Part 5: An assessment model and indicator guidance [Informative]
DTR 15504-6	Software process assessment—Part 6: Guide to qualification of assessors [Informative]
DTR 15504-7	Software process assessment—Part 7: Guide for use in process improvement [Informative]
DTR 15504-8	Software process assessment—Part 8: Guide for use in determining supplier process capability [Informative]
DTR 15504-9	Software process assessment—Part 9: Vocabulary [Informative]

OBJECTS OF SOFTWARE ENGINEERING: CUSTOMERS

In the model chosen by IEEE SESC and by JTC1/SC7, all software engineering activities are performed as a result of an agreement with a customer. Even in informal situations, within a single organization, one party has felt the need for the function to be provided by software and has initiated steps to cause it to be developed by another.

It is probably true that each of the standards to be described in this chapter could be fitted into one of the other chapters—as a process, a product, or a resource. The standards described here are those that have particular relevance to the relationship between the customer and those providing the software-related product or service for the customer. For purposes of description, three classes of customer will be distinguished: the *acquirer*, for those aspects concerning contractual agreement between buyer and seller; the *systems engineer*, for those aspects concerning the technical relationships of system and software functionality; and the *stakeholder*, for all other aspects of the software engineering project that might be of interest to parties external to the project.

Acquirer

The IEEE/EIA 12207 standard (as well as the ISO/IEC version) is premised on a relationship between an acquirer and a supplier of a software engineering project. As explained in Chapter 13, the 12207 standard specifies three classes of processes: *primary, supporting,* and *organizational*. The primary processes identify the processes of *acquisition* and *supply* as well as the engineering processes of *development, maintenance* and *operation*. In the model chosen by the standard, an acquirer and a supplier enter into an agreement for the completion of a particular product or service. The supplier then executes one of the other three primary processes to perform the development, maintenance, or operations appropriate to the performance of the agreement. Both versions of 12207 as well as some other standards useful to the acquirer/supplier relationship are listed in Table 95. The distinction between the two versions of 12207, along with descriptions of their respective guides, is described in Chapter 13.

Table 95. Standards Relevant to the Acquirer-Supplier Relationship

Standard	Title
IEEE/EIA Std 12207.0-1996	Software life cycle processes
IEEE/EIA (P1448.1) 12207.1	Guide to software life cycle processes—Life cycle data
IEEE/EIA (P1448.2) 12207.2	Guide to software life cycle processes—Implementation considerations
ISO/IEC 12207:1995	Software life cycle processes
ISO/IEC DTR 14759	Software life cycle model tailored for mockup and prototype
ISO/IEC DTR 15271	Guidebook for software life cycle processes
EIA/IEEE J-Std-016-1995	Software life cycle processes—Software development—Acquirer-supplier agreement
IEEE Std 1062-1993	Recommended practice for software acquisition
ISO 6592:1985	Guidelines for the documentation of computer-based application systems

For some software development projects, it may be more appropriate to apply EIA/IEEE J-Std-016 as the standard defining the relationship between buyer and seller. That standard is particularly useful in relationships where contractual oversight is appropriate; it is described as an important alternative in Chapter 15. IEEE Std 1062 focuses specifically on acquisition practices. It may be used to detail the acquisition process of ISO/IEC 12207 or may be applied in conjunction with other standards. ISO 6592, currently being revised by JTC1/SC7, can be regarded as a "checklist" of possible documentation on which the acquirer and the supplier should reach agreement. In major software developments where documentation is an issue, it can play a role in framing an agreement between acquirer and supplier regarding appropriate deliverable document products.

12207 Acquisition Process

The acquisition process of 12207 begins with the "definition of the need to acquire a system, software product or software service." It specifies five activities:

- *Initiation*: description of concept or need, system requirements and, optionally software requirements analysis;

make-buy-contract decision; acquisition planning; and acceptance strategy

- *Preparation of the Request for Proposal (RFP)*: documenting requirements, scope of work, and contract terms; defining contract milestones

- *Contract preparation and update*: supplier selection; contract negotiation; contract change control

- *Supplier monitoring*: application of the 12207 supporting processes to monitor contract performance, including Joint Review, Audit, Verification and Validation as needed

- *Acceptance and completion*: acceptance review and testing

The contract-oriented language of 12207 may seem inapplicable to less formal procurement methods, but the standard is intended to be useful even for the least formal of agreements. The standard was written in contractual language from the conviction that it would be easier for users to interpret formal provisions for less formal purposes rather than the other way around.

IEEE Std 1062—Software Acquisition

This is the key IEEE standard for the software acquisition process. It was approved in 1993 as a "recommended practice," meaning that its provisions are generally recommendations rather than requirements. The 37-page document provides a set of practices that are useful in the management and execution of software acquisition. Software is treated in three categories—off-the-shelf, modified, and fully developed—but the document claims to be better suited to the latter two categories. The practice encompasses nine steps covering a broad scope ranging from planning the overall strategy through follow-up on the use of the acquired software. A number of checklists are provided in an annex.

The document may be applied in a variety of contexts: to implement the acquisition requirements of an ISO 9001 quality management system; to detail the management process of a project that will acquire software products; to implement the acquisition side of the acquirer/supplier relationship described by the 12207 standard; or to implement the activities required by 12207 for the management of subcontractors.

The body of the document references several other IEEE SESC standards to provide detailed implementation of the steps involved in software acquisition. It also references ISO/IEC 9126 as a framework of quality characteristics that might be required in acquired software.

ISO 6592—Documentation of Computer-Based Application Systems

The original 1985 version of this standard predates the formation of JTC1 and carries only the ISO logo. A revision is currently underway in JTC1/SC7/WG2 and has reached the DIS stage. We can anticipate approval as ISO/IEC 6592 within a year or so. This description pertains to the DIS version.

The document was drafted with a simple intention—to provide a "checklist for two parties to use in agreeing on documentation content." It eschews guidance on the organization or structure of specific documents. The standard pertains to documents that are products of the software development, intended for users, operators, and maintainers; as well as process information products (see Chapter 11), intended for communication among developers with different assignments or responsibilities.

Application of the standard begins with the preparation of a document profile enumerating the requirements of the various intended users of documentation. The profile maps an overall structure for the total documentation to a set of "information items" to be treated in each document. The information items are noted as essential, conditional, or optional and are also classified by the desired level of treatment in each of the documents. A major portion of the standard consists of brief descriptions of the various information items to be considered. The acquirer and supplier should reach agreement on the document profile.

The data objectives annex of IEEE/EIA 12207.0 and the data guidelines of IEEE/EIA 12207.1 may be considered as alternatives to the application of this standard.

12207 Supply Process

Of course, the 12207 supply process is the complement of the acquisition process. It is important to note that the supply process does not directly incorporate the engineering activities of development, operation and maintenance. The supply process would invoke one of those processes to perform the engineering. The supply process is intended to factor out those common activities characteristic of being a supplier regardless of whether the product is development, operation, or maintenance.

The supply process is initiated in either of two ways: (1) when the supplier decides to prepare a proposal; or (2) when the supplier enters into a contract through other mechanisms. The process has seven activities:

- *Initiation*: review of RFP requirements; bid-no-bid decision

- *Preparation of response*: writing the proposal

- *Contract*: negotiation and agreement on the contract; change request

- *Planning*: requirements review; management planning; assurance planning; life cycle model selection; resource planning; make-buy decisions; project plan development

- *Execution and control*: executing the project plan using the 12207 Development, Operation or Maintenance process; monitoring and controlling progress and quality; subcontractor management; independent verification and validation, if appropriate

- *Review and evaluation*: reviews with acquirer; verification and validation; reporting to acquirer; quality assurance

- *Delivery and completion*: delivery and assistance in support

Again, the fact that the provisions of 12207 are written in contractual language should not be considered as an obstacle to application in less formal situations.

Systems Engineers

Software itself is incapable of executing any function whatsoever. To exhibit any behavior, it must be placed within the context of a system containing, at the minimum, a processor for the execution of the software. So, for any software, a relationship with an encompassing system is necessary. Of course, systems engineering is a discipline far more extensive than simply providing hardware for the execution of the software, but the point to be made is not the richness of the relationship, but the inevitability of it.

Software engineering standards have recognized this relationship. SESC sponsored the development of IEEE Std 1220, Standard for Application and Management of the Systems Engineering Process. ISO/IEC 12207 prescribes specific relationships between systems and software engineering processes and the working group that developed 12207 is currently at work on a complementary standard, 15288, on systems life cycle processes.

The viewpoint adopted in this section is that the systems-software relationship is orthogonal to the acquirer-supplier relationship. The systems engineering organization relevant to a particular software development may reside in either the customer's organization or the developer's organization. The described standards apply regardless.

Table 96 lists some of the standards specifically relevant to the relationship between software and systems engineering. The ones to be described in this section are IEEE Std 1220, IEEE Std 1228, and IEEE Std 1233. The SC7 systems standard, 15288, is not described because it exists only in outline form as of spring 1997. EIA/IS-632 is an interim standard on systems engineering that is currently under revision; it is described in Chapter 8. (The systems relationships prescribed by ISO/IEC 12207 are also described in Chapter 8.)

Table 96. Standards Relevant to the Systems-Software Relationship

Standard	Title
EIA/IS-632	Systems engineering
IEEE Std 1220-1994	(Trial Use) Standard for application and management of the systems engineering process
IEEE Std 1228-1994	Standard for software safety plans
IEEE Std 1233-1996	Guide for developing system requirements specifications
ISO/IEC DIS 15026	System and software integrity levels
ISO/IEC WD 15288	System life cycle processes

IEEE Std 1220—Application and Management of the Systems Engineering Process

This SESC standard was approved as a "trial use" standard in 1994 and is currently being revised, based on reports of trial usage, for promotion to full-use status. The 96 page standard describes the interdisciplinary tasks that are required throughout a system's life cycle to transform customer needs, requirements, and constraints into a system solution are defined. It applies to a performing activity within an enterprise that is responsible for developing a product design and establishing the life cycle infrastructure needed to provide for life cycle sustainment. It specifies the requirements for the systems engineering process and its application throughout the product life cycle. The requirements of this standard are applicable to new products as well as incremental enhancements to existing products.

The standard is useful in providing a view of systems engineering processes that is consistent with the software life cycle processes used in IEEE and other standards. This view provides a contextual anchor for software activities—like V & V, architecture, requirements engineering, integration, and qualification testing—that necessarily relate to systems-level engineering activity.

The standard makes normative references to IEEE standards 1012 and 1233. When applied, its reference to a quality management standard should be updated to ISO 9001 or, equivalently, ASQC Q9001.

IEEE Std 1228—Software Safety Plans

This SESC standard, approved in 1994, applies to "the plan used for the development, procurement, maintenance and retirement of safety-critical software; for example, software products whose failure could cause loss of life, serious harm, or have widespread negative social impact." Probably due to liability considerations, the document does not state when such a plan is appropriate, nor does it claim that its provisions are sufficient to ensure software safety. An annex is devoted to five types of software safety analyses.

Although the 24-page document deals with only the safety aspects of software, its provisions cut across all of the subjects of interest to SESC, including management processes, product characteristics, and architectural aspects of the system enclosing the software.

A detailed description of the software safety plan required by 1228, and its relationship to other standards is provided in Chapter 10.

IEEE Std 1233—Developing System Requirements Specifications

SESC approved this 32-page Guide document in 1996 as part of its efforts to describe the system-level context that necessarily encloses any software development effort. This document is a guide to capturing system-level requirements including operational concepts, design constraints and design configuration requirements. The system requirements specification is important to the software development process because the requirements allocated to software components of the system are based on the system requirements. The 12207 standard specifically cites this connection, so 1233 is a key document in detailing the acquisition, supply, and development processes prescribed by 12207.

The guide focuses more on the activities required to write the specification than the contents or format of the specification itself, although an example outline is provided. IEEE Std 1220 is cited as the source of process requirements for the development of the specification document.

ISO/IEC DIS 15026—System and Software Integrity Levels

This document is not yet a standard, but rather a Draft International Standard under development by ISO/IEC JTC1/SC7/WG9. The final standard will probably be published in late 1997 or early 1998.

Integrity is the concept that serves as the link between dependability and software engineering practice. "Dependability" is a term relevant to the user's perception of the external characteristics of the system while "integrity" is relevant to the developer's view of the internal design of the system and processes employed in its development. The determination of integrity level is based on dependability risk analysis. As a result of determining integrity level, software integrity requirements are derived and levied on the software developers.

This document forms the bridge between the dependability discipline and the software engineering discipline. It provides normative references to both IEC 300-3-9, describing risk analysis, and ISO/IEC 12207, describing processes which might be used for implementing integrity requirements. The standard establishes requirements for the determination of system and software integrity levels.

More explanation regarding the role of 15026 in the context of dependability can be found in Chapter 9. Additional material can be found in [Tripp96].

Stakeholders

During the 1970s the emphasis on software process improvement was placed on rigor. Generally, it was believed that the disciplined development of a requirements statement followed by the disciplined development of the implementing software would result in the completion of satisfactory software. Despite success in these two objectives, software development projects nevertheless often failed to satisfy the user of the software. More modern thinking has centered on communications rather than rigor. The premise is that all those with an interest in the productive deployment of the software, the *stakeholders*, should be able to suitably participate in the definition of the system. The list of stakeholders can be a long one and certainly includes the prospective users, operators, and maintainers of the intended software. In many cases, those responsible for other systems interfacing with the intended system would be included in the list. Two specific approaches to communication with stakeholders—the concept of operations and architecture—are discussed in Chapter 8 in the context of systems engineering.

Table 97 lists standards relevant to dealing with stakeholders. This section will describe the AIAA standard for the Concept of Operations document and the IEEE draft standard on the same subject. The IEEE project to develop a standard for architectural description is described in Chapter 11.

Table 97. Standards Relevant to Communication with Stakeholders

Standard	Title
AIAA G-043-1992	Guide for the preparation of operations concept documents
IEEE P1362	Guide for concept of operations document
IEEE P1471	Recommended practice for system design—Architectural description

AIAA G-043—Guide for the Preparation of Operational Concept Documents

This 29-page document was completed by the AIAA Software Systems Committee in 1992. It describes the operational concept document as "complementary" to the system specification serving as a reference during the requirements analysis and design phases. An appendix briefly describes recommended content, but the guide's emphasis is placed on good uses of the document and practices useful in preparing the document. Most of the examples are taken from aerospace.

IEEE P1362—Concept of Operations Document

This guide is currently under development by SESC. Its completion is being delayed pending final coordination with the draft IEEE/EIA 12207.1 and approval can be expected in late 1997 or early 1998. Even though the document is labeled as a guide, the reviewed draft does contain normative provisions allowing a user to assert compliance to its requirements.

The document specifies the format and content for a concept of operations document in support of a software development project. It views software as part of a larger system and considers the possibilities that a software Concept of Operations might be a separate document or might be part of a system-level document.

IMPORTANT
ALTERNATIVES

This chapter describes some important alternatives to the collections described in the main body of the book. A user might apply these standards because of sector-specific custom or regulatory requirements.

RTCA DO-178B

The purpose of this standard for Software Considerations in Airborne Systems and Equipment Certification is "to provide guidelines for the production of software for airborne systems and equipment that performs its intended function with a level of confidence in safety that complies with airworthiness requirements." It addresses the processes that should be used for the construction of software to be used in airborne systems. (There is little in the document to suggest, though, that it could not easily be modified for application to high-integrity systems in other domains.) The document is used in both the United States and Europe as a guide for the certification of airborne equipment.

This document is distinguished from the others in this book because it is specifically intended to be applied in a regulatory situation, specifically the certification process used for airborne systems. The developer reaches agreement with the "certification authority" on a "certification basis" that cites relevant regulations and special conditions. The plan for achieving certification is documented in a "Plan for Software Aspects of Certification." Because the development process is driven by the certification plan and the results are evaluated by the certification authority on the certification basis, the provisions of the standard itself are not mandatory. They provide guidance that may be ignored when agreed by the certifier.

A key concept is that of "software level," a characterization of the contribution of a software component to potential failure conditions as determined by the system safety assessment process. ("Software levels" are similar to the "integrity levels" used in other standards.) The importance of software level is that the level of effort required to show compliance varies with the contribution to potential failure. The software levels are defined in terms of the result of the failure in system function that could be caused by the software's anomalous behavior:

- *Level A*: Failure conditions that would prevent continued safe flight and landing.

- *Level B*: Failure conditions reducing the aircraft or crew's capability to the extent that there is: a large reduction in safety margins or functional capabilities; physical distress or workload increase preventing the flight crew from performing their tasks; or adverse effects on occupants including serious injuries.

- *Level C*: Failure conditions reducing the aircraft or crew's capability to the extent that there is: a significant reduction in safety margins or functional capabilities; a significant increase in crew workload; or discomfort to occupants possibly including injuries.

- *Level D*: Failure conditions which would not significantly reduce aircraft safety and which would involve crew actions that are well within their capabilities.

- *Level E*: Failure conditions that have no impact on operational capability or pilot workload.

As noted above, software level is assessed by its effects on system function, creating a strong linkage between software integrity and system safety assessment. The standard specifies other relationships between system and software life cycle processes. Some of the information passed from the system to the software processes is typical—allocated requirements, design constraints, and hardware information—but additional information is specific to this standard—notably the software levels determined as a result of the system safety assessment process. That system safety assessment process itself depends on information received from the software processes, notably fault containment boundaries, requirements and architectural considerations developed during software design, and the designation of error sources that are eliminated or detected through software methods. Thus, the system-level safety assessment and the software design are interdependent.

The description of the software processes specifies objectives and minimum required data. For each process, objectives are defined, and for each process, a description is provided of life cycle data that would demonstrate that the objectives have been satisfied. Software level is related to these objectives by a series of tables that, depending on level, label each objective by applicability and the required degree of independence. Furthermore, the degree of configuration management rigor required for the life cycle data is also prescribed based on software level. The activities described for each of the processes are merely examples of how the processes might be implemented. They are not mandatory if other methods for achieving the objectives can be formulated.

The standard prescribes neither a particular life cycle, nor particular software engineering methods; rather, it requires that they be defined during project planning. The standard does, though, describe the processes that comprise a software development project regardless of the chosen life cycle. Three categories of process are described:

- Software planning process

- Software development processes, including requirements, design, coding, and integration

- Integral processes, including verification, quality assurance, configuration management, and liaison with the certification authority

While the integral processes are active throughout the life cycle, the standard requires that the criteria for transition among the processes be established during the planning process.

The document also provides supplementary material regarding commercial off-the-shelf (COTS) software, user-modifiable code, reuse of requirements and code, and tool qualification.

The end goal in the production of airborne systems is obtaining certification of airworthiness. From this viewpoint, it should be clear that the document does not attempt to describe the best possible practices or all practices that might be applicable in various situations. Instead, it provides objectives for process and data that should be sufficient to obtain certification in most instances.

ESA PSS-05-0

PSS-05-0, Software Engineering Standards, was originally developed for use specifically by the European Space Agency but has been generalized for wider usage by their Technology Transfer Programme. The document provides mandatory requirements, recommendations, and guidance and is required for all ESA software development. It is intended to be tailored for any specific project.

Eleven additional document, designated as ESA PSS-05-01 through ESA PSS-05-11, provide additional guidance in the application of the standard.

Table 98. Relationship of ESA PSS-05-0 to IEEE Software Engineering
        Standards

Phase or Management Activity of ESA PSS-05-0	Relationship to IEEE Standards
General	Definitions are quoted from 610.12 and others.
User requirements definition	User Requirements Document is based on 830.
Software requirements definition	Software Requirements Document is based on 830.
Architectural design	Architectural Design Document is based on 1016.
Detailed design and production	Software User's Manual is based on 1063.
Transfer	
Operations and maintenance	
Software project management	Software Project Management Plan is based on 1058.1
Software configuration management	Software Configuration Management Plan is based on 828. IEEE 1042 is cited for additional guidance.
Software verification and validation	Software Verification and Validation Plan is based on 1012 and 829. Reviews are based on 1028.
Software quality assurance	Software Quality Assurance Plan and SQA activities are based on 730.

The standard recognizes that software development takes place in the context of a software life cycle that, in turn, is part of a larger system life cycle. Although system engineering activity is not prescribed by the standard, it does describe a User Requirements Definition phase that forms a bridge between systems and software engineering.

The standard describes a software life cycle that includes development, operations and maintenance. There are no requirements for operation, however, and few for maintenance. A life cycle model is provided and structured into phases and "management activities," similar to the supporting processes of ISO/IEC 12207. It is a responsibility of the project to map the standard life cycle model into a "life cycle approach" for the particular project. Three example approaches are described: waterfall, incremental delivery, and evolutionary development.

The phases of the life cycle model are generally bounded by the production of one or more documents and the completion of a review. For each phase, the standard specifies inputs, outputs, and activities. The overall development approach emphasizes top-down decomposition, but specifically notes the existence of both functional and object-oriented decomposition approaches.

It is interesting that the standard was based on several IEEE standards that are referenced within its text. The relationships among those standards are shown in Table 98.

EIA/IEEE J-Std-016

This standard[64] is best regarded as a "demilitarized" version of Mil-Std 498[65]. (A brief history appears in Chapter 13.) It describes a set of software development activities and related products performed in the context of a two-party agreement, specifically an agreement providing for oversight of the development activities by the acquirer. The version reviewed for this book was the 213-page Interim Standard, Standard for Information Technology—Software Life Cycle Processes—Software Development—Acquirer-Supplier Agreement, approved in 1995. During 1997, comments resulting from trial use will result in revision (hopefully including the jaw-breaker title), and promotion to a full use standard.

The introduction claims several advantages over its predecessor, Mil-Std 498:

- It is usable with any development strategy rather than being biased to the waterfall.

- It is usable with any development method including object-oriented techniques.

- It is compatible with the use of CASE tools rather than requiring formal paper documents.

---

[64]There is unfortunate confusion related to the designation of this standard, illustrating the hazards of paying inappropriate attention to draft standards. In the presumption that this standard would be superceded, early drafts of the document that became IEEE/EIA 12207 were labeled as draft revisions of J-Std-016. The document that became J-Std-016 is also variously known as IEEE P1498 and EIA IS 640.

[65]A detailed accounting of the differences between Mil-Std-498 and J-Std-016 can be found in [Sorensen96].

- It is compatible with software reuse practices.

- It supports the use of software management indicators.

- It emphasizes software "supportability."

- It recognizes that software exists within a system context.

Like Mil-Std 498, the document makes a clear cut and long-needed distinction between requirements and high-level design decisions. The concept of requirements is given an operational definition, those characteristics that are conditions for acceptance [Charles96].

Like its ancestors, this standard inherently requires tailoring. Because its writers intended it to suffice for standalone application in a software project, it had to say everything that might be relevant to any project. Without tailoring, its requirements would be excessive for any specific project.

The standard's immediate ancestor, Mil-Std 498, was intended for contractual imposition rather than voluntary adoption. Although some of the most egregious instances have been removed, the standard still retains vestiges of a unilateral approach to decision making, belying the phrase "two-party agreement," where specific requirements are levied on the supplier while only good intentions are required of the acquirer.

An important part of the standard are more than 130 pages of "software product descriptions,"[66] descriptions of the format and content of documents that could be created during the development of the software. The standard does not require any of these documents, but instead suggests careful consideration of which ones should be delivered.

As a matter of policy, the DoD has forsworn contractual imposition of process standards and, for most voluntary applications, this standard is superseded by IEEE/EIA 12207. Nevertheless, voluntary application of the standard is still appropriate under some circumstances [Moore97]:

- When a reference is desired for practices that were initiated under predecessor standards

- When a project is a continuation of one covered by the previous standards or is so strongly related that the same structure of documentation is appropriate

---

[66]Intended as a more neutral term than its predecessor, Data Item Descriptions (DIDs), a term that came to be associated with excessive formal documentation requirements.

- When an enterprise has instituted organization-level practices based on the provisions of the predecessor standards

The focus on the development project is both a strength and weakness of the document. On the positive side, the document is self-contained and comprehensive if users are willing to devote appropriate time, effort, and expertise to negotiation of a careful tailoring. On the negative side, today's most enlightened view of software development suggests that its processes should be firmly embedded in organizational-level practices, a relationship vulnerable to sabotage by project-level tailoring.

CATALOG OF SOFTWARE ENGINEERING STANDARDS

This appendix provides reference information for many of the standards mentioned elsewhere in this book. The standards are listed in numerical order regardless of the name of the organization that created them or any other alphabetical information that may prefix the number. The ANSI label is omitted from the designations of the standards. To shorten the often tedious titles of the standards, various terms, obvious in the present context, have been omitted; for example, "information technology," "IEEE," and "standard."

Existing standards have a date in the first column. As in the other tables and diagrams of this book, documents existing only in draft form are marked with the use of italics in the first column. Standards under development or revision have some entry in the column labeled "Status"; the meaning of the label is specific to the organization performing the effort.

For many standards, the specific (sub-) organization responsible for the development or maintenance of the standard is indicated in the column labeled "Committee."

Some of the standards are described, rather than merely mentioned, in the "Context" or "Object" chapters (Chapters 5-10 and 11-14, respectively). In such cases, the column labeled "Chapter" identifies the chapter by number.

In many cases, the standard is also described in the context of its containing collection. The column labeled "Committee" will assist in identifying the description in Chapters 3 and 4. Some of the software engineering standards not treated in this book are described in [Magee97].

Standard	Comm-ittee	Status	Title of Standard	Chap-ter(s)
PMI [No Number] (1996)			A guide to the project management body of knowledge	7
ISO/IEC [No Number]	SC7	NWI	Reference model for software engineering environments	
ISO/IEC [No Number]	SC7	NWI	Categorization of system and software events	
ASME NQA-1 -1989			Quality assurance program requirements for nuclear facilities	
ASME NQA-2a -1990			Quality assurance requirements of computer software for nuclear facility applications	
ESA PSS-05-0 [Undated]			Software engineering standards	15
IEEE Std 7-4.3.2 -1993			Standard criteria for digital computers in safety systems of nuclear power generating stations	10
AIAA G-010 -1993	SS		Guide for reusable software: Assessment criteria for aerospace applications	11
AIAA R-013 -1992	SS		Recommended practice for software reliability	9
EIA/IEEE J-Std-016 -1995	G-34 / SESC	PN-3764	Software Life Cycle Processes—Software development—Acquirer-supplier agreement [1995 version is an interim EIA standard and a trial use IEEE standard]	15
AIAA G-043 -1992	SS		Guide for the preparation of operations concept documents	8, 14
IEC 50-191 (1990)	TC1		Vocabulary—Chapter 191: Dependability and quality of service	
ANS 51.1 -1983 (R 1988)			Nuclear safety criteria for the design of stationary pressurized water reactor plants	
ANS 52.1 -1983 (R 1988)			Nuclear safety criteria for the design of stationary boiling water reactor plants	
RTCA DO-178B (1992)	SC-167		Software considerations in airborne systems and equipment certification	15
IEC 300-1 (1993)	TC56		Dependability management—Part 1: Dependability programme management	9
IEC 300-2 (1995)	TC56		Dependability management—Part 2: Dependability programme elements and tasks	9

Standard	Comm-ittee	Status	Title of Standard	Chap-ter(s)
IEC 300-3-1 (1991)	TC56		Dependability management—Part 3: Application guide—Section 1: Analysis techniques for dependability: Guide on methodology	
IEC 300-3-2 (1993)	TC56		Dependability management—Part 3: Application guide—Section 2: Collection of dependability data from the field	
IEC 300-3-3 (1996)	TC56		Dependability management—Part 3: Application guide—Section 3: Life cycle costing	
IEC 300-3-4 (1996)	TC56		Dependability management—Part 3: Application guide—Section 4: Guide to the specification of dependability requirements	
IEC 300-3-6	TC56	FDIS	Dependability management—Part 3: Application guide—Section 6: Software aspects of dependability	9
IEC 300-3-9 (1995)	TC56		Dependability management—Part 3: Application guide—Section 9: Risk analysis of technological systems	9
CAN/CSA Q396.0 -1991			Guide for selecting and applying the CAN/CSA-Q396-89 software quality assurance program standards	6
CAN/CSA Q396.1.1 -1989			Quality assurance program for the development of software used in critical applications	6
CAN/CSA Q396.1.2 -1989			Quality assurance program for previously developed software used in critical applications	6
CAN/CSA Q396.2.1 -1989			Quality assurance program for the development of software used in non-critical applications	6
CAN/CSA Q396.2.2 -1989			Quality assurance program for previously developed software used in non-critical applications	6
IEC 557 (1982)	SC45A		IEC terminology in the nuclear reactor field	
IEEE Std 603 -1991			Standard criteria for safety systems for nuclear power generating stations	10
IEEE Std 610.12 -1990	SCC	(R)	Standard glossary of software engineering terminology	11
EIA/IS 632 (1994)	G-47		Systems engineering	
EIA 632	G-47	PN-3537	Processes for engineering a system	

Standard	Committee	Status	Title of Standard	Chapter(s)
IEC 643 (1979)	SC45A		Application of digital computers to nuclear reactor instrumentation and control	10
EIA/IS 649 -1995	G-33	PN-3721	National consensus standard for configuration management	7
IEEE Std 729	SESC	P	Standard for software engineering— Fundamental terms	11
IEEE Std 730 -1989	SESC	(R)	Standard for software quality assurance plans	6, 13
IEEE Std 730.1 -1995	SESC		Guide to software quality assurance planning	6, 13
IEC 812 (1985)	TC56		Analysis techniques for system reliability—Procedure for failure mode and effects analysis (FMEA)	9
IEEE Std 828 -1990	SESC	(R)	Standard for software configuration management plans	6, 13
IEEE Std 829 -1983 (R 1991)	SESC		Standard for software test documentation	11
IEEE Std 830 -1993	SESC		Recommended practice for software requirements specifications	11
IEC 880 (1986)	SC45A		Software for computers in the safety systems of nuclear power stations	10
IEC 880-1	SC45A	CDV	Supplement 1 to IEC 880, Software for computers important to safety for nuclear power plants	10
IEC 880-2	SC45A	NWI	Supplement 2 to IEC 880, Software for computers important to safety for nuclear power plants	10
IEEE Std 982.1 -1988	SESC	(R)	Standard dictionary of measures to produce reliable software	12
IEEE Std 982.2 -1988	SESC	(R)	Guide for the use of standard dictionary of measures to produce reliable software	12
IEC 987 (1989)	SC45A		Programmed digital computers important to safety for nuclear power stations	10
CANDU CE-1001- STD [Undated]			Standard for software engineering of safety critical systems	10
IEEE Std 1002 -1987 (R 1992)	SESC		Standard taxonomy for software engineering standards	11
IEEE Std 1008 -1987 (R 1993)	SESC		Standard for software unit testing	13
IEEE Std 1012 -1986 (R 1992)	SESC	(R)	Standard for software verification and validation plans [Revision may drop the word "plans" from the title.]	13

Standard	Comm-ittee	Status	Title of Standard	Chap-ter(s)
IEEE Std 1016 -1987 (R 1993)	SESC		Recommended practice for software design descriptions	11
IEEE Std 1016.1 -1993	SESC		Guide to software design descriptions	11
IEC 1025 (1990)	TC56		Fault tree analysis	9
IEEE Std 1028 -1988 (R 1993)	SESC	(R)	Standard for software reviews and audits [Revision may drop the words "and audits" from the title.]	13
IEEE Std 1042 -1987 (R 1993)	SESC		Guide to software configuration man-agement	13
IEEE Std 1044 -1993	SESC		Standard classification for software anomalies	11
IEEE Std 1044.1 -1995	SESC		Guide to classification for software anomalies	11
IEEE Std 1045 -1992	SESC		Standard for software productivity metrics	13
IEEE Std 1058.1 -1987 (R 1993)	SESC	(R)	Standard for software project man-agement plans [Revision will probably be renumbered as 1058.]	7, 13
IEEE Std 1059 -1993	SESC		Guide for software verification and validation plans	13
IEEE Std 1061 -1992	SESC		Standard for a software quality met-rics methodology	12
IEEE Std 1062 -1993	SESC		Recommended practice for software acquisition	14
IEEE Std 1063 -1987 (R 1993)	SESC		Standard for software user docu-mentation	12
IEC 1069-1 (1991)	SC65A		Industrial-process measurement and control—Evaluation of system prop-erties for the purpose of system as-sessment—Part 1: General consid-erations and methodology	
IEC 1069-2 (1993)	SC65A		Industrial-process measurement and control—Evaluation of system prop-erties for the purpose of system as-sessment—Part 2: Assessment methodology	
IEC 1069-3 (1996)	SC65A		Industrial-process measurement and control—Evaluation of system prop-erties for the purpose of system as-sessment—Part 3: Assessment of system functionality	

Standard	Comm-ittee	Status	Title of Standard	Chap-ter(s)
IEC 1069-4 (1997)	SC65A		Industrial-process measurement and control—Evaluation of system properties for the purpose of system assessment—Part 4: Assessment of system performance	
IEC 1069-5 (1994)	SC65A		Industrial-process measurement and control—Evaluation of system properties for the purpose of system assessment—Part 5: Assessment of system dependability	
IEC 1069-6	SC65A	CDV	Industrial-process measurement and control—Evaluation of system properties for the purpose of system assessment—Part 6: Assessment of system operability	
IEC 1069-7	SC65A	CDV	Industrial-process measurement and control—Evaluation of system properties for the purpose of system assessment—Part 7: Assessment of system safety	
IEC 1069-8	SC65A	CD	Industrial-process measurement and control—Evaluation of system properties for the purpose of system assessment—Part 8: Assessment of not task related properties	
IEEE Std 1074 -1995	SESC	(R)	Standard for developing software life cycle processes	13
IEEE Std 1074.1 -1995	SESC		Guide for developing software life cycle processes	13
IEC 1078 (1991)	TC56		Analysis techniques for dependability—Reliability block diagram method	
IEEE Std 1175 -1992	SESC	(R)	[Trial Use] Standard reference model for computing system tool interconnections	11
IEEE Std 1209 -1992	SESC		Recommended practice for the evaluation and selection of CASE tools [May be replaced by P1462, the adoption of ISO/IEC 14102]	11
IEEE Std 1219 -1992	SESC		Standard for software maintenance	13
IEEE Std 1220 -1994	SESC		[Trial Use] Standard for application and management of the systems engineering process	14
IEC 1226 (1993)	SC45A		Nuclear power plants—Instrumentation and control systems important for safety—Classification	10

Standard	Comm- ittee	Status	Title of Standard	Chap- ter(s)
IEEE Std 1228 -1994	SESC		Standard for software safety plans	10, 14
IEEE Std 1233 -1996	SESC		Guide for developing system require- ments specifications	8, 14
IEEE Std 1298 -1992	SESC		Software quality management sys- tem—Part 1: Requirements	6, 13
IEEE Std 1320.1	SESC	P	Syntax and semantics for IDEF0	11
IEEE Std 1320.1.1	SESC	P	Users manual for IDEF0	11
IEEE Std 1320.2	SESC	P	Syntax and semantics for IDEF1X97	11
IEEE Std 1320.2.1	SESC	P	Users manual for IDEF1X97	11
IEEE Std 1348 -1995	SESC		Recommended practice for the adop- tion of CASE tools	11
IEEE Std 1362	SESC	P	Guide for concept of operations document	8, 14
IEEE Std 1420.1 -1995	SESC		Software reuse—Data model for reuse library interoperability: Basic interoperability data model (BIDM)	11
IEEE Std 1420.1a -1996	SESC		Supplement to 1420.1—Software reuse—Data model for reuse library interoperability: Asset certification framework	11
IEEE Std 1420.1b	SESC	P	Supplement to 1420.1—Software reuse—Data model for reuse library interoperability: Intellectual property rights framework	11
IEEE Std 1420.2	SESC	P	Software reuse—Data model for reuse library interoperability: Bindings to HTML and SGML	11
IEEE Std 1420.3	SESC	P	Software reuse—Data model for reuse library interoperability: Model extensions	11
IEEE Std 1430 -1996	SESC		Guide for software reuse—Concept of operations for interoperating reuse libraries	11
IEEE Std 1462	SESC	P	[Adoption ballot for ISO/IEC 14102] Guidelines for the evaluation and selection of CASE tools	11
IEEE Std 1465	SESC	P	[Adoption ballot for ISO/IEC 12119] Software packages—Quality require- ments and testing	12
IEEE Std 1471	SESC	P	Recommended practice for system design—Architectural description	11

Standard	Comm-ittee	Status	Title of Standard	Chap-ter(s)
IEEE Std 1491	SESC	P	[Adoption ballot for the PMI's] Guide to the project management body of knowledge	
IEC 1508-1	SC65A	CDV	Functional safety—Safety-related systems—Part 1: General require-ments	10
IEC 1508-2	SC65A	CD	Functional safety—Safety-related systems—Part 2: Requirements for electrical/electronic/programmable electronic systems	
IEC 1508-3	SC65A	CDV	Functional safety—Safety-related systems—Part 3: Software require-ments	
IEC 1508-4	SC65A	CDV	Functional safety—Safety-related systems—Part 4: Definitions and abbreviations of terms	
IEC 1508-5	SC65A	CDV	Functional safety—Safety-related systems—Part 5: Guidelines on the application of part 1	
IEC 1508-6	SC65A	CD	Functional safety—Safety-related systems—Part 6: Guidelines on the application of parts 2 and 3	
IEC 1508-7	SC65A	CD	Functional safety—Safety-related systems—Part 7: Bibliography of techniques and measures	
IEC 1513	SC45A	CD	Nuclear power plants—Instrumentation and control for sys-tems important to safety—General requirements for computer-based systems	10
IEC 1703	TC56	CD	Mathematical expressions for reliabil-ity, maintainability and maintenance support terms	
IEC 1704	TC56	CD	Guide to test methods for reliability assessment of software	
IEC 1713	TC56	CD	Guide to software dependability through the software life cycle proc-esses	
IEC 1714	TC56	CD	Software maintainability and mainte-nance aspects of a dependability programme	
IEC 1719	TC56	NP	Guide to measures (metrics) to be used for the quantitative dependability assessment of software	
IEC 1720	TC56	NP	Dependability of software for critical applications	9

Standard	Comm- ittee	Status	Title of Standard	Chap- ter(s)
IEC 1838	SC45A	NP	Supplement to IEC 1226—Risk-based classification	
ISO/IEC 2382-1 :1993	SC1		Information technology— Vocabulary—Part 1: Fundamental terms	11
ISO/IEC 2382-7 :1989	SC1	DIS	Information technology— Vocabulary—Part 7: Computer pro- gramming	11
ISO/IEC 2382-20 :1990	SC1		Information technology— Vocabulary—Part 20: System devel- opment	11
ISO 5806 :1984	SC7		Specification of single-hit decision tables	11
ISO 5807 :1985	SC7		Documentation symbols and conven- tions for data, program and system flowcharts, program network charts and system resources charts	11
ISO 6592 :1985	SC7	DIS	Guidelines for the documentation of computer-based application systems	14
ISO 6593 :1985	SC7		Program flow for processing sequen- tial files in terms of record groups	11
ISO 8402 :1994	TC176		Quality management and quality assurance—Vocabulary	
ISO/IEC 8631 :1989	SC7		Program constructs and conventions for their representation	11
ISO 8790 :1987	SC7		Computer system configuration dia- gram symbols and conventions	11
ISO 9000-1 :1994	TC176		Quality management and quality assurance standards—Part 1: Guide- lines for selection and use	
ISO 9000-2 :1997	TC176		Quality management and quality assurance standards—Part 2: Ge- neric guidelines for the application of ISO 9001, ISO 9002 and ISO 9003	
ISO 9000-3 :1991	TC176	FDIS	Quality management and quality assurance standards—Part 3: Guide- lines for the application of 9001 to the development, supply, installation and maintenance of computer software	6
ISO 9000-4 :1993	TC176		Quality management and quality assurance standards—Part 4: Guide to dependability programme man- agement	
ISO 9001 :1994	TC176		Quality systems—Model for quality assurance in design, development, production, installation, and servicing	6

Standard	Comm-ittee	Status	Title of Standard	Chap-ter(s)
ISO 9002 :1994	TC176		Quality systems—Model for quality assurance in production, installation, and servicing	
ISO 9003 :1994	TC176		Quality systems—Model for quality assurance in final inspection and test	
ISO 9004-1 :1994	TC176		Quality management and quality system elements—Part 1: Guidelines	
ISO 9004-2 :1991	TC176		Quality management and quality system elements—Part 2: Guidelines for service	
ISO 9004-3 :1993	TC176		Quality management and quality system elements—Part 3: Guidelines for processed materials	
ISO 9004-4 :1993	TC176		Quality management and quality system elements—Part 4: Guidelines for quality improvement	
ISO/IEC 9126 :1991	SC7		Software product evaluation—Quality characteristics and guidelines for their use	12, 14
ISO/IEC 9126-1	SC7	CD	Software quality characteristics and metrics—Part 1: Quality characteristics and subcharacteristics	12, 14
ISO/IEC TR 9126-2	SC7	pDTR	Software quality characteristics and metrics—Part 2: External metrics	12, 14
ISO/IEC TR 9126-3	SC7	pDTR	Software quality characteristics and metrics—Part 3: Internal metrics	12, 14
ISO 9127 :1988	SC7		User documentation and cover infor-mation for consumer software pack-ages	12, 14
ISO 9241-x :1992	TC159	Various	Ergonomic requirements for office work with visual display terminals (VDTs) [17 parts; some completed]	
ISO/IEC TR 9294 :1990	SC7		Guidelines for the management of software documentation	13
ISO 10005 :1995	TC176		Quality management—Guidelines for quality plans	
ISO 10006	TC176	FDIS	Quality management—Guidelines to quality in project management	
ISO 10007 :1995	TC176		Quality management—Guidelines for configuration management	
ISO 10011-1 :1990	TC176		Guidelines for auditing quality sys-tems—Part 1: Auditing	
ISO 10011-2 :1991	TC176		Guidelines for auditing quality sys-tems—Part 2: Qualification criteria for quality system auditors	

Standard	Comm-ittee	Status	Title of Standard	Chap-ter(s)
ISO 10011-3 :1991	TC176		Guidelines for auditing quality systems—Part 3: Management of audit programmes	
ISO 10012-1 :1992	TC176		Quality assurance requirements for measuring equipment—Part 1: Metrological confirmation system for measuring equipment	
ISO 10012-2	TC176	FDIS	Quality assurance requirements for measuring equipment—Part 2: Guidelines for control of measurement process	
ISO 10013 :1995	TC176		Guidelines for developing quality manuals	
ISO 10014	TC176	FDIS	Guidelines for managing the economics of quality	
ISO/IEC 11411 :1995	SC7		Representation for human communication of state transition of software	11
ISO/IEC 12119 :1994	SC7		Software packages—Quality requirements and testing	12
ISO/IEC TR 12182	SC7	DTR	Categorization of software	11
IEEE/EIA Std 12207.0 -1996	SESC		Software life cycle processes	8, 9, 13, 14
IEEE/EIA Std 12207.1	SESC	P1448.1	Guide for software life cycle processes—Life cycle data	8, 13
IEEE/EIA Std 12207.2	SESC	P1448.2	Guide for software life cycle processes—Implementation considerations	8, 13
ISO/IEC 12207 :1995	SC7		Software life cycle processes	8, 9, 13, 14
ISO/IEC 12220	SC7	DIS	Software life cycle process—Configuration management for software [Has been renumbered as 15846]	
ISO/IEC TR 12382 :1992	JTC1		Permuted index of the vocabulary of information technology	11
ISO/IEC 14102 :1995	SC7		Guideline for the evaluation and selection of CASE tools	11
ISO/IEC 14143-1	SC7	DIS	Software measurement—Functional size measurement—Part 1: Definition of concepts	12

Standard	Comm-ittee	Status	Title of Standard	Chap-ter(s)
ISO/IEC TR 14399	SC7	DTR	Mapping of relevant software engineering standards—Standards relevant to ISO/IEC JTC1/SC7—Software engineering	11
ISO/IEC TR 14471	SC7	DTR	Guidelines for the adoption of CASE tools	11
ISO/IEC 14568 :1997	SC7		DXL: Diagram eXchange Language for tree-structured charts	11
ISO/IEC 14598-1	SC7	DIS	Software product evaluation—Part 1: General overview	12
ISO/IEC 14598-2	SC7	CD	Software product evaluation—Part 2: Planning and management	12
ISO/IEC 14598-3	SC7	CD	Software product evaluation—Part 3: Process for developers	12
ISO/IEC 14598-4	SC7	CD	Software product evaluation—Part 4: Process for acquirers	12
ISO/IEC 14598-5	SC7	DIS	Software product evaluation—Part 5: Process for evaluators	12
ISO/IEC 14598-6	SC7	CD	Software product evaluation—Part 6: Documentation of evaluation modules	12
ISO/IEC 14756	SC7	FCD	Measurement and rating of performance of computer-based software systems	12
ISO/IEC TR 14759	SC7	DTR	Software life cycle model tailored for mockup and prototype	13
ISO/IEC 14764	SC7	CD	Software maintenance	13
ISO/IEC 15026	SC7	DIS	System and software integrity levels	9, 14
ISO/IEC TR 15271	SC7	DTR	Guide for ISO/IEC 12207 (Software life cycle processes)	13
ISO/IEC 15288	SC7	WD	System life cycle processes	
ISO/IEC 15289	SC7	WD	Guidelines for the content of software life cycle process information products	11
ISO/IEC 15474-1	SC7	CD	Software engineering data definition and interchange—Part 1: Overview	
ISO/IEC 15474-2	SC7	CD	Software engineering data definition and interchange—Part 2: Framework for modeling and extensibility	
ISO/IEC 15474-3	SC7	CD	Software engineering data definition and interchange—Part 3: Framework for mapping PCTE to CDIF	
ISO/IEC 15474-4	SC7	WD	Software engineering data definition and interchange—Part 4: Framework for mapping IRDS to CDIF	

Standard	Comm-ittee	Status	Title of Standard	Chap-ter(s)
ISO/IEC 15475-x	SC7	CD	Software engineering data definition and interchange—Transfer format [3 parts]	
ISO/IEC 15476-x	SC7	CD	Software engineering data definition and interchange—Integrated meta-model [9 parts]	
ISO/IEC 15477-x	SC7	CD	Software engineering data definition and interchange—Presentation meta-model [3 parts]	
ISO/IEC 15478-x	SC7	WD	Software engineering data definition and interchange—PCTE schema definition sets [6 parts]	
ISO/IEC 15479-x	SC7	WD	Software engineering data definition and interchange—IRDS content modules [6 parts]	
ISO/IEC TR 15504-1	SC7	DTR	Software process assessment—Part 1: Concepts and introductory guide	13
ISO/IEC TR 15504-2	SC7	DTR	Software process assessment—Part 2: A reference model for processes and process capability	13
ISO/IEC TR 15504-3	SC7	DTR	Software process assessment—Part 3: Performing an assessment	13
ISO/IEC TR 15504-4	SC7	DTR	Software process assessment—Part 4: Guide to performing assessments	13
ISO/IEC TR 15504-5	SC7	DTR	Software process assessment—Part 5: An assessment model and indicator guidance	13
ISO/IEC TR 15504-6	SC7	DTR	Software process assessment—Part 6: Guide to qualification of assessors	13
ISO/IEC TR 15504-7	SC7	DTR	Software process assessment—Part 7: Guide for use in process improvement	13
ISO/IEC TR 15504-8	SC7	DTR	Software process assessment—Part 8: Guide for use in determining supplier process capability	13
ISO/IEC TR 15504-9	SC7	DTR	Software process assessment—Part 9: Vocabulary	13
ISO/IEC 15846	SC7	DIS	Software life cycle process—Configuration management for software [Formerly numbered 12220]	

WHERE TO PURCHASE STANDARDS

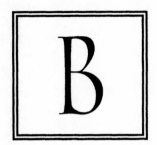

Most of the standards described in this book can be purchased from any of the following sources:

Global Engineering Documents
15 Inverness Way East
Englewood, CO 80112-5776
800.854.7179
303.397.2740 (Fax)
http://global.ihs.com/

Information Handling Services
15 Inverness Way East
Englewood, CO 80112-5776
800.447.3352
303.397.2599 (Fax)
http://www.ihs.com/

Rapidoc, Technical Indexes, Ltd (TIUK)
Willoughby Road, Bracknell
Berkshire, RG12 8DW
United Kingdom
44.1344.861666
44.1344.714440 (Fax)
http://www.techindex.co.uk/

The various standards-related organizations described in this book can be contacted at the following addresses:

AIAA American Institute of Aeronautics and Astronautics
1801 Alexander Bell Drive
Suite 500
Reston, VA 22091
703.264.7500
703.264.7551 (Fax)
http://www.aiaa.org/

ANS   American Nuclear Society
555 N. Kensington Ave.
La Grange Park, IL 60525
708.352.6611
708.352.6464 (Fax)
http://www.ans.org/

ANSI   American National Standards Institute
11 W. 42nd Street
New York, NY 10036
212.642.4900
212.398.0023 (Fax)
http://www.ansi.org/

ASME   American Society of Mechanical Engineers
345 E. 47th Street
New York, NY 10017
212.705.7722
212.705.7739 (Fax)
http://www.asme.org/

CAN/CSA   Canadian Standards Association
178 Rexdale Blvd.
Etobicoke, Ontario M9W 1R3
Canada
416.747.4104
416.747.2475 (Fax)
06-989344 (Telex)
http://www.csa.ca/

EIA   Electronic Industries Association
2500 Wilson Blvd.
Arlington, VA 22201-3834
703.907.7500
703.907.7501 (Fax)
http://www.eia.org/

ESA   European Space Agency
8-10 rue Mario Nikis
75738 Paris CEDEX 15
France
+33 1 53 69 76 54
http://www.esrin.esa.it/

IEC   International Electrotechnical Commission
                 3, Rue de Varembe
                 PO Box 131
                 Geneva, CH-1211
                 Switzerland
                 +41 22 919 02 11
                 +41 22 919 03 00 (Fax)
                 http://www.iec.ch/

IEEE   Institute of Electrical and Electronics Engineers, Inc.
                 445 Hoes Lane
                 P.O. Box 1331
                 Piscataway, NJ 08855-1331
                 800.678.4333
                 908.981.9667 (Fax, general)
                 908.562.1571 (Fax, Standards Department)
                 http://www.ieee.org/

INCOSE   International Council on Systems Engineering
                 2033 Sixth Avenue, Suite 804
                 Seattle, WA 98121
                 800.366.1164
                 206.441.1164
                 206.441.8262 (Fax)
                 http://www.incose.org/

ISO   International Organization for Standardization
(including   Case Postale 56
ISO/IEC   Geneva CH-1211
JTC1)   Switzerland
                 +41 22 749 01 11
                 +41 22 733 34 30 (Fax)
                 41 22 05 ISO CH (Telex)
                 http://www.iso.ch/

PMI   Project Management Institute
                 130 South State Road
                 Upper Darby, PA 19082
                 610.734.3330
                 610.734.3266 (Fax)
                 http://www.pmi.org/

RIG   Reuse Library Interoperability Group
c/o Applied Expertise, Inc.
1925 N. Lynn St., Suite 802
Arlington, VA 22209
703.516.0911
703.516.0918 (Fax)
http://www.rig.org/

RTCA   RTCA, Inc.
1140 Connecticut Avenue, NW, Suite 1020
Washington, DC 20036
202.833.9339
202.833.9434 (Fax)
2407254 RTCA UQ (Telex)
http://www.rtca.org/

GLOSSARY

ACE	In the context of safety, Abnormal Conditions and Events
AECB	(Canadian) Atomic Energy Control Board
AECL	Atomic Energy Canada, Ltd.
Agent	In the SESC object model, the party responsible for the execution of a process
AIAA	American Institute of Aeronautics and Astronautics
Anomaly	Any condition that departs from the expected
ANS	American Nuclear Society
ANSI	American National Standards Institute
Architecture	The highest-level concept of a system in its environment
AS	A prefix designating standards created by Standards Australia
ASME	American Society of Mechanical Engineers
ASQC	American Society for Quality Control
ASTM	American Society for Testing and Materials
Availability	The factor of dependability that quantifies the product's readiness for use on demand
Best Practice	A practice widely regarded as effective and superior to alternatives
BSR	ANSI Board of Standards Review
CAN	A prefix used on some standards created by the Canadian Standards Association
CASE	Computer-aided software engineering, sometimes extended to include systems engineering

Category A, B, and C	Levels of criticality for systems important to safety in nuclear reactor protection systems
CD	Committee Draft
CDIF	EIA's CASE Data Interchange Format
CDV	Committee Draft for Vote
CEN	European Committee for Standardization
CENELEC	European Committee for Electrotechnical Standardization
Chapeau	"Hat" in French, a colloquial term for the planned IEC 1513 standard
CM	Configuration management
CMM	Capability Maturity Model, a service mark of the SEI
Computer science	One of six contexts for software engineering standards considered in this book
ConOps	Concept of Operations, also see OCD
COS	A Committee on Standards in the AIAA
COTS	Commercial, off-the-shelf, as opposed to a product that is specially developed or modified for its intended usage
Criticality	An attribute of software related to the risk and consequences of failure
CSA	Canadian Standards Association
CSL	Computer Systems Laboratory of NIST
Customer	In the SESC object model, one of four objects treated by software engineering standards
Dependability	One of six contexts for software engineering standards considered in this book; a collective and non-quantitative term for a product characteristic that encompasses all aspects of availability performance and its factors of reliability performance, maintainability performance, and maintenance support processes
Dependability programme	The organizational structure, responsibilities, procedures, processes, and resources used for managing dependability
DID	Data Item Description

DIS	Draft International Standard
DoD	(United States) Department of Defense
DoD-Std	A prefix for standards developed by the US Department of Defense
DTR	Draft Technical Report
DXL	Diagram eXchange Language
EDEC	Engineering Department Executive Committee of the EIA
EIA	Electronic Industries Association
Engineering	The use of principles to find designs that will meet multiple competing objectives, within limited resources and other constraints, under conditions of uncertainty
ESA	European Space Agency
FAA	Federal Aviation Agency
Failure mode and effects analysis	A technique for risk analysis that identifies failures that have significant consequences affecting system performance of the application
Fault tree analysis	A technique for risk analysis that traces the conditions and factors which contribute to an undesirable event affecting the satisfactory performance of a system
FDIS	Final Draft International Standard
FIPS	Federal Information Processing Standards
FMEA	Failure Modes and Effects Analysis
FMECA	Failure Mode Effects and Criticality Analysis, FMEA extended to consider the severity of the consequences of failure
FSE	In the context of safety, Functions, Systems, and Equipment
FSM	Functional size measurement
FTA	Fault tree analysis
Function point	A measure of the size of software
G	In some SDOs, for example, AIAA, the designation for a "guide"

Guide	In IEEE, one of three types of standards documents, the one that suggests alternative approaches to good practice. AIAA has a similar usage
G-xx	Designation of EIA's standards committees
HTML	Hypertext Markup Language
ICAM	Integrated Computer-Aided Manufacturing
IDEF	Originally, ICAM Definition; now, Integrated Definition
IDEF0	IDEF Function Modeling
IDEF1X	IDEF Information Modeling Extended
IDEFObject	Alternative term for IDEF1X97, the most recent extension of IDEF1X
IEC	International Electrotechnical Commission
IEEE	Institute of Electrical and Electronics Engineers
IEV	International Electrotechnical Vocabulary, the IEC glossary
INCOSE	International Council on Systems Engineering
Integrity level, software	In the context of dependability, a range of values of a software property necessary to maintain system risks within acceptable limits. For software that performs a [risk] mitigating function, the property is the reliability with which the software must perform the mitigating function. For software whose failure can lead to a system threat, the property is the frequency or probability of that failure.
IPMC	Industrial Process Measurement and Control
IS	Interim Standard, a term used by EIA
IS	International Standard, as differentiated from a Technical Report
ISO	International Organization for Standardization
ISSB	Information Systems Standards Board of ANSI
IT	Information technology, the scope of ISO/IEC JTC1

ITI	Industry Technology Industry, the administrator of the US TAG to JTC1
ITU	International Telecommunications Union
J	The designation for a US standard jointly developed by two or more SDOs
JTC1	Joint Technical Committee 1 (information technology) of ISO and IEC
Maintainability	The factor of dependability that concerns the ease of maintenance and upgrade
Mil-Std	Prefix designating standards created by the US Department of Defense
NASA	National Aeronautics and Space Administration
National Committee	A member of IEC
NCITS	National Committee for Information Technology Standards, the committee formerly known as X3
NIST	National Institute of Standards and Technology
NP	New Work Item Proposal
NRC	(United States) Nuclear Regulatory Commission
NSA	(United States) National Security Agency
NWI	New Work Item
OCD	Operational Concept Document, also see ConOps
O-member	Observing member of an ISO organ
OMB	(US) Office of Management and Budget
Package	A complete and usable software product in saleable or deliverable form complete with documentation and cover information
PAR	IEEE's Project Authorization Request
Part	A subdivision of a single standard document
PDCA	Plan-Do-Check-Act, a concept from quality management

pDTR	Preliminary Draft Technical Report
PES	Power Engineering Society of the IEEE
PES	Programmable Electronic Systems
Pink Ballot	Colloquial name for the EIA balloting process
PINS	ANSI Project Initiation Notification System ·
PIP	Process Information Product
PMBOK	Project Management Body of Knowledge
P-member	Full, Participating member of an ISO organ
PMI	Project Management Institute
PMP	Project Management Professional, a certification program of PMI
Procedure	A series of steps to be performed, vice process
Process	In the SESC object model, one of four objects treated by software engineering standards
Process	Assignment of responsibilities to agents for enaction whenever appropriate, vice procedure
Process Information Product	A recording of intermediate information intended to be transferred from one life cycle process to another
Product	In the SESC object model, one of four objects treated by software engineering standards
Project Management	One of six contexts for software engineering standards considered in this book; a system of management procedures, practices, technologies, skills, and experience applied to managing an engineering project
PWI	Preliminary Work Item
Pxxxx	An IEEE project. The "P" distinguishes the incomplete project from the eventual standard that is produced
QA	Quality Assurance
Quality	The totality of characteristics of an entity that bear on its ability to satisfy stated or implied needs. (But ISO TC176 is considering a redefinition.)

Quality assurance	All planned and systematic activities implemented within the quality system and demonstrated as needed to provide adequate confidence that an entity will fulfill requirements for quality
Quality management	One of six contexts for software engineering standards considered in this book; all activities of the overall management function that determine and implement quality systems
Quality system	All life cycle processes that affect quality of the final product
R	A prefix used by AIAA to denote a Recommended Practice
R	A suffix used by some SDOs to note the date of reaffirmation of a standard
R	A suffix used by IEEE to indicate a project to revise a standard, for example, P1012 (R)
Recommended Practice	In IEEE, one of three types of standards documents, the one that presents procedures and positions preferred by the IEEE. AIAA has a similar usage
Reliability	The factor of dependability that determines the longevity of product performance
Reliability engineering	The application of statistical techniques to data collected during system development and operation to specify, predict, estimate, and assess the reliability of software-based systems
Resource	In the SESC object model, one of four objects treated by software engineering standards
RIG	Reuse Library Interoperability Group
Risk	In the context of dependability, a combination of the probability of a threat and the adverse consequences of its occurrence
RP	Recommended Practice
RTCA	RTCA, Inc.
S	A prefix used by AIAA to denote a Standard
Safety	One of six contexts for software engineering standards considered in this book

Safety systems	Systems critical to nuclear reactor protection, specifically those provided to ensure, in any condition, the safe shutdown of the reactor and the heat removal from the core and/or to limit the consequences of undesirable conditions
Safety, functional	Safety treated at the level of the system rather than at the level of individual equipment
Safety, systems important to	Generic term for systems related to nuclear reactor protection
Safety-related systems	Systems contributing, but not critical, to nuclear reactor protection
SC	Subcommittee of an ISO or IEC Technical Committee
SC45A	In this context, IEC Subcommittee 45A (nuclear safety)
SC65A	In this context, IEC Subcommittee 65A (systems aspects of industrial process measurement and control)
SC7	In this context, Subcommittee 7 (software engineering) of ISO/IEC JTC1
SCC	Standards Coordinating Committee of the IEEE Computer Society
SCM	Software Configuration Management
SDO	Standards Developing Organization
SEC	Standards Executive Council of the AIAA
SEDDI	Software Engineering Data Definition and Interchange
SEI	Software Engineering Institute
SESC	Software Engineering Standards Committee of the IEEE Computer Society
SESS	Software Engineering Standards Subcommittee, the predecessor of SESC
SGML	Standard Generalized Markup Language

Software engineering	(1) The application of a systematic, disciplined, quantifiable approach to the development, operation, and maintenance of software, that is, the application of engineering to software. (2) The study of approaches as in (1)—IEEE Std 610.12.
SP	An AIAA Special Projects Report
SPICE	Software Process Improvement and Capability dEtermination
SQAP	Software Quality Assurance Plan
Stack	A term used in SESC's planning, to indicate a set of standards documents that describe principles, prescribe conformance requirements, and provide application guidance in a single subject area
Standard	In IEEE, one of three types of standards documents, the one that generally contains mandatory requirements for conformance. AIAA has a similar usage
Standard	(1) an object or measure of comparison that defines or represents the magnitude of a unit; (2) a characterization that establishes allowable tolerances or constraints for categories of items; and (3) a degree or level of required excellence or attainment. Standards are definitional in nature, established either to further understanding and interaction, or to acknowledge observed (or desired norms) of exhibited characteristics or behavior.
STARS	Software Technology for Adaptable, Reliable Systems, a program of the (US) Defense Advanced Research Projects Agency
STC	Standards Technical Council of the AIAA
Std	IEEE designation for a standard
STL	Semantic Transfer Language
SW	Software
SWEP	Software Engineering Programme of ISO/IEC JTC1/SC7
SWG	Standards Working Group in the AIAA

SWLC   Software life cycle

SysRS   System Requirements Specification

Systems engi-   One of six contexts for software engineering
neering   standards considered in this book; an iterative
                     process of top-down synthesis, development,
                     and operation of a real-world system that sat-
                     isfies, in a near-optimal manner, the full range
                     of requirements for the system

TA   Technical Advisor

TAG   Technical Advisory Group

TC   Technical Committee, of ISO or IEC

TC159   ISO Technical Committee 159, responsible for
                     software ergonomics

TC176   ISO Technical Committee 176 (quality)

TC56   IEC Technical Committee 56 (dependability)

TCSE   IEEE Technical Council on Software Engi-
                     neering

Technical Advi- In effect, the chair of a TAG for an IEC organi-
sor   zation

Technical Advi- A US organization that determines national
sory Group   positions and selects delegates to represent
                     those positions to an organ of ISO or ISO/IEC
                     JTC1

Technical Re-   An official ISO product that is not a standard
port

Threat   In the context of dependability, a state of a
                     system or its environment that can have ad-
                     verse effects

TR   Technical Report, as opposed to an ISO Inter-
                     national Standard

Trial Use   An IEEE term for a standard approved for a
                     2-year period rather than the usual 5 years

V & V   Verification and Validation

WD   Working Draft

WG   Working Group (in an SDO); specifically the
                     next level down from an ISO or IEC subcom-
                     mittee

REFERENCES

[Abran96] Alain Abran, "Teaching Software Engineering Using ISO Standards," *StandardView*, Vol. 4, No. 3, Sept. 1996, pp. 139-145.

[AIAA92] American Institute of Aeronautics and Astronautics, *Standards Program Procedures*, approved 1987, revised 1990, reaffirmed 1992.

[AIAA96] American Institute of Aeronautics and Astronautics, http://www.aiaa.org/, 1996, accessed Dec. 14, 1996.

[Albrecht83] Alan Albrecht, "Measuring Application Development Productivity," *Programmer Productivity Issues for the Eighties*, C. Jones, ed., IEEE Computer Soc. Press, Los Alamitos, CA, 1981, pp. 34-43.

[Andriole93] Stephen J. Andriole and Peter A. Freeman, "Software Systems Engineering: The Case for a New Discipline," *Software Eng. J.*, Vol. 8, No. 3, May 1993, pp. 165-179.

[ANSI92] American National Standards Institute, *Guide for Submitting Proposed American National Standards for Approval*, Feb. 1992.

[April95] Alain April and François Coallier, "Trillium: A model for the Assessment of Telecom Software System Development and Maintenance Capability," *Proc. IEEE Int'l Software Eng. Standards Symp.*, IEEE Computer Soc. Press, Los Alamitos, CA, 1995, pp. 175-183.

[AWG97] IEEE Architecture Working Group, *Design Specification for Recommended Practice for Architectural Description— [Draft] IEEE Std 1471* (Revision 3), Jan. 1997.

[Baron95] S. N. Baron, "The Standards Development Process and the NII: A View from the Trenches," in Brian Kahin and Janet Abbate, eds., *Standards Policy for Information Infrastructure*, MIT Press, Cambridge, MA, 1995.

[Basili92] Victor R. Basili et al., "A Reference Architecture for the Component Factory," *ACM Trans. Software Eng. and Methodology*, Vol. 1, No. 1, Jan. 1992, pp. 53-80.

[Batik92] Albert Batik, *The Engineering Standard: A Most Useful Tool*, BookMaster/El Rancho, Ashland, OH, 1992.

[Bell94] Bell Canada, *Trillium: Model for Telecom Product Development and Support Process Capability*, Release 3.0, 1994. An on-line version of an apparently identical document can be found at: http://www2.umassd.edu/swpi/BellCanada/trillium -html/trillium.html.

[Billingsley93] Patricia A. Billingsley, "Reflections on ISO 9241: Software Usability May be More than the Sum of its Parts," *StandardView*, Vol. 1, No. 1, Sept. 1993, pp. 22-25.

[Bootstrap93] Members of the Bootstrap Project Team, "Bootstrap: Europe's Assessment Method," *IEEE Software*, Vol. 10, No. 3, May 1993, pp. 93-95.

[Bøegh95] Jorgen Bøegh, "Evaluation Modules: The Link Between Theory and Practice," *Proc. IEEE Int'l Software Eng. Standards Symp.*, IEEE Computer Soc. Press, Los Alamitos, CA, 1995, pp. 170-174.

[Brazendale95] John Brazendale, "IEC 1508: Functional Safety: Safety-Related Systems," *Proc. IEEE Int'l Software Eng. Standards Symp.*, IEEE Computer Soc. Press, Los Alamitos, CA, 1995, pp. 8-17.

[Brobeck96] Stephen Brobeck, "Consumer Participation in Standards Development," *ANSI Reporter*, Dec. 1996, pp. 5-6.

[Brooks95] Frederick P. Brooks, Jr., "The Mythical Man-Month After 20 Years," *IEEE Software*, July 1995, pp. 57-60.

[Cargill89] Carl F. Cargill, *Information Technology Standardization: Theory, Process, and Organizations*, Digital Press, Maynard, MA, 1989.

[Cargill97] Carl F. Cargill, *Open Systems Standardization: A Business Approach*, Prentice Hall PTR, Upper Saddle River, NJ, 1997.

[Charles96] John Charles, "DoD Standards Go Global, Commercial," *IEEE Software*, Vol. 13, No. 3, May 1996, pp. 98-99.

[CSA96] Canadian Standards Association, http://www.csa.ca/, Apr. 4, 1997, accessed Apr. 23, 1997.

[Davis95] Alan M. Davis, *201 Principles of Software Development*, McGraw-Hill, New York, NY, 1995.

[DEF91] *DEF 5169/T1, ImproveIT*, UK Ministry of Defense, London, 1991.

[DTI92] (UK) Department of Trade and Industry, *Guide to Software Quality Management System Construction and Certification*, 1992.

[EIA96] Electronic Industries Association, http://www.eia.org/, undated, accessed Dec. 14, 1996.

[Eisner88] H. Eisner, *Computer-aided Systems Engineering*, Prentice-Hall, Englewood Cliffs, NJ, 1988.

[Ellis96] Walter J. Ellis et al., "Toward a Recommended Practice for Architectural Description," *2nd Int'l Conf. Eng. of Complex Computer Systems*, IEEE Computer Soc. Press, Los Alamitos, CA, 1996, pp. 408-413.

[Emam95] Khaled El Emam and Dennis R. Goldensen, "SPICE: An Empiricist's Perspective," *Proc. IEEE Int'l Software Eng. Stan-*

dards Symp., IEEE Computer Soc. Press, Los Alamitos, CA, 1995, pp. 84-97.

[Fairley95] Richard E. Fairley and Richard H. Thayer, "The Concept of Operations: The Bridge from Operational Requirements to Technical Specifications," in Richard H. Thayer and Merlin Dorfman, eds., *Software Requirements Engineering*, IEEE Press, 1996, pp. 44-54.

[Fayol49] H. Fayol, *General and Industrial Administration*, Pitman & Sons, London, 1949.

[FedReg96] Nuclear Regulatory Commission, "Notices: Draft Regulatory Guides: Issuance, Availability," *Federal Register*, Vol. 61, No. 173/46834, Sept. 5, 1996.

[Fenton96] Norman Fenton, "Counterpoint: Do Standards Improve Quality?" *IEEE Software*, Vol. 13, No. 1, Jan. 1996, pp. 23-24.

[Fujii95] Roger U. Fujii and Dolores R. Wallace, "Software Verification and Validation," in Merlin Dorfman and Richard H. Thayer, eds., *Software Engineering*, IEEE Computer Soc. Press, Los Alamitos, CA, 1996.

[Gibson95] Richard B. Gibson, "The Global Standards Process: A Balance of the Old and the New," in Brian Kahin and Janet Abbate, eds., *Standards Policy for Information Infrastructure*, MIT Press, Cambridge, MA, 1995.

[Gilb96] Tom Gilb, "Level 6: Why We Can't Get There from Here," *IEEE Software*, Vol. 13, No. 1, Jan. 1996, pp. 97-98, 103.

[Haase94] Volkmar Haase et al., "Bootstrap: Fine-Tuning Process Assessment," *IEEE Software*, Vol. 11, No. 4, July 1994, pp. 25-33.

[Hall91] Patrick A. V. Hall and Maurice Resnick, "Standards," in John A. McDermid, ed., *Software Engineer's Reference Book*, CRC Press, 1991, pp. 50/3-50/21.

[Harauz96] John Harauz, "A Software Engineering Standards Framework for Nuclear Power," *StandardView*, Vol. 4, No. 3, Sept. 1996, pp. 133-138.

[Harauz97] John Harauz, private communication, Apr. 9, 1997.

[Harauz97a] John Harauz, "International Trends in Software Engineering and Quality System Standards from the Viewpoint of Ontario Hydro," *8th Int'l Conf. on Software Technology*, June 11-13, 1997, Curitiba, Brazil.

[Heineman94] G. T. Heineman et al., "Emerging Technologies that Support a Software Process Life Cycle," *IBM Systems J.*, Vol. 33, No. 3, 1994, pp. 501-529.

[IEC96] International Electrotechnical Commission, "Welcome to the IEC," http://www.iec.ch/home-e.htm, Nov. 1, 1996, accessed Jan. 2, 1997.

[IEEE95] Institute of Electrical and Electronics Engineers, Inc., *The IEEE Standards Companion*, Piscataway, NJ, 1995.

[IEEE96] *IEEE Std 100-1996, The IEEE Standard Dictionary of Electrical and Electronics Terms*, Sixth Ed., IEEE, Piscataway, NJ, 1996.

[IEEE97] Institute of Electrical and Electronics Engineers, Inc., "The IEEE Is...A World of Technology," http://www.ieee.org/ i3e_blb.html, undated, accessed Jan. 8, 1996.

[IEEE97a] Institute of Electrical and Electronics Engineers, Inc., *IEEE Standards Operations Manual*, Piscataway, NJ, 1997.

[INCOSE97] International Council on Systems Engineering, http://internet-plaza.net/incose/, Jan. 5, 1997.

[Ippolito95] Laura M. Ippolito and Dolores R. Wallace, *A Study of Hazard Analysis in High Integrity Software Standards and Guidelines*, NISTIR 5589, National Institute of Standards and Technology, US Department of Commerce, Jan. 1995.

[ISO97] International Organization for Standardization, "Introduction to ISO," http://www.iso.ch/infoe/intro.html, undated, accessed Jan. 3, 1997.

[ISO/IEC95] International Organization for Standardization/International Electrotechnical Commission Joint Technical Committee 1, *Procedures for the Technical Work of ISO/IEC JTC1 on Information Technology*, 3rd ed., Geneva, 1995.

[ISO/IEC97] International Organization for Standardization/International Electrotechnical Commission, *ISO/IEC Directives, Procedures for the Technical Work, Part 1*, http://www.iso.ch/ dire/directives.html, undated, accessed Apr. 24, 1997.

[ISO/IEC97a] International Organization for Standardization, International Electrotechnical Commission Joint Technical Committee 1, http://www.iso.ch/meme/JTC1.html, undated, accessed May 2, 1997.

[JLC96] Joint Logistics Commanders Joint Group on Systems Engineering, Practical Software Measurement, Version 2.1, Mar. 27, 1996. (Contact John McGarry, mcgarry@ada.npt.nuwc .navy.mil.)

[Jabir97] Jabir [Group], "A Search for Fundamental Principles of Software Engineering," *Computer Standards and Interfaces*, (forthcoming).

[Joannou95] Paul K. Joannou and John Harauz, "Ontario Hydro/AECL Standards for Software Engineering—Deficiencies in Existing Standards that Created Their Need," *Proc. IEEE Int'l Software Eng. Standards Symp.*, IEEE Computer Soc. Press, Los Alamitos, CA, 1995, pp. 146-152.

[Jones95] Capers Jones, "Legal Status of Software Engineering," *Computer*, Vol. 28, No. 5, May 1995, pp. 98-99.

[Kiang95] David Kiang, "Harmonization of International Software Standards on Integrity and Dependability," *Proc. IEEE Int'l Software Eng. Standards Symp.*, IEEE Computer Soc. Press, Los Alamitos, CA, 1995, pp. 98-104.

[Kiang97] David Kiang, "ISO 9000 Update," presentation to Society of Reliability Engineers, Feb. 25, 1997, Ottawa, Canada.

[Kiang97a] David Kiang, "Technology Impact on Dependability Requirements," *Proc. Int'l Software Eng. Standards Symp.*, IEEE Computer Soc. Press, Los Alamitos, CA, 1997, pp. 92-98.

[Kitson96] David H. Kitson, "Relating the Spice Framework and the SEI Approach to Software Process Assessment," *Proc. 5th European Conf. Software Quality*, Dublin, Ireland, 1996.

[Kitson97] David H. Kitson, private communication, May 1, 1997.

[Knafl95] George J. Knafl, "Overview of SRE Standards Planning Activities," *Proc. IEEE Int'l Software Eng. Standards Symp.*, IEEE Computer Soc. Press, Los Alamitos, CA, 1995, pp. 244-245.

[Konrad96] Mike Konrad et al., "Capability Maturity Modeling at the SEI," *Software Process—Improvement and Practice*, Vol. 2, 21-34, 1996, pp. 21-34.

[Koontz72] H. Koontz and C. O'Donnell, *Principles of Management: An Analysis of Managerial Functions*, 5th ed., McGraw-Hill, New York, 1972.

[Lano80] R. J. Lano, *A Structured Approach for Operational Concept Formulation (OCF)*, Tech. Report TRW-SS-80-02, TRW Systems Engineering and Integration Division, Redondo Beach, CA, 1980. Also in R. H. Thayer, ed., "Tutorial: Software Engineering Project Management," IEEE Computer Soc. Press, Los Alamitos, CA, 1988.

[Leret95] Evelyne Leret, "Safety of Computerized I&C Systems: Projects of IEC Standards with Emphasis on Power Plant Sector," *Proc. IEEE Int'l Software Eng. Standards Symp.*, IEEE Computer Soc. Press, Los Alamitos, CA, 1995, pp. 18-22.

[Ling96] David Ling and Dale Misczynski, "ISO 9001 for the Supplier and Purchaser," *ANSI Reporter*, Sept. 1996, pp. 8-9.

[Magee97] Stan Magee and Leonard L. Tripp, *Guide to Software Engineering Standards and Specifications*, Artech House, Boston, MA, 1997.

[Marquadt91] Donald Marquadt et al., "Vision 2000: The Strategy for the ISO 9000 Series Standards in the '90s," report of the Ad Hoc Task Force of ISO TC176, reprinted in [Peach94].

[Matras95] John R. Matras, "Requirements for Abnormal Conditions and Events Analysis," *Proc. IEEE Int'l Software Eng. Standards Symp.*, IEEE Computer Soc. Press, Los Alamitos, CA, 1995, pp. 4-7.

[Mazza94] C. Mazza et al., *Software Engineering Standards*, Prentice-Hall, New York, 1994.

[Moore91] James W. Moore, "A National Infrastructure for Defense Reuse," Proc. 4th Ann. Workshop Software Reuse, Reston, VA, Nov. 18-22, 1991. Also available at: ftp://gandalf.umcs .maine.edu/pub/WISR/wisr4/proceedings/ps/moore.ps.

[Moore94] James W. Moore, "A Structure for a Defense Software Reuse Marketplace," *SIGAda AdaLetters*, Vol. 14, No. 3, May/June 1994.

[Moore95] James W. Moore and Roy Rada, "Organizational Badge Collecting," *Comm. ACM*, Aug. 1996, pp. 17-21.

[Moore97] James W. Moore, Perry R. DeWeese, and Dennis Rilling, "US Software Life Cycle Process Standards," *Crosstalk,* Vol. 10, No. 7, July 1997, pp. 6-8.

[Parnas95] David Lorge Parnas, "Software Engineering: An Unconsummated Marriage," invited presentation at the *2nd IEEE Int'l Software Eng. Standards Symp.*, Montréal, Canada, 1995.

[Paulk93] Mark C. Paulk et al., *Capability Maturity Model for Software*, Version 1.1, Tech. Report CMU/SEI-93-TR-24 (DTIC No. ADA 263403), Software Engineering Institute, Carnegie-Mellon University, Pittsburgh, PA, 1993.

[Paulk95] Mark C. Paulk, "How ISO 9001 Compares with the CMM," *IEEE Software*, Vol. 12, No. 1, Jan. 1995, pp. 74-83.

[Peach94] Robert W. Peach, ed., *The ISO 9000 Handbook*, 2nd ed., CEEM Information Services, Fairfax, VA, 1994.

[Pfleeger94] Shari Lawrence Pfleeger et al., "Evaluating Software Engineering Standards," *IEEE Software*, Vol. 11, No. 5, Sept. 1994, pp. 71-79.

[PMI96] PMI Standards Committee, A Guide to The Project Management Body of Knowledge, Project Management Institute, 1996. Available at http://www.pmi.org/publictn/pmboktoc.html -ssi.

[PMI97] Project Management Institute, http://www.pmi.org/, undated, accessed Jan. 2, 1997.

[Pollak96] Bill Pollak, "The Role of Standards in Technology Transition," *Computer,* Vol. 29, No. 3, Mar. 1996, p. 102.

[Rada95] Roy Rada, "ISO 9000 Reflects the Best in Standards," *Comm. ACM*, Vol. 29, No. 3, Mar. 1996.

[Rehesaar96] Hugo Rehesaar, "International Standards: Practical or Just Theoretical?" *StandardView*, Vol. 4, No. 3, Sept. 1996, pp. 123-127.

[Royce70] Winston Royce, "Managing the Development of Large Software Systems: Concepts and Techniques," *Proc. WESCON*, IEEE Computer Soc. Press, Los Alamitos, CA, 1970.

[SC7-96] ISO/IEC JTC1/SC7 Business Planning Group, *Product Plan for ISO/IEC Software Engineering Standards*, 1st ed. (Approval Draft), 1996.

[SC7-97] ISO/IEC JTC1/SC7, "ISO/IEC JTC1/SC7 Comments on ISO/DIS 9000-3," N1703, Apr. 19, 1997.

[SC7WG9-96] ISO/IEC JTC1/SC7/WG9 N018, *Joint Product Plan*, Revised (Draft for Comments), July 1996.

[Schneidewind95] Norman F. Schneidewind, "Integrating Standards to Produce Reliable Products and Processes: Position Paper," *Proc. IEEE Int'l Software Eng. Standards Symp.*, IEEE Computer Soc. Press, Los Alamitos, CA, 1995, p. 246.

[Schneidewind96] Norman F. Schneidewind, "Point: Do standards improve quality?," *IEEE Software*, Vol. 13, No. 1, Jan. 1996, pp. 22-24.

[SESC93] SESC Long Range Planning Group, *Master Plan for Software Engineering Standards*, Version 1.0, Dec. 1, 1993.

[SESC94] SESC Business Planning Group, *Survey of Existing and In-Progress Software Engineering Standards*, Version 1.1, Aug.

8, 1994. (Updated material in greater detail can be found in [Magee97].)

[SESC95] SESC Business Planning Group, *Vision 2000 Strategy Statement* (Final Draft), v0.9, SESC/BPG-002, Aug. 20, 1995.

[SESC96] SESC Business Planning Group, *Overview of Software Engineering Standards of the IEEE Computer Society*, Version 2.2, Oct. 18, 1996.

[SESC96a] SESC Business Planning Group, *Program Plan for 1996-1998* (Review Draft), Version 0.6, Aug. 1, 1996.

[SESC96b] SESC Software Safety Planning Group, *Action Plan*, Oct. 15, 1996.

[SESC96c] SESC Architecture Planning Group, *Action Plan*, undated.

[SESC96d] SESC Reuse Planning Group, *Action Plan*, Sept. 17, 1996.

[SESC97] SESC Business Planning Group, *Program Plan for 1997-1999* (Approval Draft), Version 0.7, Dec. 23, 1996.

[Sorensen96] Reed Sorensen, "Mil-Std 498, J-Std-016, and the U.S. Commercial Standard," *Crosstalk*, Vol. 9, No. 6, June 1996, pp. 13-14.

[Spring95] Michael B. Spring et al., "Improving the Standardization Process: Working with Bulldogs and Turtles," in Brian Kahin and Janet Abbate, eds., *Standards Policy for Information Infrastructure*, MIT Press, Cambridge, MA, 1995.

[Tate95] R. J. Tate, "Assessing Software Based Safety Systems Against the Requirements and Recommendations of IEC 880 (1986)," *Proc. IEEE Int'l Software Eng. Standards Symp.*, IEEE Computer Soc. Press, Los Alamitos, CA, 1995, pp. 153-165.

[TC176-96] ISO/TC176/SC1 N149, "Key Quality Concepts, Terms and Definitions (Draft Technical Report)," June 1996.

[TC176-96a] ISO/TC176 N243 R2, "Year 2000 Family," Nov. 8, 1996.

[TC176-96b] ISO/TC176/N269, "Officers Preliminary Dispositiong [sic] of TC176 Documents/Work Items," Nov. 9, 1996.

[TC56-95] IEC TC56, "Strategic Policy Statement," undated but apparently drafted subsequent to Oct. 27, 1995.

[Thayer84] R. H. Thayer and A. B. Pyster, "Guest Editorial: Software Engineering Project Management," *IEEE Trans. Software Eng.*, Vol. SE-10, No. 1, Jan. 1984.

[Thayer95] Richard H. Thayer, "Software Engineering Project Management," in Richard H. Thayer, ed., *Software Engineering*, IEEE Computer Soc. Press, Los Alamitos, CA, 1996, pp. 358-371.

[Toth96] Robert B. Toth, ed., *Standards Activities of Organizations in the United States*, Special Publication 806, National Institute of Standards and Technology, 1996.

[Tripp95] Leonard L. Tripp and Peter Voldner, "A Market-Driven Architecture for Software Engineering Standards," *Proc. IEEE*

Int'l Software Eng. Standards Symp., IEEE Computer Soc. Press, Los Alamitos, CA, 1995, pp. 105-116.

[Tripp96] Leonard L. Tripp, "International Standards on System and Software Integrity," *StandardView*, Vol. 4, No. 3, Sept. 1996, pp. 146-150.

[Wallace94] Dolores R. Wallace and Laura M. Ippolito, *A Framework for The Development and Assurance of High Integrity Software,* Special Publication 500-223, National Institute of Standards and Technology, US Department of Commerce, 1994.

[Wegner95] Eberhard Wegner, "Quality of Software Packages: The Forthcoming International Standard," *Computer Standards & Interfaces,* Vol. 17, 1995, pp. 115-120.

INDEX

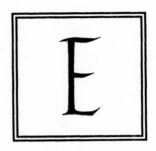

Software Engineering Standards:
A User's Road Map

by James W. Moore

is recommended by the

Software Engineering Standards Committee
of the IEEE Computer Society

as a useful guide for software practitioners
applying software engineering standards.

SESC Executive Committee